"In this compelling ethnographic account of middle-class blacks in New York City, Cassi Pittman Claytor breaks new ground in the study of black cultural capital and the complex ways her subjects use lifestyle practices to navigate race and class. A major contribution to race, consumption, class, and urban studies. A must-read and must-teach."

—Juliet Schor, author of *After the Gig*

"*Black Privilege* brings rich ethnographic detail to the study of the black middle class. Showing both the opportunities and the restrictions of black cultural expression and consumption, Pittman Claytor expands our understanding of the workings of privilege by underscoring the necessity of considering how it is racialized."

—Shamus Khan, Columbia University, and author of *Sexual Citizens*

"With compelling storytelling and exciting theoretical insights, Pittman Claytor addresses an understudied topic from a unique and creative perspective. A must-read for anyone interested in understanding how race operates in the marketplace."

—Corey Fields, author of *Black Elephants in the Room*

"A common view of consumption is that it is a source of alienation for blacks. Pittman Claytor's incisive portrait of consumption among those who are black and privileged challenges us to rethink this view. In an engaging style, Pittman Claytor shows how consumption is a resource for middle-class blacks as they navigate a world where race still matters. *Black Privilege* is an important and necessary addition to the literature on consumption and inequality."

—Patricia A. Banks, author of *Diversity and Philanthropy at African American Museums*

"*Black Privilege* is a welcome addition to contemporary research on the U.S. black middle class. What sets it apart is that it treats the marketplace as a mainstage on which members of the black middle class act out their joys and challenges in everyday life. It focuses our attention on how these actors deploy their skills, tastes, and practices—their black cultural capital—sometimes just to survive and at others to thrive."

—David Crockett, University of South Carolina

BLACK PRIVILEGE

CULTURE
AND
ECONOMIC
LIFE

BLACK PRIVILEGE

Modern Middle-Class Blacks
with Credentials and Cash to Spend

CASSI PITTMAN CLAYTOR

STANFORD UNIVERSITY PRESS
Stanford, California

STANFORD UNIVERSITY PRESS
Stanford, California

Printed in the United States of America on acid-free, archival-quality paper

Library of Congress Cataloging-in-Publication Data
Names: Claytor, Cassi Pittman, author.
Title: Black privilege : modern middle-class blacks with credentials and cash to spend / Cassi Pittman Claytor.
Other titles: Culture and economic life.
Description: Stanford, California : Stanford, 2020. | Series: Culture and economic life | Includes bibliographical references and index.
Identifiers: LCCN 2020012062 (print) | LCCN 2020012063 (ebook) | ISBN 9781503612105 (cloth) | ISBN 9781503613171 (paperback) | ISBN 9781503613188 (epub)
Subjects: LCSH: Middle class African Americans—New York (State)—New York—Social conditions. | African Americans—Race identity—New York (State)—New York. | African Americans—New York (State)—New York—Social conditions. | Consumer behavior—New York (State)—New York. | Privilege (Social psychology)—New York (State)—New York.
Classification: LCC F128.9.N3 C655 2020 (print) | LCC F128.9.N3 (ebook) | DDC 974.7/0496073—dc23
LC record available at https://lccn.loc.gov/2020012062
LC ebook record available at https://lccn.loc.gov/2020012063

Cover design: Angela Moody
Cover illustration: Fotostock32 | Adobe Stock
Typeset by Kevin Barrett Kane in 10/14 Minion Pro

For my mother, Deborah, for her unwavering love and unconditional support,
my father, Darryl, for encouraging me to break boundaries,
and my caring and devoted husband, Adam.

Contents

BLACK PRIVILEGE

Black and Privileged

1

THE SLOW BUT STEADY EXPANSION of the black middle class has led to the emergence of *black privilege*—a unique set of social experiences and entitlements that accompany middle-class status as blacks experience it. *Black privilege* refers to the experience of advantage, the benefits that accrue from having access to cultural and material capital, and the worldviews that result from the opportunities and experiences that generate such resources. But it also attends to a matrix of tastes and preferences, manifested in the habits, everyday practices, and leisure pursuits of modern middle-class blacks, that demonstrate their racial identities and allegiances.

As this book unfolds, I detail how black privilege develops and is deployed, revealing new insight that both sharpens and enriches our understanding of the black experience. The book draws from evidence collected in an interview-based study I conducted between 2009 and 2014 in the New York metropolitan area with fifty-four middle-class blacks. My analysis of the data derived from this study reveals the nature and character of black privilege and its constitutive elements—black cultural capital and cultural flexibility. What I learned illustrates the continued relevance of race in the lifestyles of black consumers who have cultural capital, credentials, and cash to spend, but still must contend with the subtle and not so subtle notions that blacks are culturally and socially inferior. From examining the daily lives of college-educated blacks, it becomes clear how, in more ways than one, they are privileged. However, being black has implications for how they experience the rewards and advantages that their middle-class status bestows.

Previous research focused on the black middle class has revealed the complexity of their lived experiences, as a consequence of both their class status and race.[1] The findings of my study add to that literature, examining the ways that consumption is a critical tool modern middle-class blacks wield in achieving the bifurcated goals of challenging cultural racism and reveling in the world's material comforts. For those who are black and privileged, born after the civil rights movement, their cultural consumption performs an essential role in the construction and display of both their race and their class identities.

Tasha, a 28-year-old attorney working in the cosmetics industry, is part of the emerging black middle class in New York City. I meet her one afternoon at a restaurant a few blocks from the brownstone where she lives in Harlem. She had agreed to tell me about her experience as a middle-class black woman living and working in New York. The restaurant Tasha chose offered a blend of Italian and Mediterranean cuisine, and its decor—modern and sophisticated, with cream-colored leather chairs and tumbled marble floors—hinted at her taste for finer things. Once we settle into a table, Tasha mentions that one of the restaurant's owners is a black woman. Tasha's choosing to meet at an aesthetically pleasing, upscale place that is also owned by a fellow black woman reflects the fact that her racial identity together with her class identity shapes her decisions about how and where to spend her money.

When Tasha leaves Harlem, heading to work each morning, she moves from a social environment in which black culture is celebrated and she feels part of a black community to a setting in which she is the exception, as one of just two black women at her company. This change in context requires cultural maneuvering. In settings like Tasha's workplace, where white culture reigns, consumption uniquely enables middle-class blacks to seamlessly cross social and cultural boundaries. And they do so frequently throughout the course of their lives. Their consumption also serves as a useful tool to manage encounters with racial stigma and anti-black bias. Like Tasha, many of the middle-class blacks in my study inhabit social worlds that diverge in their social norms and requirements, social worlds that often stand in stark contrast to one another, some predominantly black and some predominantly white. While they espouse a love for the richness of black culture, they also realize that they must maintain diverse cultural repertoires, a capacity that requires familiarity with the dominant—white—culture.

Scholars have long attempted to grapple with blacks' familiarity with and display of dominant culture and their simultaneous desire to maintain distinct black cultural practices and knowledge bases, even when black cultural practices are devalued and potentially stigmatizing. W.E.B. Du Bois famously described the fierce tension between blacks' private and public identities, which resulted in a "two-ness." He viewed blacks' "double consciousness" as a gift and a curse.[2] Mostly, though, it reflects the troublesome nature of race and the oppressive conditions that blacks face living in a racist society. For Du Bois, the internal conflict and strain that results from having to manage the disjuncture between how blacks view themselves and how they are perceived in society is a disagreeable aspect of black life that is a product of the prevailing racial order.

In more recent work, sociologist Karyn Lacy has grappled with the challenges black middle-class people face. She argues that a key aspect of the experience of being black and middle class is being able to strategically assimilate, which requires maintaining multiple public identities. For Lacy, middle-class blacks' aptitude for multiplicity is less of an encumbrance and more of a resource—an ability or skill that can be put to use in advantageous ways.[3] Similarly, Kathryn Neckerman, Prudence Carter, and Jennifer Lee describe cultural maneuvering as an attribute of minority cultures of mobility.[4] In both cases, middle-class blacks are theorized to maintain an affinity for black spaces and to place a premium on interactions with other blacks, while often operating or residing in primarily white spaces.

Others scholars have documented the purposeful work of middle-class black parents to ensure that their children have both knowledge of "mainstream, majority white practices that will help them navigate social structures and systems and African American culture," so that they can have a sense of racial pride and a connection to other blacks.[5] This skill set is not innate but often the result of parental cultivation.

The term *code-switching* is often used to describe blacks' management of their cultural duality or biculturalism. Sociolinguists define *code-switching* as a particular "verbal action," a means of communicating that develops in response to membership in multiple speech communities.[6] To use the term precisely is to refer to a linguistic capacity that entails shifting from one language, language variety, dialect, or style to another.[7] Recognizing that standard English is promoted as culturally superior and that black language varieties, accents, and ways of speaking are stigmatized, and often considered unintelligible or unintelligent, blacks resignedly code-switch. Inherent in the concept of code-switching is the idea that the two language varieties involved can rarely coexist, and thus only in black social spheres or private settings can black English be fully engaged.

For modern middle-class blacks, a core aspect of their black privilege is their cultural flexibility, and demonstrations of cultural flexibility may draw on blacks' capacity to code-switch; however, cultural flexibility is much broader in its application. Beyond the sphere of language, there are multitudes of ways in which middle-class blacks must read and respond to social and cultural cues to gain acceptance in different social situations. Using their diverse cultural repertoires, they draw upon and display, depending on the circumstances, different demeanors, behaviors, composures, knowledge bases, and even emotions, all with the goal of being understood and recognized. More than code-switching they are demonstrating an ability that relies on their cultural flexibility, and by doing so they are drawing on their *black privilege*.

Tasha is well-paid and well-versed when it comes to cultural knowledge. Both enable her to live a middle-class lifestyle. But for middle-class blacks, like Tasha, black privilege is also evident in their sense of obligation and connection to the community to which their race binds them. While they feel connected to other blacks, they also recognize that their lives are quite different from the lives of poor blacks, who not only struggle financially but often experience cumulative disadvantage.[8] In contrast, middle-class blacks often benefit from having access to opportunities, social capital, and financial resources. Researchers have shown that blacks growing up in poor neighborhoods tend to experience poverty over successive generations. Poor blacks often inherit a "legacy of disadvantage," a legacy that is almost impossible to overcome given the current political state.[9] Being college educated certainly does not guarantee blacks freedom from financial peril or downward mobility; research has shown that blacks are more likely to experience downward mobility than similarly positioned whites.[10] Nonetheless, having a college degree means that often middle-class blacks' styles of life and taste differ from those of their poorer brethren, even when they reside in the same communities or neighborhoods that are quite similar.

Yet in comparison to *white privilege*, an invisible assortment of unearned entitlements enjoyed by whites, which in many instances they are unaware of and that are a consequence of their race,[11] black privilege is restricted in terms of the rewards that are associated with it. Furthermore, most blacks who are privileged are cognizant of their relatively advantaged state, while also realizing that having both cash and credentials will not buffer them from experiences of stigmatization based on their race, nor will it always grant them preferential treatment. Unlike whites, no matter how high blacks climb, they continue to confront societal racial hierarchies that place blacks at the bottom, preventing them from capitalizing and cashing in on all the benefits that their credentials and class status should afford them.

The Constitutive Elements of Black Privilege

The members of the black middle class in my study maintain lifestyle preferences that reveal and reflect their class status, while also being deeply imbued by their race. Black cultural capital and cultural flexibility, the requisite components of black privilege, enable middle-class blacks to navigate divergent cultural and social worlds, while also maintaining a consistent and coherent sense of self.

Black cultural capital has been theorized as cultural tastes and a sense of discernment that are specific to blacks. Sociologist Prudence Carter argues that it is visible in blacks' stylistic choices in domains of culture such as language, music, and art, but also evident in how they engage in social interactions with fellow in-group members.[12] Cultural knowledge and sensibilities beyond those prized by society's dominant group prove useful for middle-class blacks, both a means of affirming their blackness and as a means of connecting them to other blacks in meaningful yet mundane ways.[13] Black cultural capital functions as the glue that bonds middle-class blacks and allows them to forge relationships with blacks across class and ethnic lines.

Processes of racial socialization—the mechanisms through which blacks develop and cultivate their racial identities—are key to the forging of black cultural capital. Racial socialization informs the development of an orientation and understanding of black culture, what French sociologist Pierre Bourdieu describes as an *aesthetic disposition*, a capacity to read, make sense of, and partake in a cultural tradition or engage with a cultural artifact in way that others would perceive as legitimate.[14] Cumulative experiences of being in and navigating black social spaces and the recurrent interactions that middle-class blacks have with different types of blacks—family members, friends, and strangers—over the course of their lives are generative of and help to reinforce black cultural capital.

Tasha grew up on a cul-de-sac in the suburbs, but she spent the weekends and summers of her youth in the city with her cousins. Formative experiences in black social settings and routine interactions with blacks—like hanging out with your cousins in the city, accompanying your grandmother to church, or going to the barbershop or beauty salon—are key to developing familiarity with various racialized rites and rituals—talking trash on the basketball court, learning to double dutch, picking up new ways to care for your hair, or becoming aware of the latest styles, songs, or slang. It is through these experiences and interpersonal connections that transpire across diverse social institutions of daily life, both in commercial and in deeply personal spaces, that middle-class blacks develop, cultivate, and refine their tastes and knowledge of their black cultural capital.

The middle-class black study participants demonstrate that black cultural capital is activated in their everyday consumption practices and aesthetic preferences—their hairstyles, wardrobe decisions, and leisure activities. Being black is not just a matter of asserting one's racial identity; it is performed and displayed through a constellation of cultural consumption preferences and practices that serve to solidify what it means to be a member of the group. Black people are connected to one another, in part, through the aesthetic preferences and cultural practices that they share. For many of my respondents, black cultural capital is deeply embedded in their worldviews and lifestyles, and it informs their ideological commitments, particularly their racial pride and desire for racial uplift.

When I ask Brittany, a 28-year-old attorney, what it means to be black, she speaks at length, detailing how black people share a rich and vibrant culture, and how their achievements and contributions have impacted U.S. society and the world. Brittany perceives that blacks have maintained racially specific cultural knowledge and tastes, which connect them. She explains, "I'm from a white suburban town and somebody could be from some all-black neighborhood in another state, but there are still a lot of things that we're going to have in common." Brittany grew up attending all-white schools, but every Sunday she accompanied her grandmother to a predominantly black church; this was part of her racial socialization. Attending a predominantly black church is a practice that she continues today, though she does not go as frequently. Her church attendance, both then and now, reflects one way that her lifestyle is distinctively black, connected to black traditions. In this way she activates her black cultural capital to maintain connections to other blacks, not all of whom share her class status.

Darryl, a 28-year-old associate at a large investment bank, is the product of an inter-ethnic black union, the son of a Ghanaian immigrant and an African American. His experience and practice of black cultural capital is exemplified by the fact that he can be found on any given Saturday night deejaying at a hip-hop

club. His deejaying and love of hip-hop culture demonstrates the bridging potential of black cultural capital, across not just class lines but ethnic lines as well.
Blacks of diverse ethnic backgrounds express support for racialized ideological
commitments, like patronizing black-owned businesses, admiring prominent
African American cultural figures, and expressing racial pride, in addition to
taking pride in their ethnic identity. Many of those I interviewed with parents
who had immigrated from the Caribbean or Africa had black friends who were
a mixture of various ethnic backgrounds, and several second-generation black
immigrants reported being members of traditionally African American cultural
institutions or social and fraternal organizations. Overall, I found support for
what sociologist Onoso Imagene has argued is a *multiethnic black middle class*, in
which social and cultural boundaries along ethnic lines are present, but incred-
ibly permeable.[15] For Darryl, black music is empowering. It is a cultural resource
that he finds energizing and affirming. As he explains, each morning before
heading to his corporate job, the first thing this hip-hop aficionado does is turn
on his music: "It gets me into the office. Got the iPod; it is always charged." Darryl
also activates his black cultural capital as he keeps his shoe game tight and makes
sure to be dressed to impress whenever he goes out. When he is not at work, his
sense of style and how to carry himself is informed by black American culture.

Examples of the utility of black cultural capital to facilitate connections
among blacks, across ethnic and class lines, emerged time and time again in my
study. Others, however, have proposed that black cultural capital functions in
an alternative fashion.[16] Sociologist Derron Wallace argues that black cultural
capital is a tool unique to the black middle class, and that this is evident in
both the U.S. and British contexts. He argues that it is illustrated in displays of
cultural tastes and knowledge that are simultaneously encoded with class and
race. For example, when blacks articulate a sophisticated understanding of the
music of a celebrated black composer or the work of a renowned black artist,
they are demonstrating an affinity for high-status culture but also a familiarity
with black culture and cultural producers. Rather than connecting middle-class
blacks to other blacks across the class spectrum, black cultural capital is, in this
conception, a means of asserting a black racial identity while simultaneously
asserting one's middle-class sensibilities. Similarly, Crystal Fleming and Lorraine Roses argue that "black cultural capitalists" among the early black elite
were those who drew upon high-status, Eurocentric tastes and artistic and aesthetic standards and applied them to black cultural products and artists. Doing
so was a means to combat pejorative views of blacks and to engage in racial

uplift, but was exclusionary of the black working classes and poor. In this way, they aimed to define and to promote " 'good' black 'culture.' "[17]

In my study, I found that black cultural capital emerged most often as a tool to forge cross-class social connections among blacks, even though at times it was manifested in ways that merged people's class and racial dispositions. For example, Tasha attended Spelman College and Harvard Law School. She describes these differing educational experiences as getting "the best of both" worlds because she has reaped the rewards of attending both types of institutions, in terms of status, pedigree, and racial prestige.

Having countless experiences with navigating both black and white social worlds, Tasha is an adroit cultural actor, who possesses not only black cultural capital but also a cultural repertoire that grants her access to and acceptance in a broader world that values and idealizes the dominant culture and mores. For middle-class blacks like Tasha, who can and do regularly and skillfully cross racial and cultural boundaries, maintaining a keen sense of when to display different kinds of cultural knowledge—cultural flexibility—has become a second, but no less critical, dimension of their black privilege.

By the time Tasha entered the workforce, she had a well-developed faculty for engaging dominant cultural schemas. She has also maintained a desire to represent her race well, and this is manifested, in part, in the things she wears and how she carries herself in white settings, such as her workplace. Being middle class and black, she recognizes that she cannot partake in black cultural traditions and rituals and express her deeply felt black pride in *all* contexts. In some settings they would simply be illegible; in other settings they might be stigmatizing. Her educational qualifications, especially her having attended one of the most prestigious law schools in the country, have helped refute negative stereotypes she might encounter as one of the few blacks in her majority white workplace, but Tasha understands that she also has to deftly deploy her knowledge of dominant culture to gain acceptance and to have her achievements recognized.

Although Darryl works as a DJ on the weekends, his primary job is as an associate at a prominent investment bank. His experience provides a telling example of how middle-class blacks often maintain black cultural capital while also demonstrating cultural flexibility. Darryl is careful and conscious not to discuss his musical tastes or his weekend pastime with his white colleagues. He curates his style and personal life to appear palatable at his majority white firm. He is confident that letting his coworkers know about his affinity for and deep knowledge of black culture and specifically hip-hop, which he personally finds uplifting and a source of profound pleasure, would undermine his professional image and could potentially put him at a disadvantage at work. At his firm, Darryl perceives that old white men—whether his superiors or prospective clients—make the rules and that they value cultural "commonalities." As he explains:

> Your boss is an older guy, probably white. So he is certainly conservative. He is not even accustomed to [hip-hop]: "What's a DJ? What kind of music do you listen to?" He then immediately thinks you are not the same conservative guy that he thought. . . . Your boss is like, do I really want to put my black associate there [in front of clients], or should I take my white analyst and put them there because at least they have some type of commonalities.

Darryl brands his colleagues and superiors as "conservative." Consequently, he believes that they are inclined to believe that his white peers, even if they have less work experience, are naturally a "better fit" for engaging with prospective clients because it is assumed that they share the clients' cultural tastes, sensibilities, and leisure pursuits. As Darryl puts it, they "all went to the same academies and play at the same golf tournaments." What Darryl references here is the idea that members of the white corporate elite often have well-established social bonds due to their participation in leisure and socializing institutions such as boarding schools and country clubs. Common institutional and organizational connections, combined with shared leisure activities (for example, golf), facilitate social solidarity and the development of shared values and worldviews.[18] Being black, Darryl faces the undue burden of demonstrating that he, too, can fit in.

Darryl hopes that his presentation of self will render whites' prejudiced and pejorative views of black men less salient. Analyzing how he strategically engages in consumption provides insight into how he works to overcome social barriers levied as a consequence of cultural racism. As opposed to explicit forms of racism, cultural racism subtly promotes racial hierarchies, based on the idea that blacks maintain distinct and often problematic cultural practices.[19] Through the lens of cultural racism, racial inequality is justified due to cultural deficits racial minorities are imagined to maintain.[20] Drawing on arguments that emphasize cultural differences, whites are able to reframe racist claims about blacks in ways that may not explicitly call out race.[21] Modern forms of racism function subtly as symbolic minefields, requiring middle-class blacks to recognize the often coded rhetoric and to adopt strategies to negate the underlying racial stereotypes that they face. Many, like Darryl, do so in part through their consumption. Darryl quite consciously manages his appearance at work, always wearing a blazer and tie even though his workplace does not require it. He does so to make visible that he knows how to play by the majority's rules.

During the workweek, Darryl does what he has to do to show that he understands the conservative culture of his workplace, but he maintains his love for black culture and displays his cultural appreciation through his work as a DJ on the weekends. The ability to judge the types of cultural knowledge and practices that are valued in particular contexts and adjust accordingly is a characteristic skill among the black middle-class participants in my study. Given the demands of cultural conformity in privileged places and the rise of cultural racism, it may very well be a skill that all non-white professionals must maintain.

Culture is often deployed strategically to respond to the demands of different social circumstances. Sociologist Prudence Carter contends that the concept of cultural flexibility refers to the cultural skills required to operate in multiple and distinct social and cultural settings.[22] Research demonstrates that people of all races possess faculties for cross-cultural participation, and different social contexts can promote or constrain the development and deployment of cultural flexibility.[23] Sociologist Shamus Khan argues that *ease* in navigating social spaces, a unique class privilege, is increasingly a defining characteristic of the American elite.[24] He argues that this ability is procured in and rewarded by social experiences in elite circles and institutions and is embodied in the way members of the elite carry themselves. Thus whites, too, may develop a capacity for cultural flexibility, particularly when faced with the demands of straddling divergent social worlds. But what makes the modern black middle class unique is the *ease* with which they can meet the cultural requirements of racially divergent social spaces. Their cultural repertoires frequently reflect racially diverse sensibilities, yet knowing when to engage or disengage their black cultural capital, and recognizing when knowledge of dominant culture is most advantageously displayed, is a skill unto itself.

Renee, a 32-year-old digital marketing manager, realizes that she has developed an ability to go between social worlds: "Having diverse experiences growing up, I mean, I know how to play the Corporate America game. I know how to blend in. I know what to say and what not to do." Renee's mother made sure that, throughout her childhood, Renee had experiences across the race and class spectrum, because, according to Renee, "she wanted me to just have different friends from different backgrounds." She grew up in the suburbs, but throughout her childhood, she attended a church in the inner-city neighborhood where her mom was raised. Renee had experiences that affirmed her racial identity and sense of black pride. She describes a program at her church that she participated in for teenagers transitioning to adulthood: it taught them lessons about "being an adult, being a black woman, celebrating your culture." She went to summer camp at the "YMCA in the hood." She went to an all-black, Baptist elementary school, then to a majority white, private middle school. She perceives that these early experiences have helped her to feel at *ease*, to "blend in" when in majority white corporate settings. A Florida A&M (FAMU) graduate and a member of the Delta Sigma Theta Sorority and the Urban League, she also feels at *ease* in settings with other blacks, particularly those who share her class status. Today, Renee continues navigating both same-race spaces and contexts where she is the only black person.

Twenty-nine-year-old Damon, a legal associate and New York native with West Indian roots, maintains both a great deal of black pride and the valuable skill of engaging in a range of other contexts. "I'm black. I'm very proud of that. I feel like it gives me actually an advantage, more so than a disadvantage. I feel like I can maneuver in worlds or in places, where others can't." He continues, "I've seen upper echelons of both societies, white, black, whatever, Spanish, and I feel like I know how to navigate both extremes. I could talk to the rich. I could talk to the poor. I talk to black, white, Spanish, whatever, and I'm accepted." Damon persuasively argues that he is capable of comfortably interacting with people across racial and class lines, and he does not believe this conflicts in any way with his sense of black pride. Also, it is important to note that his ethnic background does not supersede his racial pride, but rather they operate in tandem, facilitated in part by the fact that he sees being black as an advantage.

For Vanessa, a 29-year-old independent consultant, success for black professionals is possible only if they know how to "play the game." As she ardently declares, "It is very important to play by the rules of the game until you can write the rules of the game. You have to play by the rules until you make the rules." Vanessa believes that strategically adopting or adapting cultural displays is key: in some settings this means demonstrating cultural similarity in terms of class; in other settings it means demonstrating cultural similarity in terms of race. Like so many others, Vanessa is conscious of the cultural maneuvering that she performs. Cultural flexibility reflects pragmatism and an ability to work within the rules of a society where racism and anti-black bias is pervasive.

Black privilege, rather than being a sense of entitlement to unearned benefits, is a hard-earned ability to maintain a familiarity and intimacy with black cultural practices and institutions—black cultural capital—and also an ability to realize when black cultural capital is not valued. The challenge middle-class blacks face of having to forever evaluate social contexts to determine which circumstances might require them to "tone down" their blackness[25] and when they might be unapologetically black exemplifies the truncated nature of their privilege.

Consumption and the Manifestation of Black Privilege

Middle-class blacks' quotidian exposure to diverse social contexts, including elite white settings and same-race social spaces, as well as their social class and familial background, life experiences, social networks, and institutional connections provide them with opportunities to cultivate their black privilege. However, their *strategic* consumption is also key to the manifestation of black privilege.

Tasha feels the most pervasive stereotype she encounters is that she is poor or has been raised by a single mother on welfare in the "hood," but this could not be further from the truth. As she proudly—yet nonchalantly—reveals, "I was raised in a two-parent home on a cul-de-sac. My parents are educated and professional." Growing up in the suburbs and attending a majority white, private elementary school did not mean Tasha felt any the less black. Instead, Tasha concedes, attending a Montessori school where she was "consistently the only black child, if not in my class, in the school" taught her an important lesson. She realized early on that her home life diverged culturally from that of her white classmates because it was infused with the consumption of black culture. As she explains, "I knew that I was black and I knew that I was different." Even in the ride home from school each day, this cultural difference in preferences, tastes, and racial sensibilities was evident. As she puts it, "We're not about to go listen to rock and roll. We're putting on a hip-hop station. We listen to Power 99. When we get home we watch *Martin*." Tasha relishes the fact that growing up, her home life, from the radio station to the TV shows that she and her family enjoyed, was chock full of black culture. For members of the black middle class, like Tasha and Brittany, growing up meant living in both black and white worlds. As is true for many other middle-class blacks, their childhoods included both predominantly white and majority black settings, and each served as a training ground where they established and developed their intra-racial and intercultural competences, both their black cultural capital and cultural flexibility.

Darryl, Tasha, and Brittany all serve as examples of how middle-class blacks' consumptive decisions and cultural displays are rooted in race, rooted in class, and rooted in their contestation of cultural racism. Consumption practices critically facilitated their gaining entry to and their sustained social acceptance in the diverse social and cultural contexts they often move across and between. Consumption also provides middle-class blacks with an important means of contesting the often-invisible, yet virulent forms of modern racism. As this book unfolds, through the stories of the study participants, I illustrate how race and class together inform the consumption practices and preferences of those who are black and privileged.

The Study

The study I conducted examines the experiences of college-educated blacks living and working in the New York City area. Between 2009 and 2014 I conducted in-person interviews with fifty-four middle-class blacks. During our conversations, I asked them about their racial identity, everyday experiences of race, and consumption preferences and practices. Most interviews lasted about two hours, and my interview questions were structured around investigating their experiences and consumption as displayed in their workplaces, neighborhoods, and sites of leisure, including restaurants, retail stores, and entertainment venues.

To qualify to participate in this study respondents had to self-identify as black, be college educated, and be between the ages of 25 and 50 (adults of working age before their peak earning years). The reader will be introduced throughout to study participants, but may find the Appendix in the back of the book helpful for its outline of the key attributes of each respondent.

My respondents see themselves as black and would be categorized by others in the United States as black. Throughout this book, I use the term *black*, rather than *African American*, because black is an inclusive term that encompasses those whose racial lineage may be mixed or ethnic heritage diverse. Although defining themselves as black and categorized as such by others, there is intra-racial diversity in the sample. Three respondents are racially mixed: Crystal, whose mother is African American and whose father is white; Isaiah, whose father is Puerto Rican and whose mother is African American; and Janae, whose mother is an Ethiopian immigrant and whose father is white. Reflecting New York's ethnic diversity, roughly one-third of the participants are the children of immigrants; fourteen have parents from the Caribbean; and six have parents from African nations, including two who are the products of inter-ethnic black unions (Darryl, whose father is Ghanaian and mother is African American, and Jasmine, whose father is Jamaican and mother Nigerian). All were raised in the United States, and all but two were born here. Roughly half grew up outside the New York area. As New York has a way of drawing people from all across the country, among those not originally from New York were respondents from a wide range of places including Atlanta, Georgia; Detroit, Michigan; Fort Polk, Louisiana; Portland, Oregon; San Francisco, California; and St. Louis, Missouri.

The ethnic variation among blacks in the study is both reflective of national trends and helpful in uncovering the significance each respondent attached to their racial identity as opposed to their ethnic identity. Even with the ethnic variation in the sample, there is a great deal of convergence in terms of their experiences, attitudes, and cultural consumption. Many knew ethnic-specific cultural traditions and preferences—for example, respondents of Jamaican descent often reported that they listened to reggae and dancehall music—but they also loved Jay-Z. I found little evidence of disavowing connections to multigenerational, native-born African Americans. Often those with immigrant parents perceived blacks across the diaspora as having cultural commonalities and a shared heritage and cultural traditions. This coming together of blacks who varied in their ethnic backgrounds was evident throughout the study. Furthermore, those who were multigenerational, native-born African Americans did not draw rigid cultural boundaries or separate themselves or see themselves as wholly dissimilar from blacks of different ethnic backgrounds. There was a mutual recognition and valuing of diasporic black culture.

Middle-class status was defined by level of education. All the respondents had at least a four-year college degree, and roughly a quarter had advanced degrees. Defining class status by level of education and occupation is consistent with research that indicates cultural consumption is tied more closely to educational and occupational attainment than to income.[26] Eighty percent of those in my study self-identified as middle class.

A majority of participants in my study were millennials who came of age many years after the civil rights movement. Focusing on this younger demographic of blacks was advantageous, as research indicates that single-adult households make up a significant fraction of the black middle class.[27]

Additionally, narrowing the scope of the study by limiting the range of participants' ages reduced variation in their financial priorities, as younger adults are freer to enact their personal preferences (and less likely to be affected by concerns regarding spouses or children). Most participants were unmarried and had no children, so concerns regarding neighborhood services such as public schools were not salient. The mean and median age was 29.

As a researcher studying middle-class blacks, I occupied the position of an insider. My complexion is light to medium brown, and my phenotypical features are readily perceived as black. Having grown up in a two-parent, middle-class home, attending both a majority black elementary school and an elite, majority white preparatory school, and earning degrees from two Ivy League institutions, my personal experiences and educational background made me recognizable as a bona fide member of the black middle class. I lived in central Harlem during the collection of this data and maintained connections to black organizations, like my sorority, Delta Sigma Theta. I frequented black social events, black churches, and black salons, and I was immersed in public settings frequented by middle-class blacks, including nightclubs, restaurants, and museums.

There were advantages to my insider status, regarding both my race and class background. My rapport with respondents was easy, and our conversations were often like those between old college friends. Almost all of the people I interviewed were remarkably candid, and comfortable reliving details of their personal lives and their beliefs. With little hesitation, they told me about their experiences, views, and opinions. At times, I had to probe and ask for explanations about things they assumed I would "know." I often asked clarifying questions to get respondents to elaborate, to explain in their own words. Now, as a tenure-track professor and the only black faculty member in my department, I share the experience of navigating a majority white workplace. I also share the experience of routinely engaging black social spaces, whether that space is my neighborhood or a black-owned business. Indeed, my own position also shaped the types of questions that I asked and the ways I interpreted participants' responses.

New York, New York

New York City was a unique but ideal site for my study. With over two million blacks, it has, in absolute numbers, the largest black population of any city in the United States, and that population includes a large black middle class. Out of all the blacks in New York City who are 25 and older, 24.1 percent have college degrees. More college-educated blacks live in New York than in any other metro area; in fact, 8.4 percent of all college-educated blacks in the United States live in New York.[28] (See Table 1 for general statistics for college-educated blacks in the U.S.)

Opportunities to act as agents, producers, and consumers of culture are vast in New York, which serves as a center for cultural industries including fashion, entertainment, and media. Black New Yorkers are pioneers in cultural trends and instrumental in the development of popular culture.[29] In 2015, New York also boasted more African American–owned firms (250,890) than any other city in the country.[30]

As others have argued, the New York City area is also a particularly informative site in which to investigate race relations and the social salience

TABLE 1. The Population of Black College Graduates (25 and older) in Select Major U.S. Cities, 2013–2017 (American Community Survey [ACS] 5-Year Estimates)

	Black Population	Black College Graduates	Percentage of All Blacks Who Are College Graduates
New York, NY	3,836,411	613,054	16.00
Washington, DC	2,426,258	483,504	20.00
Atlanta, GA	2,019,969	351,770	17.41
Chicago, IL	1,631,543	224,428	13.80
Los Angeles, CA	1,224,682	204,426	16.70
Houston, TX	1,174,899	189,526	16.20
Dallas, TX	1,119,280	176,207	15.70
Philadelphia, PA	1,410,294	173,866	12.32
Detroit, MI	1,092,184	119,263	10.90

SOURCE: U.S. Census Bureau, 2013–2017 ACS 5-Year Estimates. The data reported are for the combined statistical areas (CSAs) for all cities, including New York–Newark, NY-NJ-CT-PA CSA; Atlanta-Athens–Clarke County–Sandy Springs, GA CSA; Chicago-Naperville, IL-IN-WI CSA; Houston–The Woodlands, TX CSA; Dallas–Fort Worth, TX-OK CSA; Los Angeles–Long Beach, CA CSA; Detroit-Warren–Ann Arbor, MI CSA; Philadelphia-Reading-Camden, PA-NJ-DE-MD CSA; Memphis–Forrest City, TN-MS-AR CSA; Washington-Baltimore-Arlington, DC-MD-VA-WV-PA CSA.

and significance of race. For instance, sociologists John Logan and Richard Alba argue that New York is a particularly well-positioned site because, demographically, it maintains both old and new social cleavages along racial lines.[31] In addition to its racial and ethnic diversity, racial residential segregation persists at high levels in New York. The *exposure index*, a measure of residential segregation that indicates the level of exposure of one group to another (and conversely, their isolation from each other), is 61 percent for the New York metropolitan area. This means that most blacks in this area live in neighborhoods with sizable black populations. The black-white *dissimilarity index* (another metric for accessing a city's level of segregation), which measures the percentage of a group's population that would have to move for each neighborhood to have the same proportion of that group as is found in the metropolitan area overall, was 78 percent in 2010. New York's black-white dissimilarity score qualifies it as the second most segregated large metropolitan area in the country.[32]

New York also offers a wide range of black social spaces, where black cultural capital can be cultivated and displayed. In many ways, historically and today, New York is a cultural mecca of black American life and is home to many significant, if not iconic, black cultural institutions, such as the Apollo Theater, the Studio Museum, and the Schomburg Center for Research in Black Culture. New York is an ideal site, with relevant attributes to explore and elaborate the theoretical concept of black privilege; however, it is also a unique site. The central goal of this book is to expound on the concept of black privilege as revealed in my study, which speaks to wider trends that are represented in the New York sample but are certainly not unique to it.

In the forthcoming chapters, the concept of black privilege is outlined alongside stories of respondents' experiences and cultural displays in the places where they live, work, and play. They are, by necessity, culturally strategic actors, always considering how they will be perceived and how those perceptions might threaten or enhance their social and economic well-being. At the same time, they are working to maintain and preserve a sense of dignity and agency, and aiming to be unapologetically black. Throughout, we see that common among the black middle class is a desire to consume goods and engage in practices associated with living a middle-class lifestyle as well as goods and cultural practices associated with their race. They maintain a desire to interact with black people, support black institutions, and patronize black businesses.

In the following chapter, Chapter Two, I describe the key characteristics of the modern black middle class. I provide an overview of the historical context important for its emergence and outline the demographic attributes that separate its members from middle-class blacks of the past. In Chapter Three, I hone in on the role of cultural consumption in everyday life, focusing particularly on how consumption facilitates black cultural capital and aids middle-class blacks in their quest to be unapologetically black. I demonstrate that black cultural capital constitutes a critical building block of their racial identity and allows them to maintain a distinct set of situationally deployed cultural practices and preferences.

Starting with Chapter Four, I begin to explore the places and spaces that encompass the study participants' daily lives. The central argument of this chapter concerns how neighborhoods provide their residents with a variety of services and amenities, as well as interactions and varied cultural contexts. In Chapter Five, we move to the participants' workplaces, examining how middle-class blacks adapt their cultural consumption preferences to the racial contexts of their jobs. Chapter Six examines middle-class blacks' experiences with navigating leisure settings and the marketplace. These are comparatively low-stakes settings, in which respondents' main objective is to relax and to have a good time, but even there, middle-class blacks report encountering anti-black bias and stereotypes. The same is true for restaurants and nightclubs. Black social spaces offer middle-class blacks a respite, where they can freely celebrate their black cultural tastes and proclivities.

Chapter Seven investigates how middle-class blacks, as consumers, engage in the market in ways that are informed by racialized ideologies. More specifically, it demonstrates that middle-class blacks see their collective purchasing power as a tool that can be wielded to improve the lot of the race. In the last analytic chapter, Chapter Eight, I consider middle-class blacks' aspirational consumption. This chapter depicts blacks' collective financial imagination, defying the idea that middle-class blacks are excessively materialistic as a means of distancing themselves from the black poor. Instead, I demonstrate how their *collective* orientation is maintained and revealed in their aspirational consumption.

A great deal has been written about the ways that culture reinforces and perpetuates social inequality, yet little has been written about the cultural skills necessary to transcend boundaries while simultaneously maintaining practices that connect one to a racial collective. The economically advantaged blacks in my study almost always aim to be unapologetically black. They are proud to be black, perceiving blacks as culturally distinct, and valuing the ways that black culture separates them from out-group members. Their blackness need not be in conflict with their socioeconomic privilege. The cumulative experiences of middle-class black New Yorkers, as they navigate the social settings that encompass their everyday lives, reveal that they deploy consumption as a cultural tool to manage the challenges and opportunities that arise when one is both black *and* middle class.

The Emergence of a Modern Black Middle Class

2

THE MODERN BLACK MIDDLE CLASS is composed of a new generation of blacks, the beneficiaries of the lasting legacy of the civil rights movement and the cultural transformation brought about by the Black Power movement. Some blacks driving part of the expansion of the modern black middle class come from humble backgrounds, and their experience of being middle class entails upward mobility. Others have been born to college-educated parents who participated in and gained opportunities provided by the victories of the civil rights movement. Both groups have directly and indirectly benefited from the political and economic inroads made by blacks during the civil rights era, as well as the black cultural renaissances of the twentieth century. A cultural awakening and its reverberations have resulted in racial pride permeating throughout the black middle class. That is, unwavering declarations of black pride and calls for recognition have become commonplace. As a consequence of the cultural shift and realignment of attitudes among blacks, a new normal has emerged. Members of this new generation of modern middle-class blacks simultaneously aspire to attain economic prosperity and the goods and lifestyles associated with making it in the United States and also to engage in cultural practices that reflect their race. The consensus is that to get ahead, individuals should never abandon their racial affinities, even if at times those affinities must be strategically (and momentarily) disengaged. Modern middle-class blacks do not see cultural attitudes and displays—whether they are new or long-standing practices and traditions unique to blacks—as being in conflict with their socioeconomic privilege. Instead, they experience black privilege.

The late 1960s were particularly transformative years, witnessing a notable cultural shift among blacks toward a fierce public expression of black pride.[1] The Black Power era resulted in various organizations and movements that called for political, social, and cultural transformation with the goal of liberating blacks from historically oppressive conditions.[2] Part of the legacy of the Black Power era resulted from the intensification of efforts to inspire cultural and racial pride—for blacks to celebrate their complexion and physical features and their cultural heritage and traditions.[3] It also encouraged blacks to eliminate any vestiges of internalized claims of cultural inferiority and promoted knowledge of self. It built on earlier cultural movements and traditions, including the New Negro movement of the 1920s, which also called for black pride and a collective racial consciousness.[4] The Black Power movement grew, and illustrated a growing appetite to be black unashamedly in public arenas.

Efforts to recognize and acknowledge the value and significant contribution of black people and black culture were realized and institutionalized on many fronts during this period. The black arts movement helped to establish museums and other institutional spaces where black culture and cultural works were celebrated. Especially in the late 1960s, museums dedicated to the recognition and display of African American history, culture, and art opened, exhibiting the rich, though often ignored, heritage of black people across the diaspora. Then and now, middle- and upper-class blacks have been the critical champions of such cultural institutions, serving as founders and fundraisers and maintaining active financial and philanthropic support.[5]

Both traditionally white colleges and universities and historically black colleges and universities (HBCUs) played critical roles in generating successive cohorts of middle-class blacks. Prior to the passage of civil rights reforms, HBCUs were the institutions primarily responsible for educating and creating a class of black professionals. A majority of black doctors, dentists, lawyers, and teachers were educated at HBCUs. From the late 1960s to the late 1970s, the number of blacks enrolled in college increased dramatically. In part, this was due to availability of government aid, which provided critical financial resources to pursue a college education.[6]

Many predominantly white institutions experienced profound changes in the late 1960s, in terms of both their demographic makeup, with the increased presence of black students, and also their curricular shifts as they established black studies departments. In this period, many prestigious, predominantly white colleges would experience a significant increase in the number of black students, in part as a consequence of the legal victories of the civil rights movement.[7] In 1960, Stanford University had two black students in the entering freshman class, but by 1970, there were 256 black students enrolled.[8] Harvard's class of 1969 had more black students than any prior class in the school's history.[9] At the University of Pennsylvania, the 1969 freshman class was 8 percent black, compared to only 1 percent just four years prior.[10] The significant increase in the size of the black student population, both at predominantly white institutions and HBCUs, resulted in a shift in the institutional space, driven in part by black students' demands that colleges begin to acknowledge, systematically study, and embrace blacks' heritage and culture.[11] Student protests called for the creation of black studies departments, dedicated to the examination of black history, culture, and social life, spread across college campuses around the country.[12] Between 1968 and 1971, black studies programs, departments, and institutes were established at over 500 college and university campuses.[13]

As the 1960s marched into the 1970s, college-educated blacks were able to secure positions in professional settings, signaling their entrance into the economic mainstream.[14] Movement into white-collar jobs was a departure from the economic position of the black middle classes of the past, whose status was often dependent on their role in providing professional services within the black community.[15] The 1964 Civil Rights Act led to a hard-won and dramatic opening of opportunities in professional and managerial positions from which blacks had previously been excluded.[16] As a consequence, there was an 80 percent increase in the number of blacks in white-collar jobs between 1960 and 1970.[17] Sociologist Sharon Collins draws a direct line from the black discontent and social upheaval of the 1960s to the enlargement of the black middle class in the 1970s.[18] Policies, including affirmative action, helped to fuel the growth of a new black professional class.[19]

In addition to access to new employment opportunities, the newly emergent black middle class also experienced a transformed public and commercial sphere. As a consequence of the 1964 Civil Rights Act, they now had access to sites of consumption that they were previously barred from.[20]

Many Generation Xers (those born in the period from the early 1960s to the early 1980s) and Millennials (those born from the early 1980s to mid-1990s) have parents who were among the "new black middle class," a cohort of college-educated blacks who were the first to take advantage of newly opened educational and professional opportunities, and to experience new realities available to them as consumers.[21] Modern middle-class blacks are also the beneficiaries of a cultural transformation that occurred as a consequence of the Black Power movement. A central objective of the Black Power movement was to promote black liberalization and empowerment, and this required the celebration and recognition of the value and beauty of blacks' racial and cultural distinctiveness.[22] For members of the contemporary black middle class, the idea that blacks' cultural heritage and their racial and cultural distinction should be celebrated has become increasingly normalized. They have grown up amid cultural and social organizations, and in social circles where they encountered widespread positive proclamations about the value and beauty of black culture and have often been taught to be knowledgeable about and embrace their race and heritage. Now, nearly fifty years later, a modern black middle class has emerged, and ideas about the value and utility of black culture, for many, are deeply infused in their styles of life.

The Modern Black Middle Class

Black privilege results from having economic resources in addition to the cultural tools and repertoires that broadcast a specific social position within the social hierarchies of both race and class. Blacks' access to economic resources is determined by their income and occupation. In grappling with questions of how race and class together impact the cultural consumption of members of the black middle class, it is helpful to situate them demographically in the industries where they work and the cities where they live, as well as to examine their core financial characteristics.

Scholars have used various criteria to determine who qualifies as a member of the black middle class. My study uses the attainment of a college degree as the threshold of qualification. Nearly all the blacks interviewed for my study are professionals with moderate to well-paying jobs, most earning between $50,000 and $100,000 a year. Despite the range of incomes, their cultural tastes and lifestyles are quite similar, and frequently, social and cultural factors, including their ideological beliefs and black cultural capital, together with their economic resources motivate their cultural consumption.

There are several reasons for using education as a criterion to determine membership in the black middle class. Cultural theorists have articulated the connection between level of education and cultural capital,[23] but this criterion is also consistent with a Weberian distinction between class and status. Max Weber argues that status is related to and displayed by a person's "styles of life" and worldviews; in contrast, a person's economic resources alone determine his or her class position.[24] That is, class and status are highly related, but they convey distinct aspects of social position and have different implications for social inequality. When it comes to what people consume, level of education is an important indicator of their cultural tastes: even more than income, education is correlated with patterns of consumption.[25] And because my study examines culture and consumption—ideological values, tastes, worldviews, preferences and practices—it is appropriate to adopt level of education, rather than financial characteristics, such as income or wealth, in the determination of respondents' class status. This is not to decry the importance of economic factors like income or wealth in class assignment or identification, but to acknowledge that financial characteristics alone do not drive consumption.

Furthermore, while economic inequalities are objectively measurable, status inequalities are often culturally defined. Our ideas and assessments of the social status of different types of people or groups reflects deeply held cultural beliefs about who is worthy of respect, social esteem, and honor.[26] Middle-class blacks' position in both race and class hierarchies makes them a group with a distinct social status, as assessments of their worth align to both their racial and class status.

Having a college degree dramatically improves blacks' life chances, while also conditioning their cultural tastes and consumption. There has been a tremendous growth of the black middle class since the passage of civil rights laws that barred explicit forms of racial discrimination. While only 3 percent of all blacks in the United States aged 25 or older had four or more years of college in 1960,[27] by 1992, 15.9 percent of blacks aged 25 or older had earned a bachelor's degree or higher.[28] In 2018, 31.2 percent had. In New York, 28.5 percent of blacks have some college or an associate's degree, and another 24.5 percent have at least a bachelor's degree (see Table 2).

Along with the increase in the proportion of blacks with college degrees, the number of blacks in professional occupations has steadily increased since the early 1980s, and the gap between the percentages of middle-class blacks and whites in various occupational categories has slowly been narrowing.[29] While a college education is increasingly necessary to enter into the professional class, it is also important to recognize that the economic returns on education are still

TABLE 2. Educational Attainment by Race, New York, NY, 2013–2017 (ACS 5-Year Estimates)

	WHITES		BLACKS	
	Total	Percentage	Total	Percentage
Less than high school diploma	530,806	10.1	289,619	16.5
High school graduate (includes equivalency)	1,196,967	22.8	533,533	30.4
Some college or associate's degree	1,114,914	21.2	500,095	28.5
Bachelor's degree or higher	2,406,645	45.9	430,234	24.5
Total	5,249,332		1,753,481	

Data reported are for the New York–Newark, NY-NJ-CT-PA combined statistical area (CSA).

SOURCE: U.S. Census Bureau, 2013–2017 ACS 5-Year Estimates. Sex by Educational Attainment for the Population 25 Years and Over (White Alone) and (Black or African American Alone), 2013–2017 American Community Survey 5-Year Estimates.

lower for middle-class blacks than they are for whites with similar credentials. This is particularly true for black men compared to white men.[30] Nonetheless, having a college degree is correlated with higher earnings over the life course, and it is a highly influential determinant of cultural tastes and preferences.

There are also important limitations to consider when using income alone as a criterion for defining class status among blacks. Doing so can prove restrictive because it can result in a narrower projection of who is counted as middle class, particularly as the black middle class is bottom heavy compared to the white middle class. However, a discussion of the general economic characteristics of the black middle class is warranted, given that these characteristics impact consumption. Consistent with sociologist Karyn Lacy's income categorization of the black middle-class, which separates that class into three income categories—a lower-middle-class group (individuals earning between $30k and $49k per year), a "core" group (individuals with annual incomes of $50k to $99k), and an "elite" group (individuals earning at least $100k a year)—most blacks in New York fall into the middle of the middle class (see Table 3).[31] In the New York metropolitan area, the lower-middle class represents 17.7 percent of the total black population, the core category consists of 27.6 percent of the city's total black population, and the elite category consists of 21.1 percent of the total black population. Separating out the black middle-class, the lower-middle class consists of 26.6 percent of the black middle-class and the core consists of 41.6 percent of the black middle-class. Those in the elite category in New York make up nearly one-third of the black middle-class, with 31.7 percent. The participants in my study skewed toward the higher end of the income spectrum within the black community. Their incomes place them solidly in the middle class if divided by income; most are above the black lower-middle class. Among all respondents, twenty-nine fall into the core middle-class category, and thirteen are among the high-earning elite.

Another important financial characteristic to consider when examining the lifestyles and life chances of the black middle class is wealth. Unlike income, wealth not only influences a person's livelihood and quality of life but can also

TABLE 3. Black and White Populations, by Income, New York, NY, 2013–2017

	WHITES		BLACKS	
Annual Income	Percentage of White Population	Percentage of White Middle-Class Population	Percentage of Black Population	Percentage of Black Middle-Class Population
< $30,000k	18.7	—	33.7	—
$30,000–$49,999 (Lower-middle class)	12.6	15.5	17.7	26.6
$50,000–$99,999 (Middle class)	26.6	32.7	27.6	41.6
$100,000 and above (Upper-middle class)	42.1	51.8	21.1	31.7

Data reported are for the New York–Newark, NY-NJ-CT-PA combined statistical area (CSA).
Class categories adopted from Lacy's *Blue Chip Black: Race, Class, Status in the New Black Middle Class*.

SOURCE: U.S. Census Bureau, 2013–2017 American Community Survey 5-Year Estimates.

support continued consumption during disruptions in income and prevent downward mobility.[32] If *wealth* were used as a central criterion for middle-class status among blacks, few would make the cut. Racial wealth disparities in the United States are steep and less variable over time compared to income. Black households across the board possess only a fraction of the wealth held by comparable white households,[33] and blacks tend to inherit small, if any, bequests.[34] While the median net wealth for white families in 2016 was $171,000, the comparable figure for black families was $17,000.[35] The racial wealth gap in 1962, before the passage of Civil Rights Act in 1964, was nearly the same as it is over fifty years later in 2016.[36]

Middle-class blacks, like all blacks, have little wealth to fall back on during times of economic instability. In 2005, more than 60 percent of black families had zero or negative assets, compared to 25 percent of whites.[37] The crash of the housing market that occurred between 2007 and 2009, was devastating to black wealth, and the negative impact of the Great Recession was felt more heavily among college-educated blacks. By 2009, the racial wealth gap between white households and black households, with median white wealth being twenty times median black wealth, was the greatest it had been in the most recent twenty-five years.[38] Research from the Federal Reserve Bank of St. Louis found that between 1992 and 2013, the wealth of college-educated whites increased by 86 percent, while the wealth of college-educated blacks fell by 56 percent.[39]

Despite the dreariness of the statistics on black wealth holdings, nearly all of my respondents were optimistic about their current and future financial prospects, and only a few reported being laid off or adversely impacted by the financial crisis. This aligns with findings from a 2015–2016 Prudential Financial study that more than half of the blacks surveyed felt more secure at the time of the survey than five years earlier, and 58 percent thought that the next generation would be better off financially.[40] Blacks' financial optimism supports the idea that wealth is not critical to shaping how they *think* about their status as members of the middle class, although asset poverty might considerably impact many outcomes.

Some scholars argue that a critical distinction between the black middle class and the white middle class is the degree of economic status fluctuation: that is, the likelihood of experiencing periods of economic difficulty. It is not unusual for college-educated blacks to have experienced some financial precarity during their lives. Economic fragility is a more prominent feature of black middle class life. Even blacks from wealthy families experience higher rates of downward mobility than comparable whites.[41] Additionally, middle-class blacks are more likely than comparable whites to have ties to family members, siblings, and parents living in poverty.[42] This connection to intimate others who are less well-off is consequential: compared to whites, middle-income blacks are more likely to be providing informal financial assistance to friends and family members.[43] They are also less likely to benefit from family wealth; unsurprisingly a sizeable portion of the black-white wealth gap is attributable to differences in familial network resources.[44] Familial ties affect middle-class blacks' ability to maintain their economic status. When they benefit from inter-generational wealth, their familial connections may provide them access to re-sources, but when they do not, which is most often the case, their social ties may require them to provide financial assistance.[45]

The scale of the economic resources at a person's disposal is an important factor shaping consumption, but middle-class blacks' relative economic posi-tion—having greater economic resources at their disposal than working-class or poor blacks, but fewer resources than similarly positioned whites—shapes their position on both race and class hierarchies. For example, a person earning $65,000 in 2014 was among the top 18 percent of all income-earning Americans, but in the top 10 percent of income-earning *black* Americans. Thus, blacks' subjective view of their class status is affected by which reference group they consider. If a middle-class black person's social network and relations are pri-marily black and they perceive and determine their status primarily by com-paring themselves with other blacks, then they will likely see themselves as more squarely middle class.

Similarly, occupational prestige, which is typically associated with class sta-tus, may be a less useful metric when applied to blacks, in part because pres-tigious occupations have been, historically, off-limits to blacks. Consequently, whites might consider certain occupations to be of low social rank, but the same positions might be considered respectable among blacks.[46] When con-sidering how middle-class blacks evaluate their own class status, financial resources and occupation are not sufficient determinants alone of their subjec-tive definitions of their class standing. Income and wealth, while significant predictors of blacks' well-being, may provide only limited insight about how blacks perceive themselves in terms of status. They may also be limited in what they reveal about middle-class blacks' tastes and preferences as consumers. For blacks, combining education and income yields the best predictor of their like-lihood of self-identifying as middle-class.[47]

Whether they have a little bit or a lot of money, both in the popular press and in scholarly work, blacks are frequently and prominently painted as conspicuous consumers. Both poor and middle-class blacks' consumption has been described as driven by a desire, or even a fetish, for status-enhancing goods. The pejorative yet pervasive characterization of blacks as status-oriented, conspicuous consumers ignores the complexities driving blacks' consumption. E. Franklin Frazier, in his treatise *The Black Bourgeois*, famously argued that "conspicuous consumption" was pronounced among a newly emerging, pre–civil rights era, black middle class.[48] Focusing only on middle-class blacks' desire for and acquisition of high-status goods, such as designer handbags or expensive footwear, insufficiently addresses the creative, expressive, and experiential function of their consumption, while also underplaying their *strategic* use of consumption. It ignores how blacks' consumption may be ideologically informed or oriented toward collaborative and collective rather than individualistic and competitive ends. It places a great deal of emphasis on the status signified by the consumption of particular cultural objects while ignoring the context in which goods are used, even though that context, of course, influences the perception of the goods and their possessor. We need a more expansive approach to address both the complexities of the contextual determinants shaping the meaning attached to consumption objects and the multiplicity of drivers that influence middle-class blacks' consumption.

Consumption and the Modern Black Middle Class

For members of the modern black middle class, consumption is a means to indulge their middle-class sensibilities and to display their personal style and taste. Scholars have argued that for all people, spending money—to purchase physical objects and experiences—can be a medium for pleasure, a form of leisure, and an indicator of prosperity.[49] So it is not surprising that this is true also for middle-class blacks, like Tasha and Darryl, who love to shop. Fashion is fun for them. They also have given a lot of thought to their style and self-presentation, not just for work but in relaxed settings and in the places they venture to for entertainment and amusement. Consumption offers them a way to deftly construct an image of who they are and to express their personalities.

When Tasha buys a designer handbag or pair of expensive shoes, she does so because owning them makes her feel good, and because these are things that define for her what being middle class means. For many middle-class blacks in my study, their consumption is illustrative of their middle-class taste and sensibilities; it allows them to situate themselves on status hierarchies.

Their consumption also facilitates their acquisition and display of black cultural capital. Their black cultural capital is put to use when they seek out meaningful social exchanges with other blacks—family, friends, and strangers. Whether dining together at restaurants, venturing to nightclubs, or returning week after week to the well-worn pews of their churches, having black cultural capital connects them to other blacks and to a larger racial project. Their racialized ideological commitments, but also their racial identity, importantly shapes the way they think about the power that accompanies their consumptive choices. This book builds on conversations about how ideological commitments promoting racial pride and racial uplift are displayed in a range of settings and frequently incorporated into a variety of consumption practices.[50] There are financial implications to study participants' ideological commitments. Even in their imagined future consumption, they demonstrate a commitment to racial uplift, illustrating their awareness that blacks' linked fate shapes more than just their political behavior, it also informs their consumption.[51] Many middle-class blacks in my study share in the belief that buying black—patronizing black entrepreneurs and artisans—is a critical form of racial uplift, providing an avenue to demonstrate compassion toward other blacks and to display racial solidarity. For others though, importantly, the marketplace is a sphere where they feel they should be free from obligations to fellow racial group members.

There are times when middle-class blacks' consumption is not driven by ideological beliefs, concerns about racial uplift, or commitment to the collective, though it might be driven by their racial affinities. For example, when study participants describe loving to dance and preferring to go to predominantly black nightclubs to do so, their consumption and display of black cultural capital unites them to other blacks in attendance, but dancing to the latest R&B or hip-hop song in a black club is not seen as a form of racial uplift. Similarly, the fulfilling and restorative benefits of attending a black church, which one subject describes as a combination of hearing a motivational speaker and attending a family reunion, are not necessarily a reflection of a desire to demonstrate class status. In both cases, consumption is at once tied to their racial identity but also free from social obligations to their race and the restrictions imposed by racism.

Cultural consumption allows middle-class blacks to gain purchase in predominantly black social spaces and to reflect a racialized sense of self, while also facilitating the deployment of dominant—white—cultural capital. New avenues of access and opportunity have produced an increasing presence of middle-class blacks in workplaces and commercial spaces from which blacks have historically been barred. Yet having a college or professional degree and working in a prestigious field is often not enough in itself to ensure blacks' continued advancement. That advancement is often also contingent on their ability to maneuver in majority white spaces. While blacks are now increasingly visible, they often remain underrepresented numerically, and a deep evaluation of such spaces reveals that hegemonic whiteness and ideas of white normativity are often promoted.[52] White spaces are not just spaces where whites are demographically the majority, but also spaces where white cultural tastes, traditions, ideologies, and styles are promoted as normal.[53] Material rewards are often attached to the performance of practices that are illustrative of dominant—white—cultural practices and meaning systems, though such systems are implemented in ways to appear neutral.[54] Being culturally flexible is one way of maintaining treasured black cultural practices without jeopardizing professional prospects in white dominant organizations and fields where cultural similarity is expected. This is not to say that black cultural practices and displays of black cultural capital are inherently detrimental, but to note that in a large swath of organizations, institutions, and industries, black culture is believed to be of little value.

Cultural consumption is often leveraged to combat and prevent anti-black bias and to minimize racial stigma in majority white workplace settings, where black cultural capital is often devalued. In such instances, black privilege enables middle-class blacks to play up their class-based tastes and knowledge of the dominant culture. Their unique position within race and class hierarchies also requires them to anticipate and determine what racial stereotypes might be salient and need neutralizing, and this, too, is a demonstration of their black privilege.

Outside the realm of work, as middle-class blacks engage in the leisure and other activities that make up their everyday lives, they also encounter anti-black bias. Often in these public and commercial sites their material and cultural resources can provide them with ways to protest poor service, and even at times to purchase better service. Further, these deft cultural actors are attuned to the gendered nature of stereotypes that they face: recognizing and differentiating between, on the one hand, the stereotypes that are prominent for middle-class black men and, on the other hand, those prominent for middle-class black women. Thus, their use of cultural capital to combat racism can reflect the specific, gendered ways in which they have experienced anti-black bias. Their keen knowledge of and pride regarding their racial affiliation is supplemented by a fine-tuned sense of whether, when, and how to display their black cultural capital.

Living in one of the world's fashion capitals, Tasha takes pleasure in looking put-together. Tasha believes there is no better way to confront negative perceptions of blacks and black culture than to be unapologetically black and dressed fabulously. Like many other middle-class blacks in my study, she emphasizes the importance of leaving a positive and lasting first impression. She confesses that "in a place like New York, that is very image conscious, I think the way that you dress absolutely influences the way people perceive you; it influences how important they think you are." Though she encounters racial prejudice and often anticipates having to deal with anti-black bias, Tasha still lives a full life, filled with beautiful things and noteworthy experiences that she finds gratifying. Her middle-class sensibilities, just like her racial affinities, are deeply entrenched. Being middle class, Tasha enjoys certain freedoms and revelries that come with having access to economic resources, but as an active consumer, she also contends with a consumer racial hierarchy. A middle-class upbringing, academic credentials, and money to spend have done little to buffer Tasha against racism in the market. But her consumption also allows her to defy stereotypes—particularly, that black people neither can afford nor do they deserve to own luxurious things, to be served, or to partake in leisure.

Consumption functions as a tool that middle-class black people have at their disposal to gain respect and recognition in a wide range of social contexts. Navigating social spaces that diverge in racial and class composition requires that middle-class blacks build a rapport with non-blacks (who may maintain anti-black biases) as well as with other blacks (who may not share their class position), and consumption facilitates their ability to do both. In particular, when consistent with their classed taste and sensibilities, consumption critically facilitates their entry and sustained social acceptance in white spaces. Moreover, while blacks in the United States were the focus of my study, racial meanings and stereotypes are often global. When American blacks travel outside the United States, they often find they still face racial stereotypes or stigma. Additionally, blacks living in other national contexts also encounter pejorative views of black culture, whether those other contexts are the Americas, Africa, or the Caribbean. That is, on a global scale, black culture is often seen as inferior, pathological, and threatening, while white culture is viewed as modern, sophisticated, and advanced.[55] Thus, examining the conditions and dynamics in the United States that create black privilege—that is, the ways blacks, with degrees and dollars to spend, are prevented from capitalizing on all of the benefits that their status should afford them—may shed light on the utility of consumption as it is engaged in by blacks around the world.

Unapologetically Black

3

MELODY HOBSON, President of Ariel Investments and one of the most power-ful and influential women in finance, describes arriving at the decision to be "unapologetically black."[1] Employed in an industry where blacks are severely underrepresented, making up no more than 2.6 percent of top positions at three of the largest banks,[2] Hobson uses the term to describe the centrality of being black and resisting the feeling that one must contort oneself or bend over backward to accommodate a white racial and cultural ideal. Hobson's reflec-tion on the meaning and value of race in her public and private life aptly sums a recurrent theme of my interviews. For educated and economically advan-taged blacks, altogether circumventing contexts where white cultural values and practices prevail is rarely, if ever, an option. Nonetheless, the middle-class blacks in my study aimed to be unapologetically black.

Javon is in many ways the embodiment of the modern black middle class. At the age of thirty-two, he has credentials—not only is he college educated, he has two advanced degrees. He has done well at the private equity firm where he is an associate, and his financial status lets him live a lifestyle he couldn't have imagined as a kid. Javon grew up poor in Portland, Oregon. Early on, he ad-mired black political figures. Thurgood Marshall, the first black Supreme Court justice, was his idol:

> I wanted to be Thurgood Marshall. I always wanted to be an attorney. I wanted to be
> a member of the Supreme Court because I thought that he, other than Dr. King, had

probably been the most impactful person in black American history in the 20th century. Because of his defense of *Brown vs. Board of Education* and his other NAACP
cases, and because of his membership on the Supreme Court, I really admired him,
and I wanted to be an attorney. And I knew that attorneys had to go to college.

Though Javon did not end up becoming an attorney, he was academically
driven. In his youth, Javon participated in a school busing program that enabled him to attend a magnet school across town. The student body at his high
school was predominantly white and wealthy. Other black kids at school occasionally called him out for "acting white," but Javon never doubted himself.
He loved black people and black culture; he was confident in his racial identity.

With the help of a counselor, he applied and was accepted to Georgetown University (he was familiar with Georgetown because of the university's
championship basketball team). His stellar academic performance during his
freshman year earned him a scholarship that helped to pay the costs for his
remaining years at Georgetown. After graduating, Javon went on to earn advanced degrees from two of the world's most elite universities, Columbia University in New York and Oxford University in Oxford, England. Education
has been a critical determinant of Javon's upward mobility and in shaping the
worldview he currently maintains. However, his consumption and his lifestyle
preferences are also shaped by his race.

In reflecting on his journey to this point, Javon remarks that he feels his
success is due to the support he received from his community, combined with
his academic prowess. His involvement in church growing up grounded him
spiritually, but, he says, it also "kept me out of trouble and kept me occupied."
When he enrolled at Georgetown, no one in his family had previously earned a
college degree, but the idea that *he* might go to college was a seed planted by his
mentors at the National Association for the Advancement of Colored People
(NAACP). Javon describes his membership in the NAACP's national Youth
Council as a "very important and inspirational experience for a young guy."
It exposed him to life outside his neighborhood, providing him the chance to
travel to conferences and to develop relationships with people he called "black
luminaries," such as civil rights activist and former chairman of the NAACP
Myrlie Evers, and Kweisi Mfume, the five-term congressman and former president of the NAACP. His involvement and the opportunities provided by his
participation in prominent black social organizations and institutions helped
to shape the person he is today.

Cultural consumption, and more specifically the cultivation of black cultural capital, is instrumental in establishing and maintaining middle-class blacks' sense of group position and solidarity. Javon is representative of many of the people in my study in that most express a sense of belonging to the black community and maintain a high regard for their cultural heritage. In many ways, they consciously choose to remain connected to other blacks, and indicate this choice through their displays of black cultural capital.

Some scholars propose that increasing economic differentiation among blacks will reduce feelings of racial solidarity, as political attitudes among blacks have demonstrated some divergence along class lines.[3] Those who highlight this perspective predict that the salience of middle-class blacks' racial identity will decline as their economic position improves. That is, as more blacks become permanent, multigenerational members of the middle class, they will acculturate to a white cultural ideal, becoming increasingly detached from other members of their race. Others suggest that the idea of linked fate will continue to prevail, where middle-class blacks see their "fates" as connected to outcomes for other blacks, and as a consequence, their political attitudes and preferences are shaped by their commitment to policies that they see as beneficial to all blacks.[4] The findings of my study are consistent with research demonstrating that sentiments of group attachment remain evident and are at times quite salient among modern middle-class blacks. Consistent with research suggesting that middle-class blacks maintain an attachment to their race—even as diversity among blacks increases as a consequence of nativity, region, and mixed-race status, and even in the face of intra-racial class antagonism[5]—and illustrate a robust adherence to "groupness" that stands in contrast to the experience of other racial minorities in the United States and in other national contexts.[6] Most of the middle-class blacks in my study demonstrate not only racial pride but also a collective ethos and sense of obligation to the group. Their attitudes about racial progress and belief in their role in uplifting the race are deeply enmeshed in their worldviews and are expressed in various ways even in their consumption. They also engage in and display a wide range of racialized cultural practices that constitute a form of currency in their interactions with other blacks. In this study, middle-class blacks who are upwardly mobile, like Javon, as well as those who are multigenerational members of the black middle class, do not indicate a diminished desire or capacity to draw on and deploy black cultural capital.

What I found is consistent with research that reveals that political divergence and intra-racial and even intra-ethnic divisions do not preclude blacks from maintaining common cultural orientations and ideological commitments. For example, sociologist Cory Field's research on black Republicans, who represent a small fraction of all blacks, illustrates that regardless of their political affiliation, blacks often maintain strong black identities, promote ideas about racial solidarity, and subscribe to shared racialized ideologies like uplifting the race.[7] Even if blacks differ in terms of their political attitudes and class status, they may still aim to be unapologetically black, valuing their racial identity and cultural heritage and seeing their racial distinctiveness as desirable.

Similarly, a study of black students attending elite colleges found that black students indicate a high degree of cultural nationalism.[8] Examples of cultural nationalism include seeing it as favorable that black children are surrounded by black culture, believing that blacks should patronize black-owned businesses, and viewing it as important that blacks are knowledgeable about black history. Their race, their *being black*, was central to black college students' self-concept.[9] Additional research suggests that blacks' desire to maintain cultural distinctiveness, as opposed to assimilating to whiteness, has grown over time. For example, in a national survey of black Americans conducted in 1979, 55 percent agreed with the idea that black children should learn African languages; by 1993, that number had grown to 71 percent.[10] Middle-class blacks' racialized cultural consumption preferences and practices—their black cultural capital—as well as their ideological beliefs, form a critical mechanism that unites an increasingly heterogeneous population of blacks in the United States.

While blacks today have experienced an unprecedented symbolic integration in the public sphere (evidenced most visibly in the 2008 election of President Barack Obama), they also continue to indicate a commitment to their racial group and a desire to maintain cultural distinctiveness, which connects them to other blacks, including those across class lines. Their desire to be unapologetically black represents a shift from middle-class blacks in earlier eras in how they view and evaluate black cultural traditions, forms, and practices. For much of U.S. history, black elites have emulated Eurocentric cultural ideals and aesthetic values.[11] Often, they have done so even while engaged in efforts to promote black artistry and highlight black creativity, using European standards as the metric to determine and evaluate the value and worth of black cultural products.[12] During the early part of the twentieth century, members of the black middle class often sought to distance themselves from the black lower class to facilitate their assimilatory aspirations.[13]

At times, members of the black middle class engaged in the *politics of respectability*, a term used to describe a highly conscious, purposeful, and fervent belief regarding neatness of dress and dignified presentation of self.[14] Often this meant upholding racialized norms that favored white cultural tastes and traditions over black cultural tastes and traditions, with the goal of being seen as social equals to whites.[15] Respectability politics served as a cultural response to a "history of stigmatization."[16] A great deal of historical work examining the relevance of respectability politics among blacks has demonstrated that it was a central dimension of black public and private life during the early part of the century, and the idea of dignified presentation of self and of careful and strategic management of public displays continued to operate throughout the civil rights era.[17] Blacks' aesthetic dispositions and standards impact their consumption; however, blacks' cultural preferences and values are not static. They are informed by traditions, but they are also modified in response to the contemporary cultural moment.

With the emergence of a modern black middle class, whose members must often appear before and address racially and cultural divergent audiences, new questions arise. How do middle-class blacks maintain a desire for cultural and racial distinction while navigating a world where cultural racism prevails? How do they combine their desire to enjoy all the benefits that accrue to middle-class status with their desire to engage in unique traditions and a cultural heritage that is racialized and often stigmatized? The cumulative experiences of interviewees navigating the complexities that result because of their race and their class status reveal that consumption is key to their ability to display their black cultural capital and to demonstrate cultural flexibility while striving to be unapologetically black.

A Constellation of Cultural Consumption Preferences and Practices

All people maintain a complex web of interrelated and flexible consumption preferences (tastes, dispositions, proclivities, and attitudes) and consumption practices (behaviors, actions, engagements, and performances).[18] Consumption, then, is about financial decisions—how people spend their money—as well as about the types of services and experiences people seek out and partake in, the cultural heritage and traditions they celebrate, and the meanings they attach to their everyday practices. Consumption is a process of acquiring and using, as well as disposing of, discarding, and ceasing to use, a good or service.[19]

Like other groups, middle-class blacks maintain diverse cultural tastes and partake in an assortment of cultural consumption practices. Black cultural capital is constituted and evidenced as middle-class black consumers demonstrate their distinct racialized cultural tastes and sensibilities. Their black cultural capital is a product of their combined knowledge of blacks' distinct history and cultural heritage. It is revealed in the plethora of racialized cultural practices they engage in. It is also evident in practices that they avoid or deem distasteful. Black cultural capital is a tool that helps blacks to draw cultural boundaries around who is and is not a member of the group. But it is also helpful in determining allies and those who might be considered *black adjacent*, a slang term that describes those who have respect and appreciation for black culture, and actively participate in its consumption, but who are not black.

I find that middle-class blacks' cultural preferences and practices, which constitute their black cultural capital, grant them an avenue to be unapologetically black. This builds on work of previous scholars who have articulated the ways that middle-class blacks maintain racialized consumption preferences, which serve as important vehicles used to express their racial identities.[20] From the way they style their hair to the language they use and the organizations and institutions they are members of, the majority of the middle-class blacks I interviewed both acknowledge blacks' distinct cultural heritage and also engage in black cultural practices, and thus their consumption in these different domains reflects their race.

Black Hair

Black hair care is a ritualized and racialized practice with no shortage of political and cultural significance. But more than anything else, middle-class blacks' knowledge not just of how to care for and style their hair but also of when and how to modify a style to gain acceptance in both white and black settings represents their black privilege.

Black hair care and grooming standards are nuanced, context specific, and often evolving, but in almost all cases, my interviewees' grooming practices, including how to care for and style their hair, require specialized know-how. As Amare, a 30-year-old financial analyst, bluntly explains: "I want a black person to cut my hair because I'm black." Any barber who might cut his hair, first and foremost, needs to be black. For him, as for many middle-class blacks, it is just common sense that black people have matchless experience and knowledge regarding how to care for black hair. This specialized knowledge constitutes an important form of embodied black cultural capital.

Hairstyles can serve as racial markers and signify the embodiment of racial differences. Donning certain styles can be an expression of black pride, and a rejection of dominant aesthetic preferences, expectations, and appearance norms.[21] But black hair can be modified and manipulated so that it adheres to white ideals. Not surprisingly, research has demonstrated time and again that blacks' hairstyles and grooming practices maintain symbolic and cultural weight.[22] Blacks' grooming practices and the ways they decide to style their hair for work or pleasure can be telling examples of how black cultural capital is managed and modified, and can also reveal how middle-class blacks illustrate their cultural flexibility.

Alysha, a 26-year-old financial analyst recalls adjusting to her transition from an all-white private school to a large, majority black public school. One of the first things Alysha did was alter how she wore and cared for her hair. She felt she had to up her hair game at her majority black high school by donning a straight hairstyle. Alysha consulted with her hairdresser about straightening her hair, which she hoped would help her come across as mature and prissy. Her hairdresser explained that if she wanted to wear this new style, she would have to begin the nightly routine of wrapping her hair to prevent damage. Alysha sensed that the added upkeep was worth it—as it would pave the way to popularity at her new school.

The differences in the cultural and racial contexts between her schools, she realized, were consequential for her consumption, as she explains that her fashion choices changed as well:

> I went from Abercrombie and Doc Martens to, like, "I need to get my hair wrapped. I need to get some Guess." I know that sounds terrible, but in the ninth grade when all of your friends are wearing that, and everybody's like, "What's that on your feet?" You're like, "let me get some Air Force Ones. I cannot wear these anymore."

Some might interpret her flat-ironing her hair as an indication of a desire to model herself after white beauty standards, yet this is not consistent with how she thought about her decision. Alysha's fashion choices, from head to toe, were part of a strategic effort to gain social acceptance by demonstrating that she was aware of what black people her age perceived was fashionable. For her, straightening her hair was a means of aligning herself to the appearance norms embraced by her black classmates. It meant she was old enough to sport an adult hairstyle, one that required care and maintenance. Straight hair enabled her to fit in at her predominantly black high school.

Keeping up with black hair trends—hair norms internal to the black community—can serve to represent one's racial allegiance and racial identity. Even though immense diversity in personal care practices exists among blacks, and popular preferences and stylistic choices change over time, that does not reduce the fact that blacks' choices and the meaning they attach to how they adorn their hair are informed by and woven into the larger framework of racialized tastes and practices.

Trends in the black community and the gendered and classed associations that other blacks attach to different hairstyles importantly factor into middle-class blacks' preferences and practices when it comes to their hair. In the past, straight hair has signaled middle-class status among blacks.[23] In recent years, interest in natural hairstyles, styles that accentuate blacks' tresses more or less unaltered, has increased, and new products and virtual communities have emerged to equip black women with knowledge and tools to explore and experiment with a range of styles and techniques that embrace their natural textures.[24]

Caring for their hair creates avenues of connection to the black community for middle-class blacks. Ties to barbers and beauticians and the hours spent in barbershops and beauty salons are valued. Many men in this study indicate that their barbers are close friends and the barbershop is a place where they go to reconnect, demonstrating one way that black hair and its care helps middle-class blacks to establish and maintain bonds with other blacks.

Despite its versatility and the rich and creative ways in which it can be styled, black hair is often deemed undesirable. Blacks' hair care and management is often subject to reprimand and ridicule when it does not comply or conform to white beauty and appearance standards. This is part of a longstanding tradition evident even in the times of slavery, as overseers and slave owners shaved blacks' hair as a means of denying them freedom and pride.[25] What in the past was the coercive management of black hair as a tool of oppression, is reproduced today in the stigma attached to certain styles that do not comply with white appearance norms. Middle-class blacks in my study are quite conscious of the ways in which their decisions regarding their grooming and hair might subject them to marginalizing treatment in white spaces. Decisions regarding their hair are complex and at times cumbersome, in part because styles they might find liberating and aesthetically pleasing might be deemed unattractive to the broader public and seen as unprofessional in workplace settings. However, the interviewees also revealed that their views on black hair are far more complicated than arguments that assert that donning certain styles indicates simply the desire to emulate whites or, conversely, is an expression of black pride.

Middle-class blacks in my study, and particularly black women, indicate that they have experimented with lots of different styles. Black hair is enormously versatile, granting black people a plethora of stylistic possibilities.[26] At times, their hair might reflect their mood, or it might be styled for convenience. In many instances, their choice of hairstyle reflects the social contexts and circumstances of their lives. They might have a natural hairstyle in one setting or at one stage in their lives, but modify their hair in another setting or at another time.

Bryson, a corporate attorney in his early thirties, provides a telling example of how contextual factors can impact a person's presentation of self and choice of hairstyle at particular times in their personal and professional life. Before entering corporate America, Bryson worked as a teacher in inner-city Baltimore. During this time, he wore his hair in locs (also referred to as dreadlocks, dreads, or locks), which are often seen as a symbol of Afrocentric values and black pride or as an appreciation of natural hair (additionally, some wear them as part of their adherence to the religion of Rastafarianism).[27] While locs can be a symbol of racial identity or deeply held spiritual beliefs, they can also be attached to negative stereotypes.[28] Blacks who wear locs can be seen as uncouth and uncivilized, and possibly involved in a countercultural movement.

The stigma attached to locs was evident in Bryson's experience with wearing them. As he puts it, "people reacted to me differently." He found that white people were particularly standoffish. For example, on his commute each day, he noticed that "even though I had a shirt and tie on, I'd be the last person that somebody would sit next to on the bus." Even though he was college educated and professionally dressed, strangers in public spaces made him feel stigmatized because of his race and his hair. Bryson emphasizes that he always made sure his locs looked neat, which required a great deal of maintenance. In addition to using various creams and oils and other hair products, he had to get his roots tightened regularly, which took up a significant amount of time. In the end, maintaining locs was just too much work for him. Plus he was planning to change careers, leaving teaching and entering the corporate world, where he felt his locs would not align with "professional" appearance norms. Bryson now sports a low-cut fade. Currently, as one of the few blacks at his corporate law firm, Bryson feels compelled to look, as he puts it, "presentable." This means being polished both in how he dresses and how he wears his hair.

Bryson's beliefs about the necessity of a neat appearance are attuned to the politics of respectability, but he is also attuned to the dominant corporate mores of his workplace. He found it "irritating" when one of his fellow black attorneys wore his hair in locs that Bryson deemed "wild" and unkempt. He strongly believes it is important to represent the race well, particularly in elite, white settings, and describes this black associate as not adhering to the norms of dignified self-presentation. Even after the other black attorney cut his "really crazy looking dreds," Bryson observes that his colleague did not get regular haircuts and his hair would often knot up, appearing "sloppy" according to Bryson's standards. In trying to make sense of why this colleague seemed unaware of the standards of self-presentation that Bryson feels are key for middle-class blacks, Bryson reasons that this coworker is from California and "may have hung out around a lot of white people growing up," and as a consequence he lacks the appropriate racial knowledge of how to appear in white spaces, and does not understand how to adhere to blacks' ideas about how to wear natural hair in ways that still comply with the ideal of neatness. For Bryson, locs are not a problematic hairstyle and he does not altogether disapprove of locs, but for him, they do not symbolize racial pride when they are unkempt and "wild" (especially in a context where there are only a few blacks). For Bryson, his black colleague's egregious error in judgment is an affront to efforts to advance the race and to contest negative stereotypes about blacks, stereotypes that are best disarmed by the dignified presentation of self that the politics of respectability demand.

On the surface, it may seem that Bryson's views on locs are contradictory. He had experienced mistreatment when he wore locs but continued wearing them; yet he is disapproving of his black colleague wearing a similar hairstyle. Deeper inspection, though, reveals the importance of black cultural capital. Bryon's neat and well-maintained locs, worn while teaching in a majority black school, in a majority black neighborhood, are to his mind, altogether different from the unkempt and uncombed natural hair his black colleague dons in an elite, majority white corporate setting. Locs might be a marker of one's racial identity, a means to bond with other blacks and to affirm one's black culture. But whites might perceive them altogether differently. For one thing, whites might not distinguish the care and attention that results in locs worn with pride from when they are uncaringly styled, resulting in "crazy looking" locs.

Rules about black hair are not absolute. Often, they are conditioned by context. Bryson's understanding of how to read social settings for their underlying racial logics, and to adjust one's practices accordingly, is a display of embodied black cultural capital and a demonstration of cultural flexibility.

For middle-class blacks, the styles they choose, the frequency with which they change them, and even practices they engage in to maintain the health of their hair, might draw unwarranted and unwelcome attention. Such attention could make negative racial stereotypes salient, reifying race in undesirable ways. In public settings, especially at work, others in my study are like Bryson in their emphasis on hair that is well-kept and styled to appear neat and tidy. In majority white workplace settings, styles that accentuate racial difference—afros, braids, twists, or locs—are often perceived as unconventional, and those who have donned them are aware of the ways their hair has made them stand out.

Styling one's hair may seem a mundane task; however, for middle-class blacks, hair takes on a multitude of meanings and can demonstrate adherence to deeper value systems. Bryson recognizes the relevance of social context: in one setting, a hairstyle like an afro or locs might serve as an expression of racial pride, but in another, that same style could be stigmatizing. Any one black person's hair, depending on the context, might have ramifications for how blacks as a group are perceived. The subtle distinctions my respondents make are indicative of a form of embodied black cultural capital. But their black privilege is also evident in their ability to manipulate their hair and their efforts to manage the meanings their stylistic choices convey.

Black Talk

Sociolinguists have long demonstrated that blacks employ racially specific linguistic tools to express their racial identity and forge connections when communicating with other blacks.[29] Many blacks speak not only Standard English but also black Standard English and African American English (AAE), an English dialect with varied "grammatical, phonological, and lexical systems."[30] While the use of black English has been the source of much contestation, it also has been a tradition celebrated by black intellectuals.[31] The middle-class blacks in my study also draw upon language as a cultural resource and as a means to signal their racial identity. *Black talk* is another part of the constellation of cultural practices and know-how that constitutes their black cultural capital.

Marcus, a 30-year-old nonprofit director and educational administrator, provides a notable example of how language is useful in connecting to other blacks. Marcus draws upon his diverse linguistic knowledge to establish clear racial boundaries, delineating in-group from out-group members. His view on when the use of black English is appropriate and when it is offensive is conditioned by race and context. Speaking black English allows him to connect and relate to the black students with whom he works, because it makes him come across as authentic. When he sprinkles slang throughout his speech, Marcus's students can hear that he, like them, grew up in Newark, that he knows, first-hand, the challenges they encounter. He also feels it subtly shows them that they can be successful while also maintaining a connection to black culture and black people. As Marcus told me, "I don't want [my students] to feel like their success depends on them being someone that they are not. So, if I am speaking in slang and being comfortable with [it], that helps them to disarm that. Then, yeah, I will continue to speak slang." Marcus's conscious choice to speak in non-standard English is a display of his black cultural capital and his desire to connect with the black youth with whom he works.

Marcus also describes an experience when he felt the use of black English was inappropriate. When he was a high school student, after he arrived at his predominantly white, New England boarding school, several white classmates spoke to him using slang. When they did so, he felt like an outsider. He found their use of black English off-putting and offensive:

> Why will you talk to me like "Yo' this" and "What's up that"? When you talk to them, you're like, "Well, hello. How are you?" You know, why? I can understand "Hello. How are you?" It's that kind of, are you putting on that act for me? . . . Are you trying to talk down to me and kind of use the culture in a sarcastic way to talk to the black kid?

Marcus questioned his classmates' intentions: were they trying to make fun of black culture? Were they trying to ostracize him? For Marcus, black colloquial speech is a cultural resource that enables him, a middle-class black man, to connect to Newark's inner-city youth; however, his own use of what he perceives as a black vernacular, demonstrates that he also adhered to unstated rules about who can use it appropriately and when.

Almost as a requisite of being black and middle class, most in my study maintain a linguistic capacity for both Standard English and black vernacular, and they are quite conscious about how they communicate and the social meaning conveyed by their linguistic choices. Bryson reveals that at work, "I talk different." He explains that his "accent changes. . . . You know, black people in the Midwest kind of have a Southern dialect. . . . I guess to an extent, I'll try to suppress it. . . . Some stuff I won't say at work, you know. Like 'y'all,' you know, like 'y'all trippin'.' I won't say that to anybody at my job. But I say it to my friends." Bryson quite consciously alters his speech patterns in recognition that corporate English is required. He readily uses black English when conversing with his friends. He sees it as expressive and understood in black circles, but at work he has to "put on a more professional, serious business front."

Similarly, Javon, who works in a predominantly white private equity firm, notes that he can fluently speak Standard English, but he has elected to communicate in a different cadence when in more intimate circles around other blacks. Outside of work, he speaks with "more of a drawl . . . maybe I drop vowels." At work, he uses "the King's English," minimizing perceptible racial differences in his speech. By speaking "the King's English" or making sure to be "articulate," my middle-class black respondents, like Javon and Bryson, actively work to distance themselves from stereotypes, such as blacks are ignorant or poorly educated, or only *able* to speak black English.

Even while many of the middle-class blacks in my study admit to modifying their language use and speech patterns in certain circumstances, they also indicate that speaking "proper English" will not insulate them from racism. As Javon notes, "if you pick up the phone and talk to me, most of the time, you'll know that I'm black, even though I speak the King's English." His comment rings true, as research suggests that Americans are able to determine the race of someone with great precision simply from hearing them say hello.[32]

Another example of how middle-class blacks use language in racially specific ways is their attitude toward and use of the "n-word."[33] Beyond comedians' bits and musicians' lyrics, in private settings, among friends, and in the company of other blacks, the middle-class blacks in my study report that they are quite comfortable using the term. Even as they work to curb their use of the n-word, as Michelle, a 28-year-old event planner, admits, "sometimes it just comes out."

In middle-class blacks' periodic use of the n-word, the complexity of the ways their race and black cultural capital surfaced in their language use becomes clear. After several interviewees spontaneously mentioned the n-word during our conversations, I began to ask respondents whether they use the word, and the context and meaning they associate with it when they do use it.[34]

Before discussing my respondents use of the n-word, it is worthwhile to first clarify what I am referencing. There are two forms of the n-word—*nigger* and *nigga*—which share a common history. Nigga (or *niggah* or *nigguh*), follows a linguistic pattern emerging out of AAE, dropping the *-er*. The pronunciation "nigga" conveys a different meaning from "nigger," which tends to be seen as a racial slur. As Harvard law professor Randall Kennedy points out, the n-word "could be said in many ways, put to many uses, and mean many things."[35] Subtle changes in pronunciation distinguish a racial epithet that has been described as one of the most offensive words in the English language[36] from a self-referential marker of in-group status.[37] However it is pronounced, the n-word has many rules governing its use and is generally considered taboo in public discourse, as it is taken as a racial slur that "discredits, slights, smears, stains, besmirches people of black African descent."[38]

Many of the middle-class blacks in my sample indicated that they use the n-word (with the dropped -er ending). This is consistent with research: despite its negative connotation and troublesome history, the term is employed and considered acceptable by some in the black community.[39] Analyzing its deployment by middle-class black professionals reveals that its use is a racialized cultural practice that requires knowledge of the term's varied meanings and context-specific rules governing when it should be uttered. Even when they dislike using the n-word or try to avoid it, in most cases, across ethnic lines, they still understand what the term conveys and who can use it. In particular, middle-class blacks consider its use strictly prohibited around whites and by whites.[40]

The use of the n-word by the middle-class blacks in my study is undoubtedly class-inflected. The black comedian Chris Rock elaborated on this distinction in his 1996 comedy special "Bring the Pain," as he explained what separates "black people" from "niggas." Rock described "black people" as blacks who uphold middle-class values—working hard, taking care of their families, and valuing education—whereas "niggas" are ignorant, lazy, and have criminal tendencies. Black people, according to Rock, hate "niggas," because they poorly represent the race and validate negative stereotypes that adversely impact blacks who are trying to get ahead. Nearly all of the study respondents who use the n-word, reported using it to convey this class distinction. It is almost always applied when describing blacks who are poor representatives of the race, or those who engage in behavior perceived as crude and foolish.

Most middle-class blacks who reported using the term did so to refer to other blacks in a derogatory or negative light. That is, they use the term when joking about or ridiculing another black person. In contrast to research that suggests empowering and positive usage, in reference, for example, to someone who bravely fights against racial oppression ("one bad n-word") or as a term of endearment ("you my n-word"), the middle-class blacks in my study often use the term, but almost exclusively derogatorily. Ashlee, a 28-year-old human resources administrator, uses it to describe a "crazy, black person," and Lori, a 28-year-old recruiter for a large nonprofit, said she uses the n-word "when I'm calling somebody stupid." Leah, a 32-year-old who works for the local government, uses the term when she mocks her husband: "N-word, are you crazy?" With notable nuance, I found consensus that the n-word conveys negative characteristics or qualities. For the middle-class blacks in my study, an "n-word" is a black person to be avoided; they are loud, uncouth, and classless. A person might be acting like an "n-word" when their behavior is out of control or foolish.

To Lance, a 30-year-old tax preparer, the word means, "you know, ignorant. The ignorant, bringing black folks down, setting black folks back 100 years type of person." Eric, a 27-year-old director of business strategy at a start-up, calls it "being less than what you ought to be." For example, Eric might say, "That's some real n-word shit that you just did," to express his disapproval of what he sees as disgusting and undignified behavior. Larry, a technician at a research library, says he uses the n-word to describe someone who is "basically just unruly, no manners, just ignorant," and Tatiana, a 31-year-old broker and contract specialist, suggests the term refers to someone who lacks manners and is "ghetto." She sometimes calls her sister-in-law "a real n-word," when she comes over to Tatiana's house, eats, and then leaves, which Tatiana finds both annoying and rude.

Whether multigenerational, native-born blacks or second-generation children of immigrants, my respondents share a raced and classed understanding of what the n-word conveys and when it might be put to use. Lance and Leah, whose parents are West Indian, maintain the same use and understanding as Lori and Larry, whose parents are African American. This importantly demonstrates that black cultural capital—in this case manifested in knowledge of the meaning of the n-word and the circumstances in which to use the n-word—connects blacks regardless of their ethnic identities. They all express a similar familiarity and rationale for its use.

Middle-class blacks recognize the expressive potential of the n-word, and share an understanding of what it, in some sense, succinctly conveys, even when multiple meanings are attached to it. But they also share an understanding that the term is not to be used in mixed company and that it is unacceptable for whites to use it. Sheila, a 47-year-old clinical researcher, notes that when she gets together with her girlfriends, they use the n-word all the time. She giggles as she imitated her girlfriends describing the men in their lives and recounting to each other, "You know what that n-word did?" But these women would *never* use the word in white settings, as Sheila makes clear, "because it's negative. It's derogatory. It would stereotype me." She finds it not appropriate to use what she recognizes could be an incendiary idiom in all settings. Among her friends, it may be put to use liberally as a linguistic tool used to bond over the trials and tribulations of dating. As she explains, "in private, we let our hair down." Using the n-word allows her to display her insider knowledge, but Sheila feels strongly that use of the n-word should be relegated to intimate social settings among blacks—it is *never* to be uttered in white contexts where its meaning could be misconstrued.

James, a 39-year-old firefighter, indicates that he is careful about the n-word, even restricting the music he listens to while at work. He plays only the "clean," censored versions of songs at the firehouse. He hopes that doing so will prevent his white colleagues from accidentally repeating the n-word as they sing along: "My job is predominantly white, so as I listen to music, I'm very conscious of what I play and who is around me. If I purchase singles, it's always clean." James wants to be recognized for his professionalism, and he believes that if his white coworkers state the n-word, even innocently while singing a song, a conflict would surely ensue.

William, a 32-year-old high school teacher and administrator, avoids the n-word in public, particularly around his mostly black students. These students are not only familiar with the term but also use it frequently. However, from William's perspective, this demonstrates that they lack respect for the word. The young black kids at his school do not understand the unwritten rule that it is a term to be used in private or intimate settings. He does not condone their using it in everyday speech in public and mixed-race settings, and finds it frustrating that they overuse the term and use it so carelessly in formal settings. So, while he uses the n-word at home, he could not do so at work, lest he risk indicating approval of his students' negligence and apparent disregard of the rules that govern the term's use.

Whites' use of the n-word is always and unequivocally deemed offensive by study respondents. This is consistent with the idea that when deployed by a white person, the n-word is "the nuclear bomb of racial epithets."[41] Michelle grew up in a Jamaican American household and does not recall being familiar with black American culture until college, where, through relationships and friendships with black Americans, she became familiar with the n-word and the rules surrounding its expression. Rule number one: the n-word is off-limits for whites. Michelle makes it clear that she understands and enforces this rule when she recounts a story about a white colleague spurting out the term in conversation. The incident occurred at work: "She was talking to me about something, and she was like, 'Yeah, girl, and that *nigga* was like. . . .' I didn't hear anything else she said. I didn't hear anything else. I was just like, 'Hmm.' I had to leave." Michelle was so upset by the incident, it took her three days to calm down. Only after many conversations with friends did she feel ready to speak to her colleague. She describes her white female coworker as "one of those people that just, she thought she could just . . . She was very much into black culture or African-American culture, to be specific, and she listens to certain things, and I don't know if she just felt like because she did that, and she had a couple of [black] friends, that it was cool." Appreciation for black culture did not constitute a pass for this white woman to use the n-word. When Michelle confronted her, the woman explained she felt justified in using the n-word because "they use it in rap songs." Michelle, like others, acknowledges the contradiction, but still subscribes to rule number one—white people should never use the n-word. When whites use the word, even if they drop the -er ending, it makes salient the term's problematic roots and contemporary meaning as a racial slur.

That some middle-class blacks avoid saying the word, or use it with considerable hesitation, does not mean that they do not understand its nuanced social meaning. Many report that they are increasingly unlikely to use the n-word because they think there is no way to escape its problematic racial history. Crystal, a 29-year-old executive assistant, hates it when her friends use the word in her presence. To her, it conjures up a tormenting image of "slavery." She strongly believes that blacks need to "leave that word in the past." In 2007, at the 98th annual convention of the NAACP, that civil rights organization held a symbolic funeral to put the n-word to rest,[42] so the sentiment Crystal expresses is not unusual. Others' objections stem from not wanting whites to feel comfortable saying the word; they think it is thus necessary to censor their own use of it, not just around whites, but in general. Jeff, a 28-year-old sales manager, told me that he quit using the word after an incident on the dance floor, when a white woman yelled the n-word while singing along to the Biggie Smalls' song "Juicy." He was beyond startled. He thought it was "crazy" that the young woman had used the term "so freely in a happy way to me like I was gonna be OK with it."

Because the n-word "is so acceptable amongst our own people," Jeff told me, non-blacks feel authorized to use the term and do not comprehend blacks' disapproval. He expects that whites think, "Why do you get so upset? What's the big deal?" but Jeff believes that words are powerful. To him, the n-word has symbolic power, especially when used by whites, and he is not willing to risk making them think it is ever OK to say it.

Overall, the use of the n-word among some middle-class blacks provides a provocative illustration of how they know the rules governing its use—the who, how, and why of the n-word. However, it also shows that they draw on black cultural capital, in this case, linguistic structures, in their intimate interactions with fellow in-group members. There are aspects of their daily lives that are preserved just for blacks. Most perceive the use of the n-word as a freedom afforded those who are black, no matter their ethnicity, even though they mostly use the term to distinguish and demarcate what they see, through class-coded lenses, as the cringeworthy behavior of *other* blacks.

Black Institutions

Black colleges, churches, sororities, fraternities, and other black social and professional organizations are important avenues for middle-class blacks to connect with other blacks and to affirm their blackness. Kendra, a 28-year-old account executive, has social involvements that reveal her love and pride in her people: in addition to her sorority, Delta Sigma Theta, Kendra is active in the alumni association of Florida A&M University (FAMU), a historically black university. Altogether, nine of my respondents were graduates of HBCUs, and their degrees constitute a form of institutionalized black cultural capital. HBCUs play an outsize role, producing nearly 20 percent of all black college graduates though they make up only 3 percent of the country's colleges and universities.[43] There are unique benefits for those like Kendra who have earned a degree from an HBCU. Not only are they part of an extensive social network of other college-educated blacks, but through their institutional connection, they are bound to black traditions and part of a lineage of high-achieving blacks. In the long term, social connections formed on campus are repeatedly drawn on in their social and professional lives.

Kendra's black organizational involvements do not end with her sorority and the New York City alumni chapter of the HBCU that she attended. She is also an "Emerging Leader" for the Museum for African Art[44] in New York and sits on the board of a foundation that aims to connect minority and female businesses owners with private equity firms. Her organizational involvements and institutional connections align with both her race and her class identities. Many museums dedicated to celebrating black culture and institutions that aim to capture and preserve black history exist because of the efforts of middle-class blacks.[45] Thus Kendra with her work with the Museum for African Art demonstrates the long-standing practice of philanthropic involvement and dedicated service on the part of middle-class blacks in their efforts to establish and support organizations that promote black culture.[46]

Vanessa, the independent consultant, also maintains deep connections to black organizations and social and cultural institutions. Throughout her life, she has moved back and forth between different racial spaces. She was raised in a majority white suburb, and nearly all of the educational and professional settings she has experienced have been predominantly white. In contrast, the social and voluntary organizations she has been involved with and even her church have been composed of other blacks. Vanessa, like other middle-class blacks, sees her various memberships and institutional involvements as ways to connect with and foster meaningful interactions with other blacks. Often, they provide an opportunity for blacks to give back and engage in racial uplift. At times, ties to black organizations connect them to their family history and traditions.

Vanessa, like her mother and many women on her mother's side of the family, is a member of Alpha Kappa Alpha. She joined the sorority "to keep the tradition going." Vanessa is an active member of her church, holding several leadership positions. She is proud to have "revolutionized" the Joshua Ministry. A fundraiser she organized brought in over $40,000 for a nonprofit the church sponsored that was dedicated to "fighting poverty in Ethiopia through sustainable economic development." Vanessa's involvements contribute to her sense of black pride and help her to feel embedded in a black community. They also provide relief from the challenges that come from being a black woman in a starkly white workplace and industry. For her, church is a refuge: "There were two black males out of 120 to 200 investment bankers, so, for me, going to church was the only time I would see black people. I would actually go early, like an hour early, and just hang out with all of the old women that sat in my section." Church is "wonderfully spiritual" but also "social," though Vanessa admits she rarely sees her favorite parishioners outside of church services. Going to church is such a critical part of her weekly routine that she makes sure when she is traveling to return home in time to go. Vanessa makes every effort to never miss a service.

Vanessa privileges the black church experience as a means of embedding herself in a long-standing practice and style of worship in the black community. She describes how blacks' religious life has long affirmed their worth and dignity in the United States. She believes that black churches provide a place of solace for blacks, no matter their class status:

> You know, you may be just a plantation worker, whatever, the rest of the week, but on Sundays, you might have been a deacon or in church singing. It was a very important part of African American life, and African American history, and I think continuing to present your best self to God—which is what you are going after, and what they were going on, with their best shirts and best shoes—I think it is important to still present your best self to God.

Taken altogether, Vanessa feels bound to the members of the church she attends, but she also cherishes the *idea* of the black church and the symbolic role of the black church as an institution in the lives of the black community.

For many of my interviewees, attending a black church maintains a special racial meaning. Many had grown up going to a black church, and like Vanessa, see their continued church attendance as an opportunity to connect to black people and black traditions. But they are not driven simply by tradition, nor do they see all black churches as the same. Even in all-black settings, they have to read social cues and determine what is acceptable. How they dress for church reveals a particular sort of cultural flexibility. Dressing up reflects their often ingrained understanding, learned from their parents or grandparents, that church is a sacred place and that they should always "give God their best," but they also adjust their style according to the context. If they attend a church where the pastor tells congregants to "come as you are," they tend to dress casually, recognizing that it is OK to put tradition aside.

Attending church serves multiple functions. It is often uplifting and a time for contemplation. Beyond the spiritual dimension, the black church is an important vehicle for social connection and an institutional conduit to blacks' history, heritage, and traditions. Black cultural capital enables my interviewees to bond with blacks across the class spectrum. Church is a place where they report feeling at home.

While connections to black institutions and organizations are valued by some respondents, middle-class blacks like Vanessa also believe that their ability to maintain middle-class advantages is contingent on social connections to whites. So, despite the long lineage of HBCU graduates in Vanessa's family—her grandfather was a Morehouse man; her mother a Southern University graduate—she decided to attend Princeton. There, Vanessa felt compelled to develop relationships with non-black students:

> I cannot imagine going to Princeton and not having done something social with the general population. . . . No one sent anyone to Princeton to only know people that look like them, as long as we're trying to progress. . . . Black people have a lot of great ideas and a lot of things that we can do and want to do, but we don't have access to capital by a long shot. So the people who have capital, a lot of them are related to our peers, so it makes sense to get to know them.

For Vanessa, attending an elite, predominantly white college bestowed a key advantage, an opportunity to build ties to those who have access to social and economic capital. Her experience at a traditionally white university would also prepare her for a career where she would be one of few black women, if not the only one, on the job. After graduating, she completed a successful stint at an investment bank as an analyst and then as an associate at a private equity firm, both positions in which her success was contingent on her ability to establish connections in a majority white working world. She values black cultural capital, institutionalized in terms of organizational ties. Having such ties is important. But she also believes in the importance of understanding both how to relate and associate with whites and how to appear relatable to whites. Her black privilege is evident in her active cultivation and engagement of her black cultural capital, but also in her cultural flexibility, which contributed to her success in the world of work.

Javon similarly values his past and present connections to black church communities. He even attributes attending church as a youth with keeping him out of trouble: "church was the separating factor for me from the other factors that could have had a negative influence on my life." Javon has an active religious life as an adult because the ritual of attending church was ingrained in him as a youth: "I go out of tradition." Yet he also has a deeply personal connection to the black church: "Church saved my soul in more than one way. And so I'm grateful for that, and so that's become part of my personal life, part of my personal ethos." Interestingly, earlier in our conversation, he had remarked that college was not part of his family's "ethos," but church, well, that was a whole other matter. As he stresses, "My parents, grandparents—very, *very* religious people."

Just as Javon learned the habit of going to church, he learned how to dress for church. Today, it's always a suit and tie:

> When I go to my church, which is more traditional, I wear a suit and tie. I think it's good to wear a suit and tie to church because we all need a place that is for reverence, and that takes us out of ourselves. It shows a respect for the institution and for the people in the institution. So I think wearing a suit and tie to church for black people is very important because it reminds us that this is ours.

> . . . We don't have a whole bunch of multi-million-dollar corporations. We've got church. If you put the African Methodist Episcopal Church up, if you put up all of its real estate, you'd have a multi-billion-dollar, African-American Episcopal Church. The AME Church is the oldest . . . black church in America. You'd have billions of dollars' worth of real estate.

For Javon, the black church is a powerful institution in the black community. It is a place where black people should appear dignified, in part because it is a place where blacks are respected. But he also notes that the black church is powerful because of the economic power it wields.

While Javon feels at home in terms of the style of worship and the culture of the church, as his black cultural capital enables him to bond with his fellow church members, this is not enough to erase class differences. The diverse socioeconomic makeup of his church is at times a source of discomfort for him. Giving an example, he feels this tension as he leads the church's real estate investments:

> I'm in charge of my church's real estate development initiative, and to get people who have never owned a home, or never owned or run a business, to think about multi-million-dollar real estate decisions is challenging. To have a long-term strategy like you would in business for a church, it's challenging for people who don't get it.

When it comes to the church's wealth-building strategies, Javon feels his fellow congregants often lack financial know-how—an indicator of their working-class status. He, by contrast, has an MBA degree, and large-scale financial transactions are part of his day-to-day life. While shared racial traditions draw him to the church, and he profoundly appreciates the role of the black church in providing all blacks a place where they might be revered, he also acknowledges the class divisions, which at times produce friction in the governing of the church.

Kendra's, Vanessa's, and Javon's stories illustrate the myriad ways that black cultural capital is constituted and the role it plays in the everyday lives of modern middle-class blacks. From how they dress and style their hair to how they speak and where they worship, being black informs middle-class black Americans' cultural preferences and practices. The use and usefulness of black cultural capital unfolds throughout their everyday lives, as they actively work to remain connected to other blacks through cultural practices, traditions, and shared understandings. These racialized aspects of their cultural consumption provide them with a critical site for the production of a black racial identity, and serve as a tool for managing the tensions and challenges that they face because of racial stigma and racial stereotypes. Middle-class blacks in my study, maintain connections to black people, black culture, and black institutions and organizations even as they navigate settings where black cultural capital is not valued.

Part of being unapologetically black is not only recognizing and understanding how to put into play a diverse assortment of cultural practices but also knowing when one is free to engage in those practices. Context conditions the display of black cultural capital and its meaning.

Beyond acknowledging their comfort with and competence in black cultural engagement, many of the middle-class blacks in my study have to navigate diverse social, cultural, and institutional spaces. While they aim to be unapologetically black, they also have to maintain a cultural repository that grants them continued access and acceptance in a wider world that values and idealizes dominant culture and mores. Javon makes this clear, as he states confidently, "I can be both authentically black and successful and accessible to other people." While this is not always easy, my interviewees illustrate that they have not only diverse cultural knowledge but also a sense of when to deploy which cultural skills, revealing their black privilege in their cultural flexibility.

Represent Your Hood and Your Hood's Rep 4

NOT ONLY DO OUR *HOODS* HAVE REPUTATIONS, being spaces encoded with meaning, they are also central sites of consumption: the places where we shop, dine, view art, attend concerts, hang out with friends, and engage in a wide variety of other social and cultural activities.[1] Cultural theorists argue that people maintain systems of tastes and preferences, and the decision of where to live is not enacted in isolation from these preferences.[2] Choosing a place to call home is a decision that reveals middle-class blacks' cultural inclinations and reflects their lifestyles and preferences. Access to financial resources empowers middle-class blacks in the marketplace, granting them opportunities to move into high-status neighborhoods with lots of amenities, but they do not always choose to do so. Sometimes middle-class blacks prioritize their class status in their neighborhood selection, and at other times they prioritize their race.

The same underlying cultural tastes and preferences that are evident in their listening to hip-hop, speaking black English among friends, and partaking in organizational and social life as members of black Greek fraternities and sororities or black churches, also undergird middle-class blacks' attraction to living in a black neighborhood. In my study, black neighborhoods are considered desirable by the middle-class blacks who choose to live in them because they fulfill social and symbolic functions that facilitate the formation and cultivation of their racial identities.[3] They are also places where middle-class blacks are free from the constraints of operating in a white world. In their classic work *Black Metropolis*,

St. Clair Drake and Horace Cayton highlight this function of Bronzeville, the black Chicago neighborhood they studied, describing "having a good time" as a central axis of life in the neighborhood. Avenues of pleasure available in Bronzeville and pursued by its black residents were sources of relief from the stressors of everyday life and the burdens they faced. As Drake and Cayton poignantly state: "When work is over, the pressure of the white world is lifted. Within Bronzeville Negroes are at home. They find rest from white folks as well as from labor, and they make the most of it."[4] For many respondents in my study as well, black neighborhoods continue to fulfill this important function today. This is consistent with other studies of middle-class blacks' residential choices, illustrating that for some modern middle-class blacks living in a black neighborhood continues to be a meaningful decision, one that serves as a reflection of their racial identities.[5]

Living in a black neighborhood presents middle-class blacks with an opportunity to realize their membership in a symbolic black community and facilitates the expression of black cultural capital, but their choice often comes with added and unforeseen costs. It means dealing with the fact that the amenities—stores, shops, and restaurants—that appeal to their middle-class tastes are not easily accessible. In contrast, living in a well-off white neighborhood means having a variety of services and amenities nearby that satisfy their middle-class tastes. At the same time, living in a predominantly white neighborhood also exposes them to racial stigma and stereotypes.

There is an affective dimension to neighborhoods that is generated from our sentiments toward and attachments to the places where we live, such that we often *identify with* the communities which we call home.[6] But where we live can also either enable or constrain our consumption. The findings presented in this chapter demonstrate that middle-class blacks consider both race and class-based preferences when deciding where to live, and rarely find a place that meets both criteria perfectly. Their neighborhoods may be either closely aligned with their class-based taste or reflective of their race-based proclivities. Examining where middle-class blacks decide to live, as well as their experiences in their neighborhoods, makes it clear that middle-class blacks face trade-offs whatever choice they make.

Majority black neighborhoods with few class-based amenities and prestigious majority white neighborhoods with lots of such retail and commercial options, represent only two types of neighborhoods; they do not encompass all of the possible choices in New York City—or even a run-down of the varied types of neighborhoods in which black middle-class people choose to live.

Instead, they represent opposites along a spectrum of potentially desirable neighborhoods. Just as importantly, many of New York's iconic centers of black residential life have been transformed since the interviews for this study were completed; the experiences of study participants reported here may not reflect the realities on the ground today in specific places. People move and neighborhoods change. However, the mechanisms by which race and class inform the symbolic meaning middle-class blacks attach to their neighborhoods may remain evident.

What's Good in the (Neighbor)Hood?

Tasha moved to Harlem after years living in Boston. The young attorney selected her neighborhood purposefully, and she describes Harlem as a special, almost magical place. It offers "soul that you just don't get anywhere else." She speaks of her neighborhood in glowing terms:

> I really love living here. I love living in a black neighborhood. I love going through the C-Town [a local grocery store chain] and they're playing Beyoncé and songs that I like, songs that I sing along to and then I feel just a certain sense of . . . I don't know, pride 'cause there's so much history here. When I walk down 125th Street . . . I'm like, this is one of those streets that everyone knows. Nationwide. If you're black, you've heard of 125th Street. You've heard of Sylvia's Soul Food and that's around the corner from my house, and the Apollo Theatre is around the other corner from my house, so those kinds of things. . . . I love the spirit of it [all].

Tasha rejoices in the shared cultural understandings that come to life in the everyday interactions that she has in her neighborhood, daily interactions that help to cultivate a sense of community. She finds comforting the exchange of greetings among strangers passing on the street—it is a simple form of human acknowledgment, yet for her, this quotidian experience is a tribute to the unique character of black neighborhoods. As Tasha remarks:

> There's community. There's a man who plays the Casio keyboard on Lenox, right up the street, Lenox between 126th and 125th. Every day, he says good morning to me, every day. In Chelsea, the bums wouldn't speak to me. I just feel like there's a sense of community even though it's like the doctor and the drug dealer, but they both know each other, and say, "what's up?" when they pass on their way to wherever they're going.

Living in a black neighborhood, for Tasha and many others, is one way to literally and figuratively be a part of a black community. A community where black people across the class divide recognize each other's humanity. Tasha sought out her neighborhood for its racial symbolic currency. Her choice to reside there reflects the value she places on black spaces and her desire to regularly engage with other blacks.

Tasha enjoys being in the company of other blacks, and often seeks out such opportunities for the pleasure and sense of community such interactions generate. She attended a high school where she was one of the few blacks in her honors classes, but when it came to college, she chose Spelman, a college founded to educate black women in the heart of black Atlanta. Attending a historically black college was a family tradition; both her parents were HBCU graduates. She was drawn to the South's warm climate and the fact that she would be around "black people like me." Young people who were black and "smart, hard-working, and ambitious." After graduating college, Tasha once again found herself in a majority white world, attending a prestigious and elite school, Harvard Law. After graduating from Harvard, she moved to New York City, settling in Harlem and taking a job as an in-house attorney for a cosmetics firm (where she has few black coworkers). Tasha's decision to live in a predominantly black neighborhood is part of a matrix of cultural consumption preferences and practices that reflect her black cultural capital.

Unlike Tasha, Jasmine, a 30-year-old teacher, lives in a place that she sees as consistent with her class status. She recognizes Harlem's reputation as an iconic center of black cultural life. Nonetheless, she finds that neighborhood unattractive as a place to live. "I didn't like Harlem. It wasn't as classy. I guess I am a snob. I don't know, it just felt different. . . . I didn't even consider Harlem; it would have been cheaper . . . but I wanted classier, I guess." She seems uncomfortable admitting her distaste for Harlem out loud, but in all honesty, she does not see Harlem as a suitable place to live, in character or appearance. Living on the Upper East Side, now *that* is consistent with the way she sees herself. While Jasmine lives in a place that she finds aesthetically pleasing, a neighborhood associated with high social esteem, she also describes times when she feels slight discomfort due to her race in her neighborhood. While her neighborhood is "classy," she does not always feel that she fits in:

> The first two months I lived here I was very aware that there were [few] blacks or Hispanics, [and] there are a lot of Asians and a lot of Caucasians. . . . I was kind of curious to see if it was really as [few] as I was expecting and it was as

little; there were like no black people. . . . I'm always aware that something is
different—and it's me.

Jasmine spent her formative years in a mostly white, upper-class suburb in up-
state New York, enrolled in a majority white school, and even today has mostly
white friends. Despite her familiarity with and affinity for white people and culture, she still feels like an outsider at times in her majority white neighborhood,
a neighborhood that the most recent census figures indicate is less than 2 percent
black. While she sees her neighborhood as consistent with her tastes and class
status, because of her race she does not always feel at home where she lives.

Some middle-class blacks in my study, like Tasha, opt to live in majority
black neighborhoods. In describing the meaning they attach to their neighborhoods, they indicate the ways in which their race and desire to be part of a
symbolic black community influence their experiences where they live, making
those communities places of respite. Other middle-class blacks, like Jasmine,
opt to live in high-status neighborhoods with few black residents but lots of
shops, trendy bars, and upscale amenities; nonetheless race still shapes their
day-to-day experiences living in their neighborhoods, even if it is not at the
forefront of their decision to live there.

The middle-class blacks I interviewed revealed that there is meaning encoded
in their decision to live in a particular place. At times, their preference is due to a
neighborhood's racial and social-interactional character—rooted in black culture
dictates and shared social mores. At other times, their preference for a particular neighborhood is explained as a consequence of the economic and social status associated with the neighborhood—rooted in notions of status and prestige.
The former choice, living in a black neighborhood, facilitates the development,
maintenance, and display of black cultural capital and the realization of racialized
ideological commitments. The latter choice, living in a majority white neighborhood, allows access to a diverse array of amenities, including those that cater to
the tastes of the elite and carry prestige. Housing choices are among the most important consumptive decisions people make. Middle-class blacks' choices reveal
that being black and privileged often means being able to satisfy only one aspect
of their identity when selecting a neighborhood in which to settle.

Being Black and Middle Class and Living in a Black Neighborhood

Living in a black neighborhood makes being black—engaging in black cultural capital—easy. In my interviews, black neighborhoods were described as

distinct from other kinds of neighborhoods, not just because black people are concentrated there but because that's where black culture is celebrated. Black neighborhoods are viewed as maintaining two dimensions that reflect racial symbolism. First, they are distinct cultural spaces, spaces that are symbolic due to their associations with black people, and they are places where black people and culture are recognized and prized. Second, they maintain a social-interactional dimension, being places where middle-class blacks can shore up their sense of group membership and belonging. The concentration of black cultural institutions and black-owned businesses in black neighborhoods means they are places where blacks have ample opportunities to enjoy mundane interactions with in-group members. Living in a black neighborhood promotes an atmosphere in which middle-class blacks can satisfy their affinity for other black people and affirm their racialized ideological and cultural commitments (for example, to engage in racial uplift). Together, these underlying symbolic and social dimensions contribute to the desirability of black neighborhoods for some middle-class blacks.

The stories of middle-class blacks living in black neighborhoods, however, also show that doing so comes with trade-offs. Selecting to live in a neighborhood where they can engage their black cultural capital, also means that they are burdened by, first, the perception that their neighborhood is inherently an undesirable, low-status, and stigmatized place; second, the fact that there are few neighborhood amenities and services that satisfy their class-based tastes, so they are unable to fully and locally live their middle-class lifestyles; and third, the discomfort they sometimes feel as a consequence of their class status (and for women, their combined class and gender status). Their class and gendered identities are occasionally highly salient; when this occurs, middle-class black men and women often feel out of place. These encumbrances take away from the pleasure of living in a black neighborhood; however, they do not deter my respondents from seeing their black neighborhoods in an overall positive light.

The Racial Symbolism and Cultural Dimensions of Black Neighborhoods

Black neighborhoods often get a bad rap in the press, and research consistently reveals that Americans see black neighborhoods as undesirable and low-status places. Not only are blacks the least-preferred out-group to have for neighbors,[7] but researchers also regularly find that people are often unwilling to move into predominantly black neighborhoods and that these neighborhoods are ranked as the least desirable among all possible places to live—even when controlling for the income and socioeconomic status of their residents and social conditions, such as school quality and level of crime.[8] Even when poor physical conditions are absent, black neighborhoods are perceived as low-status, "disreputable areas."[9] Why then would a subset of middle-class blacks opt to live in a majority black neighborhood?

A central reason to live in a predominantly black neighborhood articulated by the middle-class blacks in my study is that they value black neighborhoods as black spaces and see them as maintaining symbolic significance. These neighborhoods are perceived as places where blacks can actualize feelings of attraction and affection for other blacks, can talk black, and let their hair down (or out). According to Kendra, the account executive living in the heart of Harlem, living in a black neighborhood means you can demonstrate to others your "love for your people." Not only does living in a black neighborhood allow for the display of black cultural capital, but it also creates opportunities to actualize ideological commitments to "uplift the race." In this way, my respondents see their real estate choices as a means of "giving back," of displaying and cultivating their black cultural capital and being an active part of the black community that they value. This is consistent with the foregrounding work of sociologists Mary Pattillo and Karyn Lacy, who have demonstrated that for some middle-class blacks, living in a black neighborhood is a central avenue to demonstrate an allegiance to the race and also to regularly and routinely enjoy the company of other blacks.[10]

Amare, a lifelong Brooklynite, notes that living in Crown Heights "means that I'm close to my people." Damon similarly notes about living in Harlem, "I like the vibe; I like the community; I like being around this many black people." For Heather, a 29-year-old deputy director at a local government agency, whose parents own one of the historic brownstones on Harlem's Strivers Row,[11] her residence connects her to Harlem's celebrated black intellectuals of the past. With elation in her voice, she proudly divulges, "I can walk four blocks and be in front of where Langston Hughes used to live or Zora Neale Hurston used to hang out." Harlem's rich artistic and literary legacy deeply resonates with her. She admits that this is likely because she was "brought up to appreciate and understand" the neighborhood's historic significance. Like Tasha, Heather relishes the chance to celebrate, through sheer proximity, the cultural roots of Harlem's past and its vibrant present.

Several people told me they did not even *consider* searching for housing in neighborhoods that were not predominantly black. Kendra, who lives in Harlem, reveals that she is suspicious of black professionals who do not live in black neighborhoods. Racial affinity and affiliation are paramount for Kendra and some others, and living in a black neighborhood is seen as a central way to illustrate the regard you have for your race.

Bryson, a Morehouse man working at a downtown, white-shoe law firm, also lives in Harlem and takes pleasure in the interactions with other blacks that living there affords him. Bryson deeply believes in the power and brilliance of black people, especially in light of the challenges they have had and continue to face. Before attending Howard University Law School, which boasts such preeminent black graduates as Supreme Court Justice Thurgood Marshall, he was a teacher in an urban public school system. Though Bryson has switched careers, he remains deeply committed to racial uplift. It is not surprising then that he quite consciously made the choice to move to Harlem "to live around black people, regular black people." Further, his deliberate choice is deeply symbolic: black youth, he explains, "don't really see a lot of professional black people." For this Detroit native with a slender build, a fresh haircut, and impeccably tailored clothing, his mere presence in the neighborhood, as a polished, professional black man heading to work each day, serves as an example of what is possible. Though he no longer works with black youth, he remains committed to serving as a role model. His residential choice reflects his sense of obligation to give back and to uplift the race.

Middle-class blacks also value black neighborhoods because of their long-standing black cultural and religious institutions, as well as there being a concentration of black-owned commercial services that cater to a black clientele. Lori lives in Harlem and describes its cultural, commercial, and religious institutions as neighborhood "staples." Part of the neighborhood's appeal, for her is how easy it is for her to support and patronize such institutions, which are clustered within black neighborhoods rather than dispersed across the city. As will be discussed at length in Chapter Seven, study interviewees' support of black entrepreneurs and black-owned establishments is also a part of their effort to advance the race.

Lance, a native New Yorker, lives in a neighborhood in the Bronx that he describes frankly as having "a lot of black people, no white people." He draws on his relationship with his barber—which is both commercial and familial—as an example of why his neighborhood is not just a place where he sleeps, but a place he sees as "home." "I have a barber that I've been going to for fifteen years. I have his phone number. I know his kids." Lance boasts that he can call his barber and get his hair cut at any time, day or night. Like others, Lance believes black service providers, like his barber, are uniquely qualified to care for black hair and thereby cater to blacks' needs. Living near black commercial establishments makes engaging in consumption of racialized services convenient.

Beyond commercial spaces, black churches are powerful and prominent institutions operating within black neighborhoods. Marcus, who grew up in and returns to Newark as an adult, attends church every Sunday to make sure, as he puts it, that his week gets off to a positive start. The experience is uplifting, like "a family reunion with a motivational speaker." Going to church means receiving an inspirational message in the company of "people that I've known forever." Marcus's neighborhood church is a convenient place that helps to ground him and connect him to the black community. For several respondents, black churches celebrate and reinforce black cultural traditions, and some, like the Abyssinian Baptist Church located in Harlem, are honored institutions due to their storied histories. The presence of black churches is just one more factor that contributes to the symbolic and social value middle-class blacks attach to living in black neighborhoods.

Living in a black neighborhood also allows my interviewees to cultivate cultural skills and develop and display their black cultural capital. Recall, for example, Tasha's comment quoted earlier in which she notes that in her neighborhood "the doctor and the drug dealer" greet each other on the street by saying "what's up?"—illustrating how black language is incorporated freely in communications across class lines between blacks who live in black neighborhoods. Black talk is part of the everyday public discourse in black neighborhoods.

Damon values living in a black neighborhood because he sees such neighborhoods as places where black culture can thrive, they are "pockets of black culture." Others, too, note the tremendous value of living near iconic black cultural institutions, such as the Apollo Theater and the Schomburg Center for Research in Black Culture. People can engage their black cultural capital by attending neighborhood events and cultural celebrations like the Dance Africa festival in Brooklyn or the Harlem book fair. Living in black neighborhoods, middle-class blacks can enjoy a vibrant black cultural life.

The Social Dimensions of Black Neighborhoods

What does it mean to be a part of a community? What characteristics of neighborhoods afford people a sense of being part of or included in a symbolic community? Respondents who choose to live in black neighborhoods perceive the opportunity to have daily interactions with other blacks as a fulfilling aspect of their neighborhood experiences. It is these mundane, causal interactions with black neighbors that affirm their sense of being a part of both a real and an imagined black community.

Sharon, a 27-year-old advertising executive, lives in central Harlem. After growing up in a majority white suburb of Washington, DC, attending a majority white college, and working in the advertising industry, which is known for its lack of diversity, Sharon feels "it is just nice to be around black people":

> I like waking up in the morning and seeing black people and, you know, I like people calling me "sister." It's a sense of community to me. A sense of the older, grandma, grandpa people; I literally look at them like grandma, grandpa status. So them, even randomly, inviting me over for Easter, giving me ham. That is so, it is just so communal to me.

For Sharon, a child of Ghanaian immigrants, these casual yet intimate exchanges—such as the generosity displayed on holidays by neighborhood elders—are deeply meaningful. It is in these small, everyday ways that living where she does enables her to feel connected to her neighbors, but also to a larger symbolic black community.

Angela, a 28-year-old attorney working at a large corporate firm, remarks that there are good and bad aspects of living in her neighborhood of Crown Heights, Brooklyn. For her, the bad is "definitely crime and drugs and all of that stuff." But the good is the "sense of community." When she leaves her majority white corporate workplace each evening and heads home, Angela feels she is truly heading to a place of solace. Other Crown Heights residents are not strangers but her *neighbors*. Speaking appreciatively about "the culture and the people" of her Brooklyn neighborhood, she admits that she feels she knows her neighbors on a personal level: "you go to church together and you know each other's kids." In comparison, when she lived on the Upper West Side, she felt disconnected from the people and the place.

Kendra, who admits to being suspicious of black professionals who don't live in black neighborhoods, similarly notes that she feels she could rely on her neighbors, that she could call on them. "I really feel that it is a community here. I feel like there are people I could trust if something were to happen [to me]." Through these easy and ordinary interactions, middle-class blacks are able to establish and sustain a sense of community and social trust with other blacks.

Robert, a 28-year-old senior associate at a bank who grew up in both Brooklyn and Queens, currently lives in central Harlem. He enthuses that he "loves it." When I ask what he loves most about the neighborhood, he quickly and succinctly replies, "the people." He sees value in living in a place where he "can come home and feel accepted and be accepted by my neighbors." He tells me that he talks to his neighbors practically every day. They greet one another, exchange "hellos" and "good evenings," and ask each other about their day. He nurtures his relationship with his neighbors through these routine social interactions. Even though he has not had to call on them for help, he believes that he could knock on his neighbors' door and ask for assistance. In comparison, at work, Robert feels he must always have his glasses on, in order to disarm his coworkers who might see him as a threat. For a black man, the idea of being accepted and safe at home in one's neighborhood is of no small significance. Indeed, research indicates that black men, in particular, report facing added surveillance when they travel in and through white neighborhoods.[12] The affirming nature of their social interactions in black neighborhoods is, to my black middle-class participants, an advantage of living in these neighborhoods.

For those who had not lived in black majority neighborhoods growing up, like Tasha and Sharon, both the racial symbolism and the chance for everyday social interactions with other blacks are seen as desirable. Having grown up in white, suburban communities, some middle-class blacks sought out black neighborhoods to procure an experience that contrasted with that of being "the only" black on the block. As Janae, a 32-year-old freelance television producer residing in Clinton Hill, Brooklyn, explains:

> I wanted to be around people that looked like me because growing up in Claremont I was the only black person on my block. In my school there weren't that many. [In] college there weren't any. . . . So I wanted to live in a community that I had not experienced. Meeting and seeing people like me everywhere, all around, like upper-, middle-, lower-class, dark people. It doesn't matter . . . all classes.

For middle-class blacks who spent significant time during their childhoods in predominantly white communities, black neighborhoods are sought out not just because they represent a new or different experience, but because they offer a respite from the rest of the world and from a lifetime of having been the token black.

Many black neighborhoods in New York are homes to diasporic black populations. Yet only a few respondents mentioned the distinct ethnic flavor of their neighborhoods. Those neighborhoods are perceived as racially distinct black places that offer middle-class blacks a range of cultural and social experiences, which function as unique racial amenities. Robert, Sharon, and Janae, the children of African and West Indian immigrants, all value black spaces in the same ways that native-born blacks do. Whether central Harlem, Crown Heights, or Williamsbridge in the Bronx, black neighborhoods are places where middle-class blacks employ their black cultural capital. They worship and are rejuvenated for the week ahead at church, freshen up in the chair of their barber, materialize their belief in racial uplift by dining at a black-owned restaurant, and serve as a role model for neighborhood youth just by walking down the street.

The Trade-Offs

Being black and middle class and living in a largely black neighborhood offers a rich combination of symbolic and social rewards. However, it also imposes distinct burdens. Two challenges middle-class blacks living in black neighborhoods report are directly related to their class status. First, their neighborhoods are stigmatized. Often, majority black neighborhoods are seen by outsiders as an incoherent choice for someone who is middle class. If people work in an esteemed profession, why wouldn't they live in a place commensurate with their standing? When they talk with others, particularly white coworkers, it is clear that these respondents' neighborhoods have reputations, being known as the "hood" or "ghetto."

Second, my interviewees also reveal that they are often unable to realize their class-based tastes and preferences because their neighborhoods lack amenities that cater to their middle-class tastes and sensibilities. They reiterate the convenience of having black-owned businesses and retail establishments that cater to black clientele nearby, but lament that their desire for fine dining or boutique fitness studios goes unfulfilled. This is a definite downside, and navigating these challenges requires economic resources and cultural flexibility. Middle-class blacks living in black neighborhoods simultaneously draw on personal resources to work around the amenities their neighborhoods lack and utilize their cultural skills to determine whether and when black spaces are perceived negatively. They then work strategically to limit the impact that the stigma attached to black places might have on them.

While respondents see their black neighborhoods as iconic centers of black culture, as places where they are accepted, and social spaces that feel familial, what they associate with their neighborhoods is often dramatically different from what they perceive outsiders think about their neighborhoods. They report that their neighborhoods are often stigmatized due to racially tinged misconceptions about and fears of their beloved black neighbors.

Marcus was raised in Newark and moved back after he graduated from college. He "felt indebted to the city," a place that he found "endearing." He proudly proclaims, "I belong here." Still, Marcus is cognizant of the fact that outsiders view Newark "in a poor light." When people think of Newark, he said, they typically "think of murders and stolen cars." He works in education and mentions that sometimes his white male colleagues or the white volunteers at his agency are afraid to go into some of the middle and high schools that his nonprofit services. Marcus is "not afraid of any of these places" and thinks others' fearfulness and disparaging views are "a little exaggerated." This child of Newark feels responsible for defending his hometown against mischaracterizations of it as a dangerous and undesirable place.

Shante, a 25-year-old marketing professional who works at a majority female, majority white media company, is proud and excited to speak about her neighborhood. She grew up in rural Georgia in a largely white town with a family that is "very community-minded." Her background influences the meaning she attaches to being black: for her, interacting with other blacks and engaging in racial uplift is a part of who she is. She explains, "as a black woman, it's my responsibility to care about black children and care about the black image and give back, doing what I can." So after college, when she moved to New York, Shante did two things: she moved to Harlem and she got involved in a mentorship program. For her, Harlem maintains an iconic status as a place where black culture thrives:

> Harlem, you think of Harlem Renaissance, and you think black people. That is the biggest thing. So I was excited to come to Harlem and definitely you find all different kinds of black people, which is nice. I grew up in a pretty white community so I didn't really interact that much with black people on a daily basis, outside of black people from my church. But there's, like, every kind here, so

that is cool. But then when you go to midtown . . . [with] people, like, coworkers or people in my industry who don't live in Harlem, it has a, it pretty much has a negative connotation, because everybody is like, it is the "hood." You know, "I'm not coming to visit you!" Which is fine.

Shante celebrates the neighborhood's reputation of being "the African American cultural capital."[13] But as her experience shows, her positive valuation of her neighborhood, diverges from that of her white coworkers. For her white coworkers, Harlem becomes a stand-in for black neighborhoods more broadly, which they see as undesirable places. This experience is common for those who live in black neighborhoods. As much as some middle-class blacks love their hoods, they find their enthusiasm is not mirrored in their non-black coworkers' attitudes toward the places that they call home. Some might argue that, with their growing white populations, these neighborhoods' reputations have improved, but at the time of these interviews, these neighborhoods had not undergone dramatic racial transition and still carried negative stigma. In some sense, this illustrates that the stigma attached to places can change, but it also underscores that an influx of white residents might be required to improve the reputation of black neighborhoods.

Sharon's white colleagues view her neighborhood as a distant place they would rarely, if ever, visit. She believes that they associate Harlem with crime—as "shoot-'em-up city, get robbed, get mugged, 'oh my gosh it's far away.'" Sharon does not feel her coworkers appreciate Harlem's charm and its unique racial and cultural attributes. In the literature on this topic, Maria Krysan and her colleagues similarly have found evidence that black neighborhoods are perceived as being distant and unfamiliar to whites, thus reinforcing their rankings as low-status or undesirable places.[14] Elijah Anderson suggests that whites perceive "black spaces" as off-limits, unfamiliar, and unsavory.[15] Those I interviewed who live in black neighborhoods perceive that their neighborhoods are viewed by outsiders in ways that are comparable with these findings.

The association of crime with black neighborhoods is particularly prevalent. Damon assumes that his coworkers, who are nearly all white, conflate crime and drugs with the racial makeup of his neighborhood: "When I say 'Harlem,' they just assume probably a bunch of black people and crack-heads running around." While respondents rarely mentioned being fearful of crime or that crime is a highly salient characteristic of their perception or experience living in black neighborhoods, they recognize that their neighborhoods have good and bad areas. Unlike outsiders, they are more confident in their ability to judge which parts of their neighborhood are truly unsafe and off-limits. That, in itself, is proof of how their choice to live in a black neighborhood reinforces an insider status—only those in the know would know where not to go. Lance, who describes feeling at home in his neighborhood in the Bronx, notes that his coworkers see his neighborhood as simply "the hood":

> Bad, like you don't want to [be] walking here after a certain time of night. Which is the other reason why I consider it home because while some people might feel unsafe walking there at a certain time of night, I'm like, well, it's my block. I'll be fine. Although there's certain parts within my neighborhood, I'm not walking in. After twenty-something years of living there, I'm still not walking there.

Lance notes that rather than simply decrying the entire place as dangerous, *he* is able to discern areas that are safe from those are not. He does not condemn the entire place, but he is also not blind to potential danger.

For middle-class blacks, the knowledge that their black neighborhoods are stigmatized places is also evident in others' surprise that they have chosen to live in such neighborhoods. There is a perceived status mismatch. Angela, the corporate attorney, describes the sense of shock when she reveals where she lives to others at her firm. She says that, when it comes up in conversation, after telling her coworkers where she lives, there is always an awkward silence. It is as if her choice to live in Crown Heights leaves her white coworkers speechless. Angela often runs into people from her office in her neighborhood, but only the support staff, like the secretaries and folks who work in the mailroom. Even they are surprised to see that she lives in the same neighborhood: the firm's attorneys are supposed to live in "fancy" neighborhoods, not majority black ones.

Given the negative stigma attached to black neighborhoods, many middle-class blacks are concerned that their neighborhoods' reputation might affect how they are viewed. Sociologists Robert Sampson and Stephen Raudenbush classify the negative perceptions attached to neighborhoods that are then extended to the residents of those neighborhood as "ecological contamination."[16] Middle-class blacks living in predominantly black neighborhoods are aware of the risks and negative reputational repercussions of being "contaminated" by a neighborhood's stigma, and so they draw upon a number of cultural maneuvers to limit the negative social and reputational costs that might arise. In many ways, this is similar to their strategically *not* engaging in black cultural capital in majority white workplaces. Their choice to live in a black neighborhood reflects a desire to materialize their black cultural capital, allowing them to actualize racialized ideological commitments and feelings of racial belonging, but it also makes their racialized preferences evident. In particular, it is often seen as inconsistent with their middle-class status as it does not match pervasive ideas about the type of neighborhood consistent with a middle-class lifestyle.

One way of avoiding the negative reputational costs that might result from middle-class blacks' housing choice is simply to not disclose it to whites, and this happens often with white coworkers. Shante, who values black neighborhoods as unique cultural spaces, remarks, "I don't tell many people where I live who aren't black or cool." Some respondents report referring to a larger area or a proximate, but less stigmatized area. For instance, instead of revealing that they live in Harlem or the Bronx, they will tell people they live "near the Upper West Side" (which typically means the area just south of Harlem) or "Uptown." This sort of cultural maneuvering, deciding when and with what specificity to denote where they live, demonstrates their ability to engage strategically. By doing so, they demonstrate their cultural flexibility, recognizing when their neighborhood is perceived negatively, then describing where they live in coded terms.

At times, middle-class blacks who live in black neighborhoods take a more defensive stance. They openly confront those who might question their neighborhoods and their choice to live there. They do so to inform people, whom they perceive as "ignorant," of the many points of pride that come with living in a majority black neighborhood. Robert, for example, feels that he should never have to justify his decision, but also that he has a duty to "educate" the misinformed.

Managing negative views about their neighborhoods or mitigating the effects of "ecological contamination" requires cultural maneuvering. While at work, middle-class blacks might not discuss with their colleagues or boss where they live with any precision or great detail. At the same time, living in a black neighborhood might be a point of pride and shared experience among black coworkers, those whom they perceive as appreciating black culture, or as Shante suggests, those who are "cool." Often respondents reported that they entertain black coworkers in their homes, but not white coworkers. Black coworkers tend not to exhibit an aversion to visiting them nor do they judge their decision to live in a black neighborhood negatively.

These black coworkers also often share their cultural tastes and partake in similar types of leisure activities outside of work. Many of the respondents' black coworkers live in the same or similar neighborhoods, and appreciate a black neighborhood's social-interactional character and recognize its cultural amenities as attractive features. Nonetheless, this cultural maneuvering is indicative of the recognized necessity for the respondents of avoiding racial stigma—the bad reputation of one's hood—while also knowing when to express the pride they maintain in the places they call home and often feel most comfortable.

Another highly salient trade-off for respondents is their inability to satisfy their class-based preferences because their neighborhoods lack services and amenities that would satisfy their middle-class tastes and proclivities. When I ask if she shops in her neighborhood of Crown Heights, Angela replies, "There are not a lot of places to shop." Middle-class blacks who live in black neighborhoods complain of a lack of diversity among vendors and also find the products that are locally available to be of poor or inferior quality. Enacting their race-based neighborhood preferences often means traveling to other areas to actualize their class-based tastes and preferences.

They, for instance, dine out in other neighborhoods because there are so few "nice" options close to home. As Tasha laments, "There's no Thai restaurants here. . . . If me and my boyfriend are, like, let's go out to eat, we don't go out to eat in Harlem. If we go somewhere, we go downtown or to [the] Upper West Side." While her neighborhood now has a number of new restaurants and establishments, changes in the neighborhood's racial makeup seem concurrent with the new commercial landscape. My respondents also note a lack of variety in businesses catering to diverse patrons. Often, they don't just complain, but vehemently express their frustration about the lack of retail and commercial conveniences in their black neighborhoods. Vanessa is outraged at the number of fried chicken takeout spots in Harlem, which she calls "nutri-cide." For her, the dearth of nutritious and healthy options makes the neighborhoods' residents susceptible to untimely death. Similarly, Amare describes his experience of living in but *not* dining in Crown Heights:

> Yeah, I don't dine [in my own neighborhood] because . . . all the food is fatty and greasy. And . . . it's just not good for you. You know, like whatever happened to chicken Caesar salad, or like a turkey sandwich, or things like that. Those things are lacking in my neighborhood; there's no real diner where I can go and eat.

> And if there was one that I thought was reputable, I would go there and patron-
> ize them. But like it's just lacking.

Amare would like to support restaurants in his neighborhood, but can't bring himself to subsist on the "fatty and greasy" fare available nearby. Others believe the grocery stores in their neighborhood sell fruit and vegetables that are quick to rot or suspect meat, and in general, food that is of poor or inferior qual-ity. Consistent with research that shows comparatively fewer shops and retail spaces in black neighborhoods, these middle-class blacks often head outside their neighborhoods to make even simple purchases.

Many black neighborhoods suffer from poor food availability as a conse-quence of what some scholars have called "grocery store redlining,"[17] so it is not surprising that this is a frequent complaint. But middle-class blacks also observe a lack of breadth in other retail sectors, such as the types and styles of clothing available for purchase in their neighborhoods. Darryl, who lives in West New York, New Jersey, reports that his neighborhood shops "don't have the kind of clothes that I'm looking for," and Lance states nonchalantly, "I don't shop in my neighborhood anymore because they don't, they don't re-ally offer what I want to buy. I mean the only thing I usually would buy in my neighborhood was maybe a fitted hat. . . . Maybe summertime I'll shop for a white tee to go to a barbecue or some socks." Beyond shops with basic goods or streetwear, there are few places Lance could go in his neighborhood to find clothing that suited his class-based taste. The styles sold in his neighborhood would be "unacceptable" and would make him feel out of place in many of the venues where he likes to socialize. As he puts it, "the clothes that they sell in my neighborhood is for, you know, basically if you were sitting on the corner":

> There's no, no Men's Wearhouses. You can't find a trench coat. You can't find a nice
> decent coat that . . . you don't feel uncomfortable going to work in. If I went to
> work in anything that they sold in the store, of course I'd be the typical black man.

By "the typical black man," Lance means that he would be perceived—in ac-cordance with a stereotype—as criminal or idle. Wearing the clothes sold in his neighborhood to work, would stall any chance of advancement there. Middle-class blacks living in black neighborhoods find it frustrating that it is nearly impossible to satisfy their class-based tastes and inclinations in their neighbor-hoods, across consumptive domains, whether shopping for food or clothing.

This means they often leave their neighborhoods to procure items that they want. Sometimes they pay for services that deliver goods to them. Before a new grocery store opened up, Kendra used to order her groceries online and have them delivered. She avoids the neighborhood grocery store near her apartment because it is expensive, "dirty," and has "the worst produce." She believes the store continues to operate despite its poor condition and the poor quality of its products because "the people who live there can't afford to shop anywhere else." She, however, could and does seek out better options:

> They didn't have to have fresh anything essentially, because everyone who lived in the neighborhood shopped there and the prices were higher. So essentially what I was ordering from FreshDirect was almost the exact same prices I would have spent at C-Town minus one or two things. So, for me, I will pay somebody to drop off my groceries at my house and I know that everything that comes out of that box is fresh versus shopping at C-Town just because it's down the street.

Kendra put her middle-class sensibilities to use and found a work-around to get the products and services she finds satisfactory. She does not mind spending more to get better quality groceries, but she is simultaneously aware that not everyone has the resources to do the same.

Vanessa sees her ability to shop outside the confines of the neighborhood as a luxury. She comments that she is bothered by the prevalence of obesity in her neighborhood and attributes it to a dearth of healthy, nearby options:

> I've been here for six years, and a decent grocery store just opened on my block this year. Which I am extremely excited about. Before I would always go to Fairway, or go food shopping outside my area, but for other parents who don't have that luxury, who have to go with what's closer or most convenient, you know there is a very significant struggle for them to feed themselves and to feed their families.

Kendra and Vanessa know they benefit from their class status when it comes to consumption. They are cognizant that options afforded to them are not options for others in their neighborhood. And they enact their class-based preferences by venturing outside the neighborhood when they have to.

Neighborhood Discomfort

Most middle-class blacks living in black neighborhoods seek out these areas for the sense of community they bestow. Still, a few of my respondents who live in majority black neighborhoods describe their class status as becoming highly salient in ways that make them feel, at times, out of place. Part of their discomfort results from being exposed to different interactional codes and class-coded social norms.

Some study participants feel that they wear their class status on their sleeves; their clothing being an important marker of that status. How they dress for work, to adhere to professional dress code standards, serves to differentiate black professionals as they travel each day on their daily commutes from their majority black neighborhoods to their workplaces.

Damon is fully invested in his neighborhood—he has recently bought a condo—and he relishes "being around this many black people." He feels a part of what Du Bois dubbed the "talented tenth," an exceptional class of blacks charged with the task of advancing the race.[18] Sometimes, though, he feels a bit out of place as one of few black men dressed in a suit and tie on his way to work: "When I go to work in the morning . . . because I am a black man dressed up going to work . . . like, you feel the eyes on you. It's like, 'It's not Sunday. What you wearing that for? Got your church suit on, on a Tuesday.'" Other black men say the same: wearing a suit, the expected attire in their workplaces, is a marker of class status that makes them stand out in their neighborhood.

In contrast, black women's class status is not as easily determined by their clothing. This may be because business attire for women could be associated with many different positions. For example, a woman who wears a black sheath dress, pearls, and black pumps may be a CEO or an executive aide. While middle-class black women's class position may not be discernible through their attire, these respondents describe how their gender is often highly salient in their interactions with male strangers on the street in ways that made them, at times, feel uneasy.

"Hey, Baby, hey Mama, let me walk with you"; "How you doing, hello, how are you? Can I talk to you for a minute?"; "Ay, yo!"; "Hey Chocolate, hey sexy, can I talk to you for a second, can I get your number?" These are examples of the catcalls that female interviewees living in black neighborhoods report experiencing almost daily. Not only are these interactions galling and gendered, they can be an affront to these women's class sensibilities. As Alysha, a financial analyst, explains:

> These young groups of boys, they just get a little reckless and it's just like, not I'm so much fearful that they would hurt me, but just I'm coming home from work and I'm tired, please don't try to strike up a conversation with me and keep it going . . . like you can bet money that [as you] walk past them somebody's got something to say!

Most black women living in black neighborhoods perceive street harassment, as Alysha does, as a mere annoyance. Alysha calls attention to the status mismatch, which often is enveloped in these interactions, between her arriving home to her neighborhood from work and the "young boys" hanging out and playing around. Several women describe wearing earbuds to both drown out catcalls and make it evident they are not listening. Sharon calls it "operation turn-up-the-iPod," stating that she uses her iPod and visible earphones "to drown out any of the comments that might make [me] feel uncomfortable or [that I don't] know how to respond to."

Some women's responses to catcalls are class-imbued. Janae, the freelance producer who grew up in a majority white neighborhood, says she knows street harassment is "harmless," but she usually "ends up walking the other way." She explains, "it is a difference in culture in a way; I didn't grow up around it," implying that she does not share in the interactional norms that might deem this type of street harassment tolerable because she grew up in a predominantly white, middle-class neighborhood.

Being exposed to everyday street harassment might seem to be a huge burden, but that is not how the black women who encounter it describe it to me. There are positive and affirming interactions that transpire in their neighborhoods; catcalls are an added and unfortunate cost, but they are not seen as a reason to avoid living in a black neighborhood. However, the pervasiveness of street harassment indicates that black women experience predominantly black public spaces differently as a consequence of their gender. Interestingly, this type of experience is not mentioned by middle-class black women living in predominantly white upper-crust neighborhoods. It is often assumed that all black people experience black neighborhoods similarly, but as the reports of middle-class black women reveal, their multiple identities combine to shape their experience of place.

Being Black and Middle Class and Living in an Upper-Class White Neighborhood

Middle-class blacks who live in predominantly white, high-status neighborhoods talk about the ease of access and the prestige attached to the places they call home. Residing in these types of neighborhoods makes living a middle-class lifestyle stress-free, with plentiful parks, parking, and luxury shops. For them, the trade-offs include being subject to heightened visibility, racial stereotypes, and social isolation, all consequences associated with being a racial token.[19]

Jasmine, who lives on the Upper East Side, describes her neighborhood as "classy." Others use the words "wealthy" and "expensive" to describe their majority white, upper-class neighborhoods. Often, these middle-class blacks recognize and value the social prestige, perceive exclusivity attached to these locales, and contrast their positive reputations with the stigma attached to predominantly black neighborhoods. Lisa, a 32-year-old with a Stanford MBA, who is the managing partner for a start-up, has experienced this firsthand: "New Yorkers are very conscious of [the city] block by block. . . . They're able to make a lot of assumptions about your life based on the corner that you live on." Since moving from a largely minority neighborhood to a majority white one, Lisa has noticed a difference in how people respond when they learn where she lives. She finds that mentioning her old neighborhood generally elicits remarks from whites like, "oh, that's far," or it tends to halt the conversation altogether. Whites' silence in the midst of a conversation about the place where one lives is interpreted by middle-class blacks as disinterest or disdain, a devaluing of majority minority spaces. Now that Lisa lives in Gramercy, not only are whites interested and willing to engage in a conversation about her neighborhood, they are *excited* to do so. Conversations about where she lives now elicit questions about her experience in the neighborhood and discussions about local restaurants or shops. Lisa's observations suggest high-status white neighborhoods make a positive impression, signaling cultural similarity to whites, while minority neighborhoods are seen as unfamiliar, signaling dissimilarity and distance.

Upmarket Amenities

In addition to the prestige, middle-class blacks who live in wealthy, white neighborhoods place a premium on lifestyle conveniences. They value boutiques, high-end shops, luxury apartment buildings, pricey gyms, easy access to parks, and plentiful paid parking. Brittany, the attorney who lives on the Upper East Side, likes having an abundance of amenities:

> There are so many things I can get within a two-block radius of where I live, whether it'd be shoes, clothes. There's even a Petco. I had a fish for a little while. It was so convenient. . . . There's a lot of little nice brunch places. There's a lot of little nice lunch places. So it's a variety, and it's a very busy area. . . . I mean there's even two bars right on my block, so there's people outside all times of night. . . . I just felt like even though it was expensive, it was just me. I could afford it, and so I was there.

Brittany mentions that there are places to shop for clothes and shoes, while, in contrast, Lance remarks that there are no places in his neighborhood where he might shop for clothing, unless he needs something to wear to a cookout. Brittany likes having ample places where she can engage in leisure, with brunch and lunch spots close by and even two bars on her block. The convenience of it all makes living out a middle-class lifestyle easy.

Stacey, a 28-year-old who works in the advertising industry and lives on the Upper East Side, notes that she likes living near Central Park, where she regularly walks her large dog. She is happy to have a pet supply store near where she lives. The fact that these majority white, upper-class neighborhoods are accommodating to pet owners, with pet stores and parks, is indicative of the presence of not just more amenities but also specific amenities that cater to the tastes and sensibilities of the middle and upper classes. In their research, marketing scholars Sonya Grier and Vanessa Perry found that the presence of coffee shops and dog parks is indicative of the class character of a neighborhood.[20] Similarly, researchers have found that affluent people favor neighborhoods that cater to dog owners.[21] A huge benefit of residing in a majority white, prestigious neighborhood for my study respondents is the effortlessness of access and proximity to places where they can engage in their middle-class tastes and proclivities.

The Trade-Offs

Living in "privileged" places with lots of conveniences also exposes middle-class blacks to racially alienating experiences, consistent with the social costs of being a token. Their experience of race in their neighborhoods is unlike the experience of those who choose to live in black neighborhoods, where they believe black people will feel at home and black culture is celebrated. Those who live in majority white, high-status neighborhoods report feeling invisible or ignored, or hyper-visible but in ways consistent with racial stereotypes.

When middle-class blacks describe what it is like to be the only black on the block, certain types of encounters come up repeatedly. Often, they detect that their neighbors are hypersensitive to their race. For some, this emerges in the sense that they are out of place in their surroundings or do not totally belong. Black men often report encountering racial stereotypes and micro-aggressions, even an association with criminality. Isaiah, a 31-year-old entrepreneur living in a luxury building in New Rochelle, Connecticut, explains:

> I feel like, certain people are just looking at me [and thinking] how the hell can he afford this car and this apartment, what does he do? . . . So my neighbor,

he would already try to talk all like, "Yo, whuz up, brother, still workin' hard?" Yeah, "Keep hustling."

Not only are some of his neighbors baffled that he could afford to live there, this particular white neighbor thought that he must be a "hustler" or sell drugs. As a young black entrepreneur who owns multiple businesses and investment properties, Isaiah finds the presumption that his financial success could only be ascribed to criminality insulting, to say the least.

James, a mild-mannered man in his late thirties living on Staten Island, senses that his neighbors were initially frightened by him. Speaking in the third person, he imitates his neighbors' initial assessments of this black man in their midst: "probably been in jail, that he didn't graduate from school, that he didn't work, and would have a whole bunch of women coming in and out of his place." James thinks his neighbors' anti-black biases are driven by several stereotypes that are indicative of cultural racism. Only after he revealed that he was a New York City firefighter did he feel that his neighbors changed their perceptions. They respect firefighters and they associate them with being upstanding, so— because the fire department won't hire someone with a criminal record—*he* must be a good guy. Black women, like Brittany and Lisa, did not report feeling out of place as a consequence of racial stereotypes that associate blacks with criminality, but they did feel either invisible or hyper-visible, a racial anomaly. Thus, interestingly, gender, too, impacts the experiences of middle-class blacks in prestigious white spaces, echoing the fact that lived experiences of members of the black middle class are affected by gender, particularly in terms of the stereotypes they encounter and have to defuse.

Amid the abundant commercial spaces in their upper-class neighborhoods, my respondents find few that cater to or satisfy black patrons' racialized tastes. This is particularly true for the social scene. Predominantly white neighborhoods are not places to go out with their black friends. Brittany comments that even though her neighborhood has "a lot of little bars . . . I guess I have to honestly say I go to places where I could socialize with black people." She anticipates that even if she did go to a neighborhood bar, it would be a "different type of night." As she explains:

> The type of music that you're gonna hear in an all-black setting is maybe different than what you'll hear in an all-white setting. . . . There's a different vibe. I mean, quite honestly, I feel like I'm not really used to interacting with non-black males. Especially if I'm out at a white bar, I think I'll be less likely to interact

with males, 'cause it's outside everybody's comfort zone. And again, I'm saying all this as a single woman. This is something we encounter, and it's like if I go to an all-black setting, it'd be more likely that I will find a guy to talk to.

When it comes to going out with the objective of meeting a possible romantic partner, she ventures out of the Upper East Side, where she lives. Dive bars are a popular type of venue in her neighborhood, but these aren't places where she anticipates attracting male attention. Others mention going to black neighborhoods to get their hair styled or cut and to go to church. Renee, whose apartment is not far from Wall Street, tells me when it comes to church: "I haven't been going regularly but I would like to go more. I would like to go to Bible study. I would love to join the choir." But living downtown makes it difficult for her to get to her church, located in Harlem. Whenever she does go, she feels she is always rushing or "arriving late" because of the commute. The added travel time makes doing things that cultivate or employ black cultural capital inconvenient. So, while middle-class blacks enjoy a diverse set of amenities living in majority white neighborhoods, these amenities rarely satisfy their penchant for black culture or provide them with occasions to interact with other blacks.

Not all study respondents characterize the reason they select a neighborhood as based on the amenities, cultural or social or otherwise. Some prioritize proximity to family and close social ties. William, the high school teacher and school administrator with a young son, lives in a predominantly Hispanic section of the Bronx and rents an apartment upstairs from his aunt. Being close to family is particularly important for this single dad, who finds it reassuring that he can always call on his family when he needs help or childcare.

This is to say that, when people are evaluating and deciding on neighborhoods, their preferences reflect a complex array of considerations: affordability, the features of the housing available, the distance to work, the quality of the schools, and so on.[22] Theories that suggest that market-relevant traits, such as a person's income, are key to determining residential preferences inadequately consider that neighborhoods maintain symbolic, cultural, and social-interactional qualities that affect their perceived desirability. The findings presented in this chapter demonstrate that middle-class blacks consider both racial and class-based preferences when deciding where to live, and rarely find a place that suits both entirely.

The choice of neighborhood is an important consumptive decision because where we live can make it easy or difficult to engage our tastes and preferences. For some middle-class blacks, majority black neighborhoods are desirable, despite perceptions of such neighborhoods as low-status, stigmatized places. These respondents value black neighborhoods, seeing them as places where they can engage in cultural practices and have social interactions with in-group members that help them to realize and affirm their racial group membership. However, these same respondents report that their neighborhoods have few services and amenities catering to a middle-class clientele. In contrast, blacks who favor class-based preferences, residing in high-status, majority white neighborhoods, report doing so because they value both the prestige associated with their neighborhoods and the up-market amenities of these locations. They want effortless access to the things and experiences that they see as part of their middle-class lifestyle. But these respondents also indicate that they pay a racial cost for enacting their class-based preferences, having to contend with racial stigma and the heightened salience of their race in their interactions with their neighbors, and being unable to satisfy their race-based cultural consumption.

Middle-class blacks maintain a matrix of cultural consumption preferences and practices that reflect their black cultural capital and their middle-class tastes and style of life. As we leave the neighborhoods that middle-class blacks call home and explore their workplaces, we will see how they negotiate the maintenance of black cultural capital and demonstrate cultural flexibility in the working world, which imposes an entirely different set of cultural requirements and constraints that middle-class blacks must navigate.

Work, Work, and More Work at Work

5

DARRYL, THE PART-TIME DJ and full-time investment banker, epitomizes cultural flexibility. He acknowledges and adheres to the cultural standards of his majority white workplace, but also engages in black cultural practices that are meaningful to him in his free time. One way he conforms in the workplace is by carefully managing his appearance. "I don't have to wear a suit and tie every day, I don't have to wear a blazer every day, but I do it anyway," Darryl explains. He describes the firm's clients as "conservative," and figures that how he dresses is a visual cue that can remind his white colleagues, clients, and superiors that he is a safe bet, prepared for impromptu meetings and capable of engaging wealthy clients in a way that makes them comfortable. Like so many other modern black middle-class Americans, Darryl has a well-honed ability to recognize and to modify his style of dress, his personal grooming, and what he reveals or does not reveal about his personal life to signal cultural alignment with coworkers when he perceives it is necessary.

This chapter examines how the middle-class blacks in my study managed their self-presentation, specifically their dress and personal grooming on the job. As argued in Chapter Three, grooming and hair, in addition to styles of dress, are part of the everyday consumption practices that express (or suppress) black cultural capital, as well as an individual's class identity. In Chapter Four, we saw how choice of neighborhood allowed middle-class blacks to express either black cultural capital or class-based tastes. Recall that one of the ramifications of living in a majority black neighborhood is managing non-black coworkers' negative perceptions of such areas. This chapter builds on this theme as it relates to the consequences of maintaining and expressing black cultural capital at work. To heighten their status in the workplace, these middle-class blacks strategically display their cultural consumption and mobilize consumption practices to offset racial stigma attached not to their neighborhoods but to their blackness itself.

Many of my respondents work in majority white settings. On occasion, they can be unapologetically black, but more often they exhibit behavior consistent with the "Jackie Robinson Syndrome"—more on that later. They moderate their self-presentation, wielding cultural flexibility as they assess the racial makeup and the salience of race in their workplaces: how pervasive racial stigma and anti-black bias are among their clients, coworkers, and superiors; and the extent to which they must demonstrate their knowledge and mastery of dominant cultural mores. They carefully cultivate others' assessments of their social rank through strategic consumption. Talk about a long day at the office.

Middle-Class Blacks at Work

Research shows that workplace settings are often rife with negative racial stereotypes.[1] Middle-class blacks frequently confront negative perceptions of their racial group and barriers to full participation and incorporation in organizational life. In part this is due to institutional and organizational cultures that maintain and promote particular sets of racial meanings, and the fact that race is often embedded in workplace status hierarchies.[2]

Race impacts everything from company opportunity structures to evaluation criteria, and even individuals' display of emotions.[3] Research on corporate settings reveals that being black becomes "a conspicuous and observable characteristic that often makes them [blacks] subject a priori to negative consideration and treatment."[4] Ethnographic research, too, ranks race among the "persistent issues" facing blacks in corporate workplaces.[5] So, how do middle-class black professionals manage cultural racism and negative perceptions of blackness at work? How do they do so while also being unapologetically black?

Scholars usually use two measures to determine whether organizational settings are racially hospitable or hostile: demographic composition and institutional and organizational culture. Like most black professionals in the United States, many of my respondents were employed in workplaces and industries where blacks are in the minority. In fact, in many professional settings, blacks are hyper-tokens—that is, severely underrepresented (see Table 4).

Amare, the financial professional, uses culturally loaded language to describe his coworkers, who according to him consist of mostly "middle-aged WASPS" (white Anglo-Saxon Protestants). Other respondents describe their workplaces as "good old boy networks" or fraternity houses, even comparing them to the overwhelmingly white and male office on the AMC television show *Mad Men*. By describing their workplaces in these terms, they highlight not just a lack of diversity but a racial and cultural hierarchy in which white men rule. They also perceive their white coworkers to have had limited experiences and interactions with black people over the course of their lives. Kendra, the account executive, describes a team member as being from "suburban middle America, kind of like

TABLE 4. Blacks and Whites in Prestigious Occupations, 2018

Occupation	Total Employed (in thousands)	Percentage of Total Employed	
		WHITES	BLACKS
Accountants and auditors	1,929	75.8	9.3
Architects and engineers	3,263	79.3	6.5
Chief executives	1,573	89.5	3.5
Dentists	162	79.0	1.6
Lawyers	1,199	88.0	5.5
Pharmacists	348	67.9	7.2
Physicians and surgeons	1,094	70.8	7.6
Applications and systems software developers	1,682	58.6	3.9
Veterinarians	102	92.9	<0.1

SOURCE: Bureau of Labor Statistics, 2018, Current Population Study: Household Data Annual Averages: Table 11: Employed Persons by Detailed Occupation, Sex, Race, and Hispanic or Latino Ethnicity (Washington, DC: U.S. Department of Labor, Bureau of Labor Statistics), https://www.bls.gov/cps/cpsaat11.htm.

he can count all of his black friends on the one hand." Comments like Kendra's, convey not only that their workplaces are often largely white but also that their white coworkers are perceived as having curtailed cultural knowledge, and little to no experience of interacting with blacks.

Rosabeth Moss Kanter's theory of tokenism is useful here: my respondents report encountering heighten visibility, negative stereotypes, and social isolation when they are among the few black people in their workspaces.[6] Many scholars have outlined the adverse impact of token status, indicating that even when modulated by another social status (economically advantaged class position, for example), blackness (and other token statuses) can mean exclusion from institutional and organizational culture.[7] Managing the social and cultural requirements imposed in such settings requires additional cognitive and emotional labor.

The analysis of my respondents' experiences at work presented in this book centers not on workplace policies but on blacks' responses to workplace culture, standards, and racial stigma, across industries and workplace contexts. The degree to which they express racialized tastes through their dress and grooming is conditioned by their assessments of on-the-job cultural norms. I asked my respondents to describe their work settings, norms about clothing and hair, their coworkers, and their experiences and interactions at work as they manage their self-presentation. In majority minority spaces, middle-class blacks in my study report being freer to express themselves—having the ability to dress how they liked, to be themselves, on the job and off. But when middle-class blacks feel racially isolated, many police their own behavior and personal style, adopting practices that downplay their racial identity.

Such efforts to limit the impact of racial stigma and anti-black bias are meant to facilitate the formation of social relationships and counteract stereotypes that if unaddressed would otherwise result in experiences of social marginalization and exclusion. Such behavior exemplifies the Jackie Robinson Syndrome, described as a default double standard that requires blacks to exceed expectations, to be "superstars," outperforming whites, and to do it all without drawing too much attention to their race so that they can be looked upon as part of the team.[8]

The Jackie Robinson Syndrome

Jeff, the sales manager at a major insurance company, sees himself as the Jackie Robinson of his firm. Like the famed baseball player, Jeff feels he must exhibit exceptional composure in the face of racial stigma to ensure that other blacks

have opportunities at the management level. Jeff passionately makes his view-
point clear:

> If [Jackie Robinson] was spitting at people who were calling him the n-word,
> throwing stuff, getting mad at press conferences after the game, yeah, they would
> have been, like, "Shut it down"; "No more." However, he had to be quiet. He had
> to take the hits. He had to be docile and be, like, OK. [So that baseball teams
> would say about other blacks] "Yeah, look, they are not that bad; let them in."

Jeff, too, thinks of himself as a race representative. The team he supervises is the
most diverse in his department, and so he feels, "as a team, we have to cross our
t's and dot our i's, 'cause I don't want anyone, HR, no one, saying, or, coming up
with issues about my team." Jeff fervently believes that he cannot be mediocre
or average; his team has to come correct because the stakes involved are not
just how his team members will be judged, but how future non-white team
members will be judged.

None of my respondents reported that their work environments were racially hostile, but they note the salience of race in their interactions with their
coworkers. In majority white workplaces, they sense that they may be evaluated more harshly than their white coworkers. For the sake of their careers,
they try to be more "put together" than their white counterparts and take far
more care with their appearance. They describe wearing dress pants when their
white colleagues are wearing khakis. While they are sure to wear clothing that
is always clean and pressed, they describe white colleagues as wearing clothes
that are wrinkled or have holes. To highlight the contrast, they told me their
white colleagues dress to the minimum of the dress code, test its limits, and
wear clothes that at times can be inappropriate on the job. That isn't an option
for black professionals.

It is as if the middle-class blacks I spoke with had created for themselves a
second, more conservative dress code. Darryl shaves off his mustache and goa-
tee, for instance. William, one of the few black men at a school staffed mostly
by white women, notes that wearing his hair in cornrows means feeling hyper-
aware that his clothing must always be exceptionally "neat" and he must look
"nice." Yet, while he carefully irons his clothes, his white coworkers come to
work, according to him, wearing "some dingy ass, dirty ass t-shirt, or a sweater
with a hole in it. Flip-flops." Even if he could dress similarly without penalty,
William never would. He has too much pride to be seen at work in such undignified attire.

Alysha points out that her gender, in combination with her race, contributes to her stylistic choices for work. Being one of the few black women at her investment bank, she describes her career goals and personal dress code in tandem:

> I want people talking about my work and not what I look like. . . . I just want things to be a non-issue. I want physical things to be a non-issue. I already am one of the few [black women] on the floor, and the last thing I need is to be in some ostentatious color, or a low cut and tight outfit.

When I ask whether she feels pressure from her colleagues to dress conservatively, she indicates that the pressure, in part, comes from within; "Honestly, I wouldn't say it is from my colleagues. Because a lot of these young white girls, they push the limits a lot. But I just feel like we have different body types." Alysha simultaneously attributed her decision to dress conservatively to race and suggested that because she had "hips and [a] behind" she had to be conscious about how her clothes fit, presumably because some styles could seem overly sexy. For Alysha, gender and race were fused. This double-token status made her—and other women in my study—not just highly visible but highly aware of their bodies at work. Dressing in a way that could possibly be seen as racy is perceived as a no-no. To deemphasize their bodies, some even sought out clothes they deemed matronly: it couldn't be tight, short, show cleavage, or reveal them as being "curvaceous" or having a "big behind" (that is, as having the stereotypical black woman's body).

Managing perceptions of blackness in the office means that fit and good tailoring are absolutely essential when it comes to clothes, and neatness absolutely essential when it comes to grooming and hairstyles. Having unkempt hair or hair that the respondents describe as "lookin' crazy" is to be avoided at all cost. Of course, this is complex: black hairstyles and hair, even when neatly styled, may not conform to white cultural appearance norms. Hairstyles also serve as racial markers and are often understood to embody racial difference. Black people can also modify their hairstyles and textures to indicate assimilation or the adoption of white normative beauty standards.

Several women, especially those who interact with clients in their jobs, describe changing how they style their hair for professional reasons. Vanessa points out that to compete in her industry she simply has to do whatever it takes to make clients comfortable:

> [My clients] very well may not have a black person working for them that is not their assistant or not the janitor or whatever. And they don't see black people

out in the places they shop. They don't see them out in the street. They just don't
see black people. If I'm the only black person that you see, hum, and it's going
to make you more comfortable with me if my hair is straight, it's really nothing
you can do. We're talking about specifically client-based engagements. This is
money. . . . If you are my client and you need me to look a certain way, you are
talking about hundreds of thousands of dollars, I can straighten this [*she pointed
to her hair*]. How straight do you want it?

When interacting with whites, who live in and work in nearly all-white worlds,
Vanessa knows just her presence might make certain clients uncomfortable.
Wearing her hair naturally—in the curly, kinky afro she sported when we
met—simply might alarm them. Thus, Vanessa willingly straightens her hair
when she perceives doing so might help her to get and keep clients.

If black cultural capital is instantiated in hairstyles like two-strand twists,
braids, or a curly afro, my respondents' assimilatory styles suggest that on-the-
job displays of black cultural capital could accrue penalties. Lisa, the managing partner of a successful start-up, says frankly, "I've had braids in my life.
I've never had braids in my corporate life." And Sharon, the advertising professional, told me she got rid of her braids for job interviews, "because I was
thinking that I might look too quote-unquote ethnic and angry black woman,
Black Power-esque." A hairstyle that could be seen as demonstrating racial
pride risked eliciting negative stereotypes about black women and black culture. Braids could signal an unwillingness to conform and possibly a critical
stance. Any of these might negatively influence hiring committees' assessments
of whether or not a black candidate would fit in.

Recently, the New York City Commission on Human Rights issued protec-
tions that grant black workers freedom from being fired due to their hairstyles.
Guidelines issued in February 2019 provide some legal recourse to individuals
who have been harassed, punished, or fired because of the style of their hair.[9]
However, the legal precedent at the federal level still extends little protection
for blacks who are penalized because their natural hairstyles are perceived as
failing to conform to workplace aesthetic policies. Blacks can even be fired,
given the precedent established in the 1981 *Rogers v. American Airlines* case. In
that case, Renee Rogers sued American Airlines, her former employer, charg-
ing the company with racial discrimination based on a grooming policy that
prohibited employees from wearing an all braided hairstyle. In deciding the
case, the federal district court ruled in favor of American Airlines, arguing that

the "grooming policy applies equally to members of all races" and that an all braided hairstyle was not an immutable racial characteristic, and hence was undeserving of legal protection. This decision allows employers to legally impose formal rules that prohibit braids, twists, and dreadlocks. In 2018, the U.S. Supreme Court refused to review a case in which a black woman, Chastity Jones, had refused to cut off her locs and was subsequently not hired for the position that had been offered to her.[10] Until further action is taken in the courts to protect black workers, failing to conform to workplace rules, even racially biased ones, can result in adverse action, such as being fired or, as in Jones's case, having an offer rescinded.

Evidence that some middle-class blacks in my study feel compelled to modify their appearance, even if doing so is not their preference, supports claims that firms often demand "deep-level" cultural alignment.[11] Lauren Rivera argues that hiring committees select candidates they perceive as culturally similar, those who display characteristics consistent with the firm's "personality," indicated by "the typical extracurricular interests and self-presentation styles of their employees."[12] Many firms actively cultivate "country club" or "fratty" reputations, and it is easy to imagine that for a black person to land a job at such a firm, they would have to minimize their displays of black cultural capital to be read as someone who would fit in.

Sticking out because of their race often results in middle-class blacks' feeling that they are considered representatives of their race, a feature consistent with research on the social costs of token status. As Bryson, the corporate attorney, remarked, white coworkers might attribute *his* behavior to *all* black people. Many of the study's respondents who work in majority white workplaces feel that they are subject to surveillance—they are watched more closely than white colleagues. Renee shares in this sentiment: "I don't ever want to be perceived as being unprofessional, because I'm being looked at more closely than others are." Yes, it can be good to be noticed by your superiors, but feeling *watched* is an entirely different experience. It took respondents lots of extra work to ensure getting noticed for the right reasons.

Tasha's firm primarily employs white women, and she considers her behavior in light of this fact:

> In general, being a black woman, I'm careful because I don't want to be the one to keep them from ever [again] hiring another black girl. I want them to be, like, "she was fabulous," "she was great," "we are sorry to see her go." Because for me, at least, in the back of my mind, you never know how much their perception of

you is based on who you are as a person, or who you are as, like, judgment based on your skin color.

Professionals like Tasha and Jeff believe that they are, in part, responsible for ensuring opportunities for other blacks who may be hired after them. Even if they do not engage their black cultural capital at work, their behaviors are guided by a sense of obligation to the race and their sense of black pride.

Regardless of their credentials and professional standing, college-educated blacks often feel stereotypes are evident at work. Amare is aware of the pervasive perception that black men are violent and aggressive, and he actively works to refute that stereotype: "I don't want to ever be seen as the overly aggressive black guy. The angry black man or, you know, I don't want to get stigmatized." Consequently, he manages not only his appearance but also his social interactions and emotions. He makes sure to "never really get too animated, never really too excited, never really raise your voice, because you don't want that stigma." He perceives this is necessary because, as he explains, "You know, some of these people have never really dealt with black people before." Like Kendra, who believes her white colleague can count his black friends on one hand, Amare intuits that his coworkers have had few, if any, previous interactions with black people and might fear him for no other reason than his race. "I'm a joyful guy. I'm not really that big; I'm only six feet tall, two hundred pounds. But to a five-foot three-inch woman, you can look big and aggressive." Indeed, when he first started, his white coworkers seemed visibly uncomfortable around him, and as a consequence he feels, "you gotta play it low key." He explains: "I just know that I have my limitations of what I can do and say. Where other people would not have to. But I'm OK with that. I work within those boundaries. . . . I know that I can't be that animated." Tasha adds a gendered inflection to this management of emotions. She actively works to avoid being seen as a black woman with bad attitude, and she does not want to be thought of as difficult to work with. She quite consciously controls her emotions at work; if ever frustrated, she aims to still appear upbeat and agreeable. So at work, she notes, "I'm not aggressive; I'm not loud; I'm not confrontational. I'm generally not those things anyway, but I'm also aware that things that I may not let slide on a personal level, at work I'm just like, 'It's work, I'm going to let that go.'"

Renee observes that although her Asian colleague spoke openly about her personal life at work, she, as a black woman, cannot do the same. When I ask whether she can "be herself at work," Renee says, "I can be myself but I choose not to, you know, I try to separate personal and professional as much as possible." In contrast, her Asian coworker "will talk about her dating life. . . . She is just very transparent with her personal life, and I just choose not to be." Renee prefers not to divulge details about her personal life at work because she anticipates that being black, being perceived as engaging in certain practices would be judged by different standards. As she says, "I feel like, it could be, you know, 'she is a black woman, and she went to the club on Saturday,' whereas one of my non-black coworkers, when they talk about going to the bar, I don't think it is perceived in the same way." Her Asian colleague might talk about hanging out, partying, and dating different men, but if she were to do the same, she might be seen as confirming a negative stereotype about black women being promiscuous.

Efforts to appear culturally similar to their coworkers often mean curtailing their black cultural capital, including not using slang, avoiding expressive hand gestures, and not disclosing too much about their personal lives as that might make their race or racialized preferences evident. This was apparent, too, as they might purposefully avoid discussing their neighborhoods (when they lived in a majority black area). Robert, the senior associate at a major financial institution, working with high net worth individuals (clients with liquid assets over a million dollars), avoids mentioning his personal background, having been raised by a single mother. Revealing this part of his life, something that he has no shame about, could prove a costly mistake, as it might arouse stereotypical views about black families being broken or dysfunctional, and thus make him stand out in an undesirable way. Robert also stresses "playing it safe," and points out, "if you see me, I'm rocking glasses." He believes his glasses can lead others to think "this guy is obviously not a threat," and he believes, like Amare, that it is critical to reduce any fears or anxieties his mere presence as a black man might cause.

Robert told me that he had observed firsthand the negative "reception" of black cultural capital at work. He is a graduate of an elite, highly ranked college, and at work this is seen as aligned with the types of schools his employer mainly recruits from. In the case of those blacks who have attended historically black colleges and universities (HBCUs), an institutionalized form of black cultural capital, Robert has witnessed occasions when they are treated adversely because they are seen as having the wrong kind of credentials:

> If you are going to be black you have to have pedigree, you have to be super smart, because if you don't, then they are not going to take you seriously. . . .

I mean you can tell from the reception when you tell them where you went to
school. . . . There is an analyst . . . she went to FAMU, and she can go to a client
meeting with another analyst on her team and the private banker will be, like
[*imitates someone speaking in an elevated and enthusiastic tone*], "Oh, here is
Alison, you know she went to Harvard, and [*speaking in a hesitant and curt tone*]
here is Elena." Pause. And it's like, OK.

For recognizes that institutional forms of black cultural capital are seen as discrediting where he works. In the matter of Elena's college, he guesses that the
private banker either "simply forgot—it's an HBCU and they are not familiar
with it and simply forgot the name of it," or it could be that the private banker
feels that an HBCU will not be seen as impressive to the client, so there is no
need to even mention it. As Robert comments:

That plays a big deal, cause they like to have people who if they bring them in
front of a client, here is the person's background, they want to be impressive
to the client, so they want people who come from certain places, have certain
backgrounds, certain experiences, go to certain schools, and going to FAMU or
Morehouse, or Howard, they feel it's not impressive.

Robert saw with his own eyes how coming from an Ivy League school is celebrated and considered noteworthy, whereas having attended an HBCU is
viewed as forgettable, if it is even recognized, but more than this, to be perceived as credible as a black person requires prestigious credentials. In such
constraining contexts, middle-class blacks often decide to forgo the display
of certain behaviors or withhold personal information owing to their understanding that black cultural capital is perceived as off-putting and undesirable.
Middle-class blacks often take proactive steps to reduce the potential negative
effect of racial stigma at work.

The need to determine when to display black cultural capital and when to
opt out is itself indicative of the cultural skills middle-class blacks often maintain. The ability to successfully evaluate when it is best to appear conservative
and culturally similar to whites, and when one can be free to engage one's black
cultural capital has implications for one's economic prospects and social mobility. For middle-class blacks, this is a critical skill. Notice that some of the
middle-class blacks studied describe making it their goal to neutralize race, to
blend in. They indicate that there is a degree to which they must modify their
racialized tastes and self-regulate their bodies.

Not all white workplaces are the same: some demand greater cultural constraint, others require some but not total omission of black cultural capital. But even in less restrictive environments, middle-class blacks aim to make their race and the presence of their bodies a "non-issue." Respondents describe how under certain conditions they are aware of the salience of their race, demarcating them as different; however, their response to the salience of race and racial stigma is to follow the rules, to try to fit in, and to "play it by the book." They recognize that being black is something that distinguishes them, but do not necessarily feel that black culture is perceived as inherently discrediting. Unlike those middle-class blacks who aim to exceed the professionalism of their colleagues, Shante, the marketing professional who works at a majority female, majority white firm, notes: "I'm the only black person and that is very common for the industry I work in. So yeah, I try to be, I am extra aware of that, so I just try to blend in as much as possible." Shante is aware that her race is salient, so she aims to minimize any additional attention that she might attract by simply blending in.

Kevin, a 27-year-old accountant, aims to be professional and to meet workplace standards. As he states, when it comes to his personal appearance, "I dress to comply with their code, with their professional code." He calibrates what is acceptable in terms of dress and grooming by observing his white colleagues, which is not difficult considering he is one of six blacks in an office of around 500 people. He believes, for example, that his mustache is OK, because no one has told him it's inappropriate and several of his white colleagues also have mustaches. Similarly, Crystal, the executive assistant, notes that she often wears slacks, as the dress code is business causal, but also wears sneakers, too, as she often is running around the office. Once she changes into her sneakers, she may continue to wear them even after she is back at her desk. In her assessment of whether this is appropriate, she looks at what her colleagues are wearing. She believes that "it's not a problem; it's not an issue" because "many people do it at my job."

In responding to race at work, these respondents believe that practicing conformity and neutralizing race is the most advantageous strategy. While they are conscious of the salience of their race, they believe that displaying a basic understanding of rules and adhering to the workplace codes and mores in a fashion similar to that of their non-black colleagues is the best way to gain acceptance at work.

An awareness of when it is best to just blend in still means black professionals moderate their style, because they are conscious that blacks might be viewed negatively in accordance with stereotypes. Whether striving always to outperform ones' white colleagues, or working to disconfirm stereotypes, or planning to just fit in, the cultural tactics that middle-class blacks in my study use are a means to contest anti-black bias. They aim to keep doors open, partly so they can develop social ties with their non-black associates but also in the hope that their own positive relations with gatekeepers and power brokers will result in fewer barriers for blacks coming after them.

Being Yourself

Kenneth, a 27-year-old, works in the advertising department of a magazine catering to a black readership with a staff that he describes as being over 90 percent black. When he discusses how he dresses for work, he reports that "there is a certain comfort with everyone" and that he feels no pressure to dress up for work to demonstrate he is competent or professional. At his firm, employees "are essentially just responsible for doing [their] job." Black hairstyles are accepted, and locs would be "totally OK" where he works. Larry, too, works in a majority black workplace. A technician at a research library, he laughs when I ask if he ever feels he must groom himself or keep his hair a certain way for work. He tells me that he has recently grown his hair in a "really, really high" afro, and says, "That was my choice; I had no problems. You know, no one had anything to say, there aren't any restrictions as far as that." Consistently, the study participants who work in majority black workplaces report that they do not feel they have to represent the race. Appearing polished at all times, wearing glasses to disprove stereotypes, or disavowing hairstyles that make race salient just aren't concerns for this group. Granted the freedom to be unapologetically black, these professionals can focus on their work. They have a sense of security: they will be judged by the quality of the work they produce and the extent to which they perform the tasks required for their positions. This does not mean being sloppy or looking unprofessional, but it does reveal that their expressions of style are a personal choice, not a tactic for navigating racial tokenism.

Interestingly, the few middle-class blacks who work primarily with working-class whites also describe feeling free to dress as they please. For example, Damon, the associate in the legal department of a major financial institution, wears a beard and, in his own estimation, barely adheres to the dress code standards. He has educational credentials and he perceives his social status sets him apart from most of his white and female coworkers, whom he describes as being like "older versions of the people on *Jersey Shore*." Damon attended one of the most prestigious private high schools in New York City, and then earned a degree from an Ivy League university. In contrast, many of his coworkers, who mostly hailed from working-class backgrounds, do not even have a college degree. In his eyes, they are not equal in terms of their class status, and so he does not feel any need to adhere strictly to the dress code. He feels his background, and perhaps his gender, gives him leverage to liberally interpret and sometimes even to disregard the rules.

Jada, a 28-year-old marketing manager who until recently was the only black woman in her mostly white and female department, describes working in "a very laidback environment" where "you can wear jeans; you can be yourself." She maintains a carefree attitude, even amid these laxer standards:

> I wear green fingernail polish. And when I started this job, I had a Mohawk, and I wear bright colors. And, you know, my response to them, which I have said, is, "when my green fingernail polish and my Mohawk stop making you money, then we could talk."

Jada does not feel pressure to conform, because she has produced results and feels she has earned her place in the company, therefore she feels that she should be granted the freedom to express herself in terms of her style. However, she has still experiences being "singled out" in the workplace because of her race. This was the case on one occasion when her department was hiring. She had advocated for greater diversity and encouraged her colleagues to consider hiring a qualified minority candidate. Jada did not feel at all supported: "I felt in a way alone in that sense, like, does nobody feel me? . . . I didn't, I couldn't find anyone that would see eye to eye with me." She is free to dress how she pleases, even to paint her fingernails green, but this does not mean her experiences and opinions, as one of only a few black people at her firm, are valued. Workplaces certainly ranged in the degree to which they required cultural similarities, and in the extent to which black employees perceive they must refashion their bodies and their narratives. Yet, even in the most liberal places in terms of dress code and grooming standards, in workplaces where blacks feel most freedom to be themselves, they might still face added challenges due to their race.

Black Cultural Capital and Demands of Cultural Flexibility

Most of my respondents describe ways in which their interactions with black coworkers, when they have them, are vastly different from their interactions with non-blacks. While black cultural capital is often devalued in many workplaces, middle-class blacks often acknowledge, display, and engage their black cultural capital with black colleagues without fear of stigmatization, and regardless of any status mismatches (that is, whether they are superiors to, on the same level as, or report to their black coworkers).

They discuss the NBA finals, their experiences at historically black colleges and universities, their involvement in black Greek life, and events taking place in their black neighborhoods. None of these are likely topics with non-black colleagues, and in some instances, they are consciously avoided for fear of causing an awkward silence or arousing stigma. Information about their personal lives and displays of black cultural capital might alter the professional image that their coworkers have of them, but this is not so much a risk with other blacks with whom they work.

This distinction between white and black coworkers, and how they view black people and culture, is clearly evident in discussions of black neighborhoods. Amare, like many others, reports that he has his black coworkers over to his house "all the time." He explains that "some of them live in my neighborhood . . . they grew up like me. So it's OK; this is normal for them." In contrast, he would never invite his white colleagues to Crown Heights, the area of Brooklyn where he lives. First and foremost, while they get along at work, he is not particularly close with any of his white coworkers. As he puts it frankly, "they ain't friends. I work with them, but they ain't friends." Second, he perceives that being around so many black people would be uncomfortable for them. "Most of my colleagues, they live in WASP neighborhoods in Connecticut and Westchester and even Long Island, and me, I get off my train, you know, 90 percent of my train is African American. . . . It's just a totally different environment." He guesses that many of his colleagues would be scared if they were to visit his neighborhood. He imagines the result if they came to his neighborhood: "They'll look around and all they'll see is young black people," and they will say, "Oh my god, what am I doing here?" Amare believes there are sharp racial cleavages between his white and black colleagues in how black neighborhoods are perceived. Moreover, this difference in evaluation extends beyond black neighborhoods; it applies more broadly to the utility of black cultural capital at work.

Black coworkers provide a bit of workplace respite. Black cultural capital is a key ingredient in their interactions with other blacks, helping them to forge ties, which often proves beneficial. These relationships provide emotional and social

support, but also a way to gather information and determine how best to negotiate inhospitable workplace racial and cultural climates. As Renee remarks about
blacks at her job, whether superiors or subordinates, "we are all in this together."

Paul, a 28-year-old strategist for a major health insurance company, says
of his black coworkers: "We all know each other. We don't all hang out, but
definitely, we are definitely . . . aware, and try to help out each other a little
bit more. We just lean on each other." With other black employees, my respondents often discuss how to be successful, the do's and don'ts of what to
wear, and how to engage with non-black coworkers and superiors. Through
interactions with more advanced blacks, they develop their self-presentation
strategies and are alerted to workplace norms. Many who serve as mentors see
their efforts to help other blacks succeed as an instantiation of their belief in
racial uplift. Some provide direction and advice even when it is not asked for,
owing to their sense that it is their duty to alert other blacks to unwritten rules
of the workplace.

Many middle-class blacks in my study suggested that they benefited from
the mentorship and support of blacks in positions of influence, or served as
mentors to junior colleagues themselves. In terms of how they engage with
other blacks who work in support or administrative positions, they note that
they often receive special treatment or feel that blacks working in those positions are proud of them. For example, Amare feels the support staff see him as
"a brother doing it," and so the black administrative assistants treat him kindly
and in a motherly way. Black secretaries, particularly, are seen as behind-the-
scenes cheerleaders.

As a consequence of mobilizing black cultural capital and drawing on
shared racial understandings, my respondents working in majority white
spaces report having interactions with other blacks that are more intimate and
personal than their interactions with their non-black colleagues. Many note
that they discuss personal matters with a higher frequency with their black coworkers, and often consider their black colleagues to be friends. They might
socialize outside of work or invite black colleagues to gatherings at their homes.

Building relationships with black mentors often seems natural, but it is certainly also a consequence of being able to draw on racial and cultural similarities to establish and maintain bonds. For example, Kendra, the account
executive, reports that a black executive at her firm has been instrumental in
guiding her career. Her mentor is critical in cultivating her ability to navigate
the cultural and social terrain of her majority white workplace:

I've had opportunities to have a lot of really good mentors at my company, and one of them is actually our Chief Communications Officer, who is black, and he brought me in and hired me sight unseen out of my program, and he is like my big brother. You know he's teaching me kind of how to play the game, the rules of engagement. He's exposing me to a lot of things, and I think more African American young professionals, specifically, need people like that in their corner because there are things you just don't know.

Kendra uses terms of kinship to imply that their mentorship connection is more than merely professional: he is like her "brother," and together, they are part of a larger black community. The relationship also provides Kendra with the chance to learn via "trial and error," in a way that would not be possible otherwise. Her mentor helps her to determine when to hold back her opinion and when to assert herself: "He's definitely one to pick his battles, and so that's one thing I'm learning, definitely learning from him."

A few of my respondents report distancing themselves from other blacks at work, particularly those in support or lower-status positions. Jeff, for example, mentions that he tends to avoid engaging too causally with black subordinates. He describes a "clique" consisting of black administrative assistants, mailroom attendants, and security guards, and says he thinks they view him as "bourgeois, acting white. Not keeping it real." Consequently, he avoids mingling with the clique. It is hard to say why he perceives them this way. Perhaps Jeff does not display the requisite black cultural capital, or perhaps they see his class status, evident in his carefully crafted professional image, Brooks Brothers suits and all, as not genuine. A few middle-class blacks report more conflict-ridden relationships with other blacks in lower-status positions in the workplace hierarchy. They note that these blacks view them as "uppity" or snobbish. Perceptions of class status seemed to create distance. To be sure, Jeff is not opposed to helping other blacks; though he does not engage much with the clique, he has taken it upon himself to mentor a young black woman whom he believes has promise, whose position is more aligned to his own and offers room to advance at the company. Workplace interactions are complex, race and class together affecting intra- and inter-racial relations.

Race and class identities (gender, too) are put on display and emerge in middle-class interactions at work in a variety of ways. When middle-class blacks work in predominantly white settings, they aim to neutralize their race when interacting with their white colleagues, because they anticipate that they will be evaluated first by how they look. When they perceive that their race serves as a proxy for their abilities and potential, they often stringently adhere to workplace dress codes and embrace conservative standards. They police their behaviors to avoid the threat of being stereotyped, for men, as aggressive, and for women, as having a bad attitude or being overly sensual. Most feel compelled to modify their self-presentation and even forgo their racialized tastes and preferences in order to be seen as approachable or acceptable to whites. This suggests that middle-class blacks have been "permitted entrance, but not full participation" in most workplace settings.[13] However, when a critical mass of racial minorities is present, that often frees them from belaboring cultural similarity and contesting negative perceptions of their racial group. On these occasions, they can be unapologetically black, engaging black cultural capital without fear of penalty.

Because workplace settings vary in the degree to which blacks feel free to express black cultural capital, middle-class black workers are constantly evaluating their workplaces' cultural climates and re-evaluating what styles of self-presentation and grooming are acceptable. The racial makeup of their workplaces affects whether they feel it best to reveal or conceal their taste in music, leisure pursuits, and neighborhoods, and whether they should engage or suppress racially coded cultural practices, such as wearing their hair naturally curly or in cornrows. Contextual conditions together with the firm's racial makeup circumscribe the degree to which blacks engage their racialized consumption preferences at work. And while keeping their black cultural capital hidden is indicative of their effort to achieve coordination, doing so also reveals a racial hierarchy in which blacks and black culture are perceived as inferior.

The range of cultural practices and strategies engaged by respondents at work indicates that their professional lives are attenuated by both their knowledge of embodied black cultural capital and their adherence to the cultural norms evident and valued in their workplaces. They have race-based preferences, indicated by their black cultural capital, but they do not always sense that they can comfortably display or engage such preferences while at work. To minimize the social costs imposed by racial stigma and to gain respect, blacks have had to be culturally flexible. While nearly all the middle-class blacks in my study emphasize the importance of "being professional," evidencing their recognition of "business culture,"[14] blacks working in majority non-white and/or female settings report having a wider range of no-reprisal options when choosing their attire and hairstyles. They perceive that they can be unapologetically black and still move up through the organizational ranks.

At work, consumption becomes a means of gaining social legitimation, and cultural practices and displays of cultural knowledge help to demonstrate competence and cultural similarity. Moreover, anti-black biases do not dissipate at five o'clock when middle-class blacks leave their workplaces: whether shopping, dining, or clubbing, middle-class blacks still confront disparaging views of their race. However, it is not while engaging in black cultural capital that they face discrimination, but when they engage their *middle-class* tastes and sensibilities. Even having a good time might mean *work*.

Policing Black Privilege

6

CONSUMPTION OBJECTS ARE SYMBOLIC TOOLS, but also instruments of pleasure. Through their consumption, middle-class blacks are often able to realize their ideas about what a good life entails. For Heather, who grew up in Harlem's historic Striver's Row, consumption practices and experiences are deeply embedded in her conception of a good life, where she envisions one is able

> to be financially stable, to have a room full of books and a record player, an old-school record player to play jazz, to have a cellar with wine. To be around friends and family, good food . . . to feel at ease and to get up and go to a different country at my leisure, and to be able to take care of my mother so that she can rest.

For Heather, living a good life has an economic component—it requires financial stability, including the ability to provide security for her kin (this collective orientation is a common theme that emerges when middle-class blacks envision their future consumption, and will be discussed at length in Chapter Eight). But her imagined good life also includes lots of experiential and material signifiers of status; experiences and objects that she would enjoy doing and owning: having a room full of books and a wine cellar, listening to jazz records on an old-school record player, eating good food, and traveling the world. The good life for Heather, and many other middle-class blacks represented in my study, is deeply infused with class-based consumption. When middle-class blacks attempt to realize their consumptive desires, at times, their being black may present an unwelcome challenge as the consumptive sphere is often experienced as a site of social censure. My respondents report being surveilled, receiving poor treatment, and sensing their privilege is policed while out and about trying to live the good life. Sharon says it succinctly, "Because I'm black, they think I'm going to try to steal something." In these moments, it makes no difference that Sharon grew up in a well-heeled suburb, attended one of the best colleges in the country, and is successful in her career in advertising. All that matters is that she is black. Her cultural capital is useless in the face of racism, limiting her ability to capitalize on her middle-class status. Nonetheless Sharon, like Heather, still engages in consumption in her pursuit of a rich and full life.

Historically, entertainment and leisure settings are critical symbolic sites in which middle-class blacks have fought for full inclusion and equal treatment. In part, this stems from the shared American practice of utilizing goods as signifiers of one's social position. During the civil rights movement, black communities used their purchasing power for political ends by boycotting stores, lunch counters, movie theaters, and other public venues of entertainment and leisure that maintained discriminatory policies. Protest leaders called on fellow blacks to "withhold the dollar to make the white man holler."[1] The desire of the black middle class to have unrestricted access to retail and commercial establishments, to freely engage in consumption and leisure activities, served as a crucial prompt in early civil rights era demands for equal treatment.[2] The desire to be recognized as equal included a status dimension for middle-class blacks that was revealed in the marketplace; full inclusion and fair treatment in public venues meant equal access to a "good life," in which consumption and leisure is key.[3]

Being middle class means that they have money to spend, but it does not mean that their money is welcome everywhere. Even those who are famous or national icons have not been free from discriminatory experiences when "shopping while black," as anecdotes from, for example, Oprah Winfrey and President Barack Obama have revealed.[4] Blacks' experiences of exclusionary treatment in public spaces raise an important question: Why are black consumers marginalized while engaging in leisure and trying to spend their money?

On purely economic grounds, marketers, retailers, and service providers should want black consumers' money. Yet through advertisements and practices at stores, restaurants, and clubs, they often treat black consumers as second-class citizens.[5] What some have termed "consumer racial profiling," that is, service failure experienced by black consumers, is perhaps most pronounced in retail settings. Nearly two-thirds of blacks surveyed in a 2018 Gallup Social Audit perceive that blacks are treated unfairly while shopping. For over two decades, blacks have reported that they encounter unfair treatment due to their race at higher rates while shopping than in any other context, including interactions with the police and at work. An audit study conducted in 2009 found that retailers are more likely to consider black customers suspicious and that black customers are more likely than other racial groups to be followed and monitored in retail settings.[6] Other researchers have noted that black patrons are less likely than white patrons to be helped and encounter longer wait times in stores.[7] Blacks are nearly ten times more likely than members of other races to report having experienced "consumer racial profiling."[8] In the same study, those black shoppers who were more educated were more likely than those with little education to report having experienced discriminatory treatment. Time and again, research shows that middle-class status does little to buffer blacks from discrimination in retail and leisure settings.[9]

Exclusionary treatment in the marketplace is due, in part, to social structural conditions, such as residential segregation and the organization of the marketplace. Regardless of their class composition, black neighborhoods are more likely to be retail deserts than are even poor neighborhoods.[10] As discussed in Chapter Four, middle-class blacks in my study certainly experience black neighborhoods as lacking in terms of the availability of diverse retail and commercial establishments. Persistent residential segregation has resulted in the "spatial containment of black consumers," meaning the market is structured in ways that keep blacks out of certain areas or ensure that blacks have only limited access.[11] Discrimination and restricted access to credit also contributes to blacks' unequal access to goods and services.[12] Despite their economic resources, cultural tastes and proclivities, and desire for the material objects conferring the "good life," structural conditions constrain middle-class blacks' access and options in the marketplace.

Another potential reason for middle-class blacks' second-class treatment as consumers is tied to the role of cultural goods in demarcating social and symbolic boundaries. Retail salespeople and service providers are often charged with the task of distinguishing which consumers are worthy of service and deserving of goods that might function to heighten the status of the owner. Limiting these goods and services to certain patrons can contribute to the allure of exclusivity associated with a product or an experience. In addition to creating and enforcing boundaries and signaling distinction and selectivity, such practices may also reproduce the existing racial order. Rather than rewarding blacks who are affluent, market actors may punish blacks with money to spend. To prevent the disruption of "the racial logics of white superiority and black inferiority," service workers and salespeople may regulate blacks' procurement of the kinds of objects and experiences reserved for elites and the rewarding of prestige.[13] Despite businesses' presumed objective to maximize profits, middle-class blacks often encounter an active and evident racial consumer hierarchy.

While the market is often theorized as a democratic sphere, where people are free to choose and money is assumed to be the great equalizer,[14] the policing of black privilege reveals that a consumer racial hierarchy, a system that evaluates and assigns different value and worth to different consumers based on their race, is pervasive. Retail and commercial venues operate with an ideal consumer in mind, and blacks often encounter poor treatment, which indicates that they are viewed as undesirable or unworthy, and in some cases, they are treated as if they are do not deserve to be served. The market, far from a sphere free of race, is often an interface, a site of interracial and cross-class contact and confrontation.[15] The consumer hierarchy operates in a way that can transform the performance of an ordinary task into an aggravating and inconvenient event for blacks, and it can also constitute a form of exploitation. As legal scholar Regina Austin powerfully asserts, "Blacks are condemned and negatively stereotyped for engaging in activities that white people undertake without a second thought." She argues that exploitation of black consumers is evident in two ways. First, if service is part of a consumer experience, and if "blacks pay the same prices as everyone else but get less in the way of service or merchandise, they are being cheated." Second, knowing that blacks are seen as discredited in the market, merchants willing "to deal with blacks can extract a premium for doing so."[16] Middle-class blacks operate with an awareness that every transaction has the potential to be exploitative, or at least problematic, owing to pervasive racial biases often deeply embedded in the operation of the market.

Cultural theorists argue that symbolic boundaries and social hierarchies are asserted and maintained in the marketplace. Price is not a neutral or objective indicator of value, but a product of social determinations and assignments; the price offered to a consumer may have more to do with the perceived worth of the consumer than with the value of the object or service itself.[17] Across the board, low-status consumers encounter poor evaluations and face negative characterizations that are difficult to shake.[18] Blacks, due to their perceived low status, are more likely to be viewed negatively in the marketplace, notwithstanding the price they pay, how they view themselves, or the money they have to spend. Consider that, like others, middle-class blacks may see their purchases as a way of rewarding themselves for their hard work. A store salesperson, however, may view them as buying things they cannot afford, and consider their purchases and presence inappropriate. In this way, racial hierarchies are maintained and enforced in mundane ways. Sales staff and service providers are not immune from cultural racism, and as such, it is not surprising if they view black consumers through a racialized lens that rationalizes the inferior treatment blacks receive.

I asked study participants about their consumption and leisure, including where they shop in general and for particular items (clothes for work, clothes for leisure, and so forth) and what types of activities, events, and venues they patronize when trying to have fun or seeking entertainment. I asked them to characterize their interactions with salespeople and waitstaff and to describe how they respond to poor service and unfair treatment. Their replies reveal the kinds of stereotypes that middle-class blacks frequently encounter and the range of responses they deploy when faced with racially exclusionary treatment. Even when these discriminatory events occurred long in the past, making them susceptible to errors of memory, respondents still paint a picture of the scope and scale of mistreatment that middle-class blacks encounter when they are just out and about. Yet the details of specific stories are not what is most important; rather our attention should be directed to the impact of encountering discrimination and retail racism on black consumers and their experience of the market more broadly.

Encountering Service Failure

Middle-class blacks report unfair treatment in a range of establishments: from boutiques to big-box stores, from grocery stores to furniture stores, restaurants, and dance clubs. Stores that sell high-end apparel or luxury goods are often hot spots of discriminatory treatment. However, in their reporting, many middle-class blacks absolve the establishment (store, restaurant, or club) itself of guilt, rather finding fault with the behavior of store security personnel,

salespeople, and even other customers. Their accounts reveal that racial hierarchies operate in the market, and that though economically advantaged, their
privilege is policed in many public settings.

Shopping While Black

The most common stereotype evident in retail settings is the association of
blackness with criminality—when black customers are treated as potential
shoplifters and thieves. It is also common for middle-class blacks to encounter the association of blackness with poverty, typified by the assumption that
they cannot afford a particular purchase, do not belong in a given store, or
are the wrong type of clientele for a particular service or object. At times
stereotypes about black people as poor or criminal operate separately, and
at times they appear in tandem: that is, even if service people know their
black customers have money, they might think that money was ill-gotten,
like Isaiah's neighbor, described in Chapter Four, who assumes Isaiah is a
"hustler." While workplace racial bias means countering stereotypes about
aggression (for men) and being oversexed (for women), in the marketplace
the stereotypes that are most salient have to do with blacks' presumed class
status and criminality.

Amare had not grown up in an upper-middle-class home in a majority
white suburb like Sharon, but now he works in a corporate setting and maintains a taste for high-end brands that show he has "made it." Amare is an avid
shopper, and he routinely encounters prejudicial treatment at the places he
frequents. He describes this aspect of his shopping experience vividly when
he tells me that whenever he goes into one particular high-end Italian fashion
store, "the security guard—it's like him and I are holding hands. Like, he's on
me." As described in Chapter Three, Amare spends time and money to appear
polished. He rarely goes a week without a visit to his barber. Yet he has come
to accept the fact he will always be under surveillance when shopping. This is
simply an added cost of maintaining his polished, professional image. Though
he faces unfair treatment, he still enjoys keeping up with the latest fashions.

Isaiah, the entrepreneur, also describes the expectation that if you are black
and shopping in a department store like Bloomingdale's or Lord & Taylor, you
will likely be subject to surveillance. When I ask if he has ever been treated
unfairly while out shopping, he replies, "Hell, yeah." Nonetheless, he remains
optimistic; he hopes that things are getting better as a consequence of companies being fearful they might be sued. He is also hopeful because of the impact

of several "Eyewitness News" reports that have spotlighted incidents in which black customers have been followed around while shopping. Like Amare, Isaiah takes pride in his appearance and has a flare for fashion. For both of them, getting dressed is a form of play, a source of pure pleasure and merriment. They spend a lot of money to maintain a put-together image, both at work and in their personal lives. Nonetheless, for these frequent shoppers, being black men comes with the expectation of encountering anti-black bias and being policed while engaging in consumption. Having to anticipate racism is also a component of black privilege. It is an indication not only that their experience of class privilege is curtailed but also that they must be conscious of the significance of their race across a range of public settings.

Lisa grew up with two MIT-educated parents in what she describes as an upper-upper-middle-class household; however, she, too, feels that her privilege is policed. Despite her impressive resume, career accomplishments, and extensive cultural capital, despite the fact she has attended mostly white, private schools since kindergarten and earned her MBA degree from Stanford University, Lisa is still followed around when she shops. The sales staff, she emphasizes, are not following her around to see if she needs assistance—they don't ask if she needs help. It doesn't happen every time, but she is certainly aware of occasions when her cultural capital does not translate in retail settings because she is black.

Larry, the library technician, describes being searched on the way out of a store:

> To make a long story short, I paid, and when I was checking out, you know, there was a person at the door who said, "This way." I guess one of the doors wasn't working. So she asked to see my receipt. I showed her the receipt. Then she asked to see my bag, and she just goes in my bag, and she's looking all around, you know, in my bag, so it's just, like—you know, like what is she doing? You know, she looks at the receipt, and she looks in the bag, and she gives it back to me and gives me back the receipt. And then at that moment a white guy walked through the door, and it went beep-beep-beep, and she saw him go ahead.

Larry describes having to go through the extra trouble of having to prove that he had made a purchase, while simultaneously observing that the security guard did not check the bag or receipt of the white customer. He found the whole ordeal unsettling: blatantly unfair treatment based on his race. He did not object to the practice of checking bags or receipts at the door, just to the fact that a white patron was not subject to the same practice as he was.

Even when they are not thought to be criminals, many middle-class blacks in my study reported that they are treated in accordance with the stereotype that all black people are poor, not serious about making a purchase, and unworthy of being served. Daniel, a 35-year-old training specialist for a medical firm, earns around $100,000 a year. But when he shops at a luxury department store, he is sure salespeople are thinking, "Look at this African American buying stuff that he probably can't afford." There is no way to know whether he is correct, yet he senses the sales staff do not see him as a legitimate patron with the financial acumen to spend his money appropriately.

At times, these racist tropes are made explicit. Darryl provides an example:

> I walked in, and then I asked the guy, how much something was going to cost. And I thought it was too expensive, so I was like, "Nah, nah, I'm not . . . " And I was cool about not wanting to buy it. And the guy replied, "Oh, you knew you weren't gonna buy this before you even asked me." Or like, "You know you didn't want to buy this anyway." And I was kind of, like, "Excuse me?" But he didn't want to say nothing else. So that's how I knew it was more like a racial slur.

The clerk insinuated that Darryl should not be taken seriously as a prospective customer, someone deserving of his deference and attention, and Darryl feels sure that being judged in such an unjust way is racially motivated. Sharon recalls an occasion where a salesperson made it clear that she did not want to be of service:

> I was in [a store], and the lady just straight up told me, "Yeah, I don't think you should try that on. It's 800 dollars." And I was like, "I want to try it on, thank you." So, already making assumptions from that. And that was clearly a race thing to me, because other people were trying stuff on, and it was the same price, and I didn't hear her say that.

Sharon insisted that she be allowed to try on the pricey dress, against the saleswoman's efforts to dissuade her. The staff person acted as a gatekeeper, protecting the prestige associated with the store and the goods they sold by discouraging Sharon from even trying on an $800 dress. It is not uncommon for salespeople to assume that black people cannot afford to be shopping where they are shopping. Lisa, too, has encountered this assumption, but in the form of being told the price of items without asking, or of being directed to the sale section of a store.

At times, blacks' report that poor service is evident in an unfriendly tone of voice or when other customers are helped before or instead of black customers. At other times, blacks are simply ignored or receive a poor reception. As Brittany describes, "I'll go in, and I may be the only person there, and people there, people act like I'm not there." She senses that sales staff rationalize ignoring her as they "don't really expect that I'd be able to buy anything." Considering that Brittany has multiple markers of middle-class status—she grew up in a solidly middle-class home, attended suburban schools, lives at present in a nearly all-white, prestigious neighborhood, and is an attorney—it is hard to imagine that her class status is not legible to store staff. It is as if her race makes her class—her cultural capital—a moot point.

Jeff, whose efforts to appear dignified at work were explored in Chapter Five, recalls one particular time he was shopping:

> I was walking around and trying to get help, like, "Excuse me, could I . . . ?"
> "Oh, I'll be with you in a second." And then you see them helping someone; then someone else comes over and asks them a question and they help them. . . . People were sort of, didn't care.

Occasions like this, where black customers are the last to be served or blatantly ignored, are instances where middle-class blacks perceive the red flag of racism being waved. Alysha describes a moment in which she felt keenly that her patronage was considered less desirable than that of a white female shopper:

> This woman just was not helpful, and I thought she was just an unhelpful salesperson. But then I would see . . . a fill-in-the-blank white girl comes in, and she's just like, "Oh, I'll get you this; Oh, I'll get you that," you know, as opposed to the one time [to me], "Oh, you need any help?" You know, and she wasn't as doting as she was for this other person.

Alysha is like many other middle-class blacks who remark that white women shoppers are the beneficiaries of preferential treatment. They do not jump to the conclusion that the salesperson or waitstaff must be racist, as many acknowledged it is difficult to know a person's motivation, but it is hard to ignore occasions when white customers are prioritized or preferred. Even while trying to give a salesperson or waiter the benefit of the doubt—maybe they are incompetent rather than racist—middle-class blacks indicate seeing racial bias at play when black customers are deprived of entitlements that white customers are freely granted.

Even settings that cater to an exclusive clientele, venues where all custom-ers receive personalized attention and timely assistance, are often sites of mis-treatment for middle-class blacks. Poor service in such establishments, such as high-end restaurants or luxury shops, is not only noticeable but is often seen by middle-class blacks as racially motivated. Often when middle-class blacks are un-certain of whether racism alone accounts for the poor treatment they receive, it is, as Larry described when recalling the time his bag was searched, made readily apparent when they are able to compare their treatment to that of whites.

These occasions can be humiliating and unsettling, and they remind black consumers that retail spaces are not places where they should expect to re-ceive equitable treatment. Their middle-class status guarantees no entitlements. Again, their experience of class privilege is truncated.

Dining While Black

In addition to the service failure they encounter while shopping, middle-class blacks in my study report receiving inferior service in a range of establishments. Vanessa, an active and engaged member of black organizations like her sorority Alpha Kappa Alpha and the historic black Baptist church she regularly attends, also enjoys trying out new high-end restaurants with her girlfriends. "A lot of times, me and my friends will be the only black people there," Vanessa shares. On one such occasion, the women dined at a swanky restaurant and received noticeably poor service. Vanessa was dismayed and confused when "it was re-ally difficult to get them to bring me anything." Vanessa grew up middle class, attended an Ivy League school, and works as a consultant. She enjoys good food and wine, often venturing to expensive restaurants that boast famous, award-winning chefs. And this was "a fine dining restaurant. Their check average is probably a hundred bucks a head, maybe higher." Vanessa expected highly per-sonalized, attentive service—"there are certain things that you expect when you reach a certain level of dining"—but the service she received was abysmal. Van-essa, like so many other mistreated black patrons, swore never to go back.

Vanessa's poor experience dining out is consistent with the findings of sev-eral studies that have documented an association between servers' endorsement and awareness of racial stereotypes depicting blacks as undesirable consumers and their self-reported proclivities to racially profile their black clientele.[19] Serv-ers have been found to withhold service to black customers due to stereotypes that blacks do not tip well and are discourteous, demanding, and difficult cus-tomers. Research reveals that waitstaff can go to great lengths to avoid serving black patrons, including working out agreements with the restaurant host so that blacks are not seated in their sections.[20] A 2012 study of 195 servers in North Carolina found that nearly 40 percent of participants admitted that their service sometimes varies according to their customers' race.[21] In a more recent study, conducted in 2015, researchers surveyed nearly 1,000 servers nationwide. Nearly 60 percent admitted that they do not always give their black customers their best effort, indicating that servers readily admit withholding service or providing black patrons with poor service as a consequence of anti-black bias.[22]

Clubbing While Black

Nightclubs can also be sites where blacks are subject to mistreatment, what sociologist Reuben May has termed "velvet rope racism."[23] A common complaint among my respondents is that whites are favored and feel entitled to such treatment. For example, they might move to the front of the line, by-passing black patrons. Kendra explains that she has experienced occasions when a bouncer would "let the people who were in line after me in front of me." These situations, she believes, reveal that racism is operating, even if it isn't "overt." Sharon, too, has experienced occasions when a group of white people made real her racial disadvantage as they skipped past her to the front of the line. Sharon's privileged class position did little to ensure she received the same treatment she saw whites getting on their way into a party at a nightclub.

Natalie, a 25-year-old senior banking analyst, recalls a time when she and a group of her black, college-educated friends waited in line at a rooftop bar at a hotel in New York's midtown. They had gone out to celebrate a friend's birthday, but when they arrived, they were told the lounge had reached capacity. Before they departed, the staff at the door "let in a group of white people right in front of us." Natalie and her friends asked why they couldn't come in; the folks at the door simply replied, "It's full." Natalie feels it is "very clear that they didn't wanna let us in 'cause they didn't really want black people to be in there."

Desiree, a 29-year-old marketing professional, also had a frustrating and humiliating night out with her group of close girlfriends and a few guys. When hanging out, she remarks, they did not focus on the crowd around them: "as long as I'm with good company, I'm not really focused on whatever else is going on." However, when her group was trying to get into a Manhattan nightclub for a going-away party, they met with what she terms a "racial situation":

> The bouncer and then the manager of the night, wouldn't let us in. It was really weird. We were like, "our friends have bottles in there. People are spending

money, so why aren't you letting us in?" And it was mostly because we were all black and we were trying to get in. . . . They were just being extra racist, and it was basically like they had reached their black, light-skinned, skinny quota.

In this moment, Desiree draws attention to both racial hierarchies and colorism. Black women may be ranked, categorized, and subjected to slightly different treatment contingent on their physical attributes. Those black women with physical attributes associated with whiteness, even if they are not white, in Desiree's eyes may be given a pass, but not brown-skinned black women and black men; they are seen as undesirable. When I ask her how she knows the club had reached its "quota," she tells me the bouncer stated it explicitly. Even though the group's friends were already in the club "spending money," that did not matter. She senses that they were denied entry because they did not meet the phenotype of an ideal patron—they weren't white, but they also weren't "light-skinned, long hair, skinny girls." Modern racism operates in a sophisticated fashion: blacks are not wholly and entirely barred from entry, but subject to a gatekeeper's preferences and discretion. In Desiree's eyes, the bouncer and club manager were enforcing a racialized beauty ideal in which fair-skinned black women with long straight hair are tolerable, but brown-skinned, curvy black women and black men are unwelcome, and more likely to be denied entry.

Middle-class black men indicate experiencing an even higher degree of scrutiny and gatekeeper discretion at clubs. Kevin, the accountant, says that there is basically no way to avoid discrimination in certain parts of the city. He explains that in the Meatpacking District, black people, especially men, should simply anticipate "bad treatment." He tries to avoid partying in these parts of town because, "you already know what the outcome is gonna be." Kevin does not assume that racism is always the culprit behind exclusionary treatment, but on one particular evening, a bouncer told him:

"We're not letting anybody in," and then you see a bunch of white girls, who look like they are from the Valley or something, just walk in, and they have no problem, and it's like, "Really?" I generally don't like to think that, but when you see that, it's hard not to automatically assume [racism]; it happens.

The racial hierarchy becomes undeniable when it's visibly enforced. Nightclub personnel are charged with the task of creating an exclusive environment, and to do so, they must screen out undesirable elements. Unfortunately, blacks, especially black men, have experienced occasions when their presence was deemed objectionable. This is consistent with the findings of an audit study that, using matched testers, found black men were more likely to be subject to greater scrutiny, screened out, and denied entry to nightclubs than comparable whites.[24]

My middle-class black respondents tell story after story of nights when they are out for a good time, but are told not only that they do not belong but that they cannot enter. While Jada knows she is "beautiful," she is also aware that as a black woman, she does not "fit" what is commonly considered attractive in certain settings. Jada explains there are unwritten rules about the type of person who is allowed into certain clubs with ease: "they let . . . model chicks in. You've got to be five foot ten and be wearing a rubber band, and you look like you stepped out of *Vogue*. . . . It's very much like you're about to audition for a Kanye video or something." When I ask if she thinks that race matters, she recounts an instance which, in her eyes, made clear a racialized standard of beauty. Jada and her friends, a group of black women, were denied entry by a white woman monitoring the door. When she would not allow them in, a conflict ensued. Jada describes "the aesthetic of that club" by saying that "there weren't a lot of people that looked like us up in there," and the woman was, as Jada put it, trying to "cop control" the situation. The woman made it clear that she had the power to decide who the club favored as clientele. She huffed, "You don't get in unless I let you in." Jada rationalized it: perhaps this woman did not want to offend the lounge's regular patrons by letting in a group of black women. Eventually, Jada and her friends were let in, but only after the woman spoke with Jada's friend who was hosting the private party to which they'd been invited. The host, Jada said, was Latina, but "white-looking," and she intervened, lobbying at great length with the door attendant to let Jada and the others in. That night's insult could be described as a form of policing, a means of restricting blacks and ensuring that they are excluded. The participants in my study faced such exclusionary treatment from a broad group of actors, from bouncers to club managers to other patrons. And such incidents made it plain: leisure settings, like clubs, bars, and lounges, are not universally open to all consumers with money to spend. Instead, they are places where racial hierarchies are reinforced. No matter how culturally astute middle-class blacks are or how refined their tastes and preferences might be, they are not guaranteed the right to revelry.

After all that hassle, why would Jada want to patronize an establishment where her presence and person are considered undesirable? Well, in most cases, the middle-class blacks in my study did not stay at such places. Desiree describes an insulting and embarrassing moment when a bouncer got "aggressive" and told her and her friends, "we have enough," meaning that they did not want any more black people in the club. The whole experience was unpleasant, and as a consequence, Desiree and her friends left, and she refuses to ever return. As she explains: "We just left. I was like I don't even wanna be here. And that's a place that I won't go back to, and I always say I don't care if Oprah is in there giving away her Holiday Christmas shit. I won't go back into that place. Like, no!" Exiting a shop or venue, where their presence is un-wanted emerged as a common response among study participants. They refuse to spend money where they sense their presence is unwelcome.

Middle-class blacks report feeling uncomfortable, frustrated, and dis-pleased when, instead of being given their due, they are subjected to exclusion-ary treatment in public settings. The anti-black bias they experience, including not being acknowledged as a valid consumer or being ignored, detracts from the pleasure that shopping, dining, or going to a nightclub might otherwise afford them.

Strategies to Address Racial Exclusion in Leisure Settings

Racism often puts a damper on the mood when the middle-class blacks in my study are out trying to have a good time. But they also have an arsenal of ways of dealing with such treatment and anti-black bias. They are prepared in part because many assume that being black means that status misrecognition and unfair treatment are unavoidable. Unlike the workplace, where most middle-class blacks commit to fitting in and aim to defy stereotypes by putting forth a refined presentation of self, leisure settings elicit a different set of strategies for handling racism, both overt and covert. In nearly all instances, the middle-class blacks in my study, like Desiree, deal with anti-black bias by withdrawing, refusing to make a purchase, or avoiding the establishment in the future. Some respond confrontationally, but far more often they adopt nonconfrontational strategies when managing racial stigma and protesting gatekeepers' attempts to bar them from consuming.

Jeff, who experiences racism while shopping, Vanessa, while dining, and Desiree, while clubbing, all describe occasions of exclusionary treatment, which they responded to by leaving the store, restaurant, or club. Javon takes a similar approach, confirming that after being mistreated at one store, he responded by refusing to shop there again. The poor treatment, in his eyes, was primarily because he is black but secondarily because he looks young.

Javon is one of the highest-ranking blacks at the private equity firm where he works. This means that to be dressed appropriately for his job, he must wear dress shirts and suits. Because he is one of few blacks at this firm, he makes sure his attire is impeccable and consequently, he regularly shops at stores that sell formal attire catering to the business elite. However, in certain high-end stores, the sales staff do not aim to accommodate him or guarantee that he leaves satisfied. When subjected to poor service or unfair treatment, Javon, like many other middle-class blacks, makes what he feels is the best choice, to exit the establishment and to refuse to spend his money where his presence is unwelcome.

Only a few in my study reported taking a confrontational strategy in response to unfair treatment. Withdrawing from a discriminatory episode requires far less emotional energy, and it does not impose the added burden of proving that one is a legitimate consumer with money to spend. Bryson, the teacher turned attorney, routinely dines at upscale restaurants for work events, taking new recruits out for a fancy lunch on behalf of his corporate law firm. Usually, he told me, in those instances, "I'm the only black person in the place." Being the only black diner could make him self-conscious, particularly because these are the sorts of restaurants where he so often feels he receives less than stellar service. Often, he senses that because of his race, the restaurant staff are "kind of rude or just not as attentive as they are to other customers." When I probe, inquiring how he responds to such treatment, he explains, "there's just nothing you can do. . . . I just wouldn't go back." He continues, "It's not really worth losing sleep over. . . . I don't report them to the Better Business Bureau or anything. I don't waste that much energy on it." Leaving and not returning, may not address the root of the problem, but it also requires that no additional energy be expended. It is perhaps the simplest way to minimize the toll of dealing with undesirable, yet seemingly unavoidable, racism as a black patron in the marketplace.

At the same time, merely exiting and avoiding such establishments does little to ensure black people are treated fairly in the future. A store's security staff may continue to follow black people around, waitstaff may neglect tables with black patrons, and bouncers may enforce racial quotas. Nor does avoiding businesses where one has experienced poor treatment challenge underlying processes that account for the prevalence of such incidents. And avoiding a particular restaurant, store, or club means curtailing one's options, rather than expanding them in a way that these middle-class blacks believe their finances should allow. Finally, not purchasing something or refusing to return to a specific establishment can be inconvenient. So some of my interviewees opt to speak up.

Tasha says she has vocalized her discontent on more than one occasion. Without hesitation, she has spoken out and addressed the problem head on:

> Oh, I'll call the manager in a second. . . . [One time] I called the manager . . . [and said] "I am in this section. Three of your people are sitting at the register talking and I need help, and no one's come up to me." And they wrote me a letter, like they were so apologetic, and blah blah blah blah blah. So, I mean, I will talk to someone.

Tasha also reports taking preventive steps to demonstrate that she has a history of spending money with a particular store. This has been effective, in part because she loves fashion. She loves to shop and had established a personal relationship and a history of transactions at her favorite retailers. This makes her more confident that she has leverage if she is ever treated poorly, and it empowers her to adopt a more confrontational stand:

> I tend to shop in places where I'm a cardholder. I will buy something Chanel from Saks before I go to Chanel and buy it, 'cause I feel like it gives me a little more leverage. I can be like, "I'm a cardholder, I've been a loyal customer since whatever year. . . . Like I've always shopped here." You can pull up my card savings. You see the amount of money I spend. . . . I do think it gives you a little bit of leverage if [you are being] treated differently.

Tasha could mitigate the risk of taking a confrontational stand by demonstrating her economic power in certain stores, which she believes entitles her to some assurances that she will be served and treated with respect. Being a regular patron helps her to more confidently feel that if she reports being mistreated, or raises concerns about inferior or poor service, there will be some redress.

A few middle-class blacks in my study engage in a more proactive strategy when responding to anti-black bias and racism in retail and leisure settings. They actively seek to improve retailers' and service providers' perceptions of black customers. They develop personal relationships with salespeople and service providers in the hope that social capital will buffer them from discrimination. For some, to truly have a good time and be free from racism means venturing to black events and establishments, to spaces that cater to a black clientele. They much prefer to patronize restaurants and shops that are black-owned or at least that treat black clientele, as well as others, with respect. Mainly, they know that they are least likely to deal with anti-black bias in the company of other blacks in public spaces, and also when they entertain in their homes.

Another means of responding to unfair or stigmatizing treatment, that a small number employed, is to spend money. They, at times, overspend so as to disprove negative racial associations and undermine class stigma connected with blacks. This approach is nonconfrontational, but it still contests unfair treatment. Damon, for instance, made several large purchases he did not desire to prove a point:

> There are times when I've done it, and, you know, I'll regret it, and say . . . "I really didn't need that and I'm not even sure if that person remembers me." But in my mind, I kind of say to myself, "maybe they won't treat the next guy that looks like me that way." So, maybe if I go back in there next time, they might hop to and say, "Oh, how's it going?" You know, and treat me a little different.

By making extravagant purchases (which he later regrets), Damon is flexing, demonstrating his worth as a consumer and contesting the idea that because he is black he should not be taken seriously as a consumer.

Michelle, the event planner, had done the same. She described an occasion when she went shoe shopping at Neiman Marcus, a splurge for her birthday. When Michelle arrived in the shoe department, no one greeted her. She did not leave or ask to speak with a manager. Instead, Michelle, spent her birthday money:

> I ended up walking out of there with a pair of shoes, full-priced, 'cause it was my birthday. The woman who rolled her eyes at me was so mad because not only did I purchase a pair of shoes with someone else, another sales associate who was helpful, I also opened a card, which for them is a big deal. . . . She was salty as hell, and I was like, "Have a nice day," and I'm [thinking] "Hmm, your day would've been nicer had you said hello."

Michelle passively retaliated against a store staffer's dismissal. Like other middle-class blacks who decide to spend money to prove that they belong, by establishing a Neiman Marcus charge card she aimed to challenge stereotypes linked to blacks not being credible consumers or creditworthy. Both Michelle and Damon hoped that their purchases would teach sale staff a lesson and would discourage them from treating blacks poorly in the future.

Darryl describes a similar incident that took place at a club. In general, he feels that being a "nonwhite guy" means that "bouncers want to give you flack." On this occasion, the bouncer refused to let him in, justifying his refusal by claiming that Darryl's jeans were ripped and he therefore was not dressed appropriately. When Darryl protested that his designer True Religion jeans were purposefully ripped, that it was a part of the design, the bouncer flippantly suggested he go to Gap to pick up some new jeans if he wanted to get in. Darryl was annoyed by the suggestion: "If anybody knows anything about fashion, Gap compared to True Religion is like a BMW compared to a [Honda] Civic. So I don't understand how he could tell me to do such a thing." To gain entry, Darryl and his friends decided to pay for bottle service. After that, the bouncer had no qualms with Darryl's appearance. Fashionably dressed and well-versed in what was "fresh," Darryl and his friends still had to spend more than the average patron if they wanted to be let into the club. "Money, we had money to get a table, and it was like no questions then. So, at the end of the day, why wasn't he [the bouncer] letting me in? Just goes to discrimination." As they proved their worth (net and otherwise), these professionals found having fun could sometimes prove more costly when you are black.

Sometimes, to demonstrate their legitimacy as consumers, my respondents say they bypass browsing. Rather than looking to see what's new at stores or window shopping for pleasure, they enter a store on a mission. Jada told me, "When I shop, I go where I know I'm going to get something. Even if I don't know what I'm going to get. . . . Like, I don't window shop on Madison Avenue just for the heck of it." This strategy represents a compromise in that they abstain from perusing through a store. But doing so puts them at a disadvantage in the marketplace, as browsing and window shopping are forms of information gathering. These pre-acquisition activities familiarize consumers with product prices and availability and make it easier to identify where and what qualifies as the best item or object to purchase. By limiting their window shopping they might be disconfirming the idea that blacks don't really have money to spend, but they also restrict their ability to gain the nonmaterial benefits that come from browsing.

A select few, mostly women, draw on a different preventative strategy. They actively establish ties to sales staff and make a special effort to demonstrate brand loyalty. Like Tasha who shops where she has a store credit card, Jada reports that she has developed relationships with salespeople, and this reduces her experience of poor service. Since for her, "the service is just as important as the product I'm buying," Jada works to build strong connections with sales staff to mediate against negative perceptions of blacks and to assure that she has a positive and enjoyable shopping experience. This is equivalent to becoming a regular, returning time and time again to places where you are treated right.

Most middle-class blacks are less invested in demonstrating their worth and attempting to disprove negative stereotypes while in leisure settings. Even though many feel that their clothes influence the service they receive, they do not feel that they must always appear polished. When it comes to their self-presentation in their free time, they are driven by a different set of motivating factors. To the extent that they play up their style, wearing high-status brands or being impeccably dressed, it is for the feeling of confidence it generates. Looking good, feeling good. Nonetheless, they are cognizant of the role of clothing as a communicator of status and anticipate that perceptions about their race, combined with how they are dressed, will affect how they are treated.

Curtis, a 34-year-old who works in politics and is image-conscious at work, told me that he dresses down, even when he shopping at high-end department stores. He realizes that being a black man dressed casually might mean being treated poorly, but as he explains, "I don't really care about what I'm dressed like when I'm not trying to make a power move or something. . . . I just dress for comfort. I'd wear slippers to [a high-end department store] to buy whatever I'm looking for." Curtis, like most of the middle-class blacks in my study, concedes that his clothing has a limited ability to protect him from racial stereotypes or class misrecognition in public spaces, so he does not employ the strategy of managing his appearance, except while at work or when trying to "make a power move."

Vanessa, in contrast, likes to dress the part when she is out shopping. That is, she aims to appear suitable to be served: "I like to prevent against poor service. If I'm ever out shopping and I pretty much, I'll know I'm gonna be out shopping because I hate it so much. . . . I will try to look like I belong to be shopping there." She looks like she belongs by "wearing something a little more designer. Having on really fabulous shoes. Just being more high-end in general." For Vanessa, looking the part means, in general, wearing expensive clothes. Tasha also mentions that how one is dressed impacts how one is treated, particularly in stores that sell high-end goods:

> If I was to go into Saks, and I just had on my flip-flops and sweatpants, and you know, like a cheap leather bag that I bought at Walmart, the service I get is a lot different than if I go into Saks and I'm all put together, and they can tell from my handbag or from my shoes, like I'm that kind of shopper.

Tasha, like Vanessa, perceives that dressing the part, using markers of class status to convey the caliber of service you should receive, might reduce the chance of encountering unfair treatment.

Tasha, however, is also aware that even when adorned with high-status goods, being black one might still be denied equal access. She told me the story of an evening out with a group of friends in the Meatpacking District (the same area where Kevin and his friends had experienced discrimination). Even though Tasha and her friends wore sleek, fashionable dresses and heels and were in the company of several professional football players—which she reveals meant that they were "not coming just to buy ginger ale, they're coming to buy bottles and spend money"—the bouncers would not allow them in. She remembers that "a million and one random white people that look like they're from New Jersey or Long Island just walk right up to the door and get in with no problem," implicitly categorizing white patrons from places like New Jersey or Long Island as low status, nonetheless they entered the club effortlessly. Racism in such instances is obvious. As Tasha puts it, "you don't have to be a rocket scientist to put two and two together." The limitations of black privilege are apparent on such occasions, when even being dressed to impress does not do much to help dispel negative perceptions of blacks.

Vanessa also recognizes that dressing up does not prevent misrecognition—that is, being incorrectly classed on sight—in all instances. She recounts an experience at a high-end department store where another customer made assumptions based on her race:

> I was actually in [a high-end store] one day in a suit, just on my lunch break from work, and I got in an elevator, and these other two women got in [the] elevator, and one of them was like, "Oh, do you know where the bathroom is?" I was like, "Oh, no, I don't." And then she gets irate, and she's like, "Oh, my gosh, how come you don't know where the bathroom is?" And I was like, "I don't know.". . . . And then the other one, she was like, "She doesn't work here." So I was like, oh. 'Cause I'm black.

Even while adopting the strategy of trying to display one's class status, middle-class blacks might encounter status misrecognition.

Robert, who works in finance, reports that if he shops while wearing a suit, he gets asked whether he works at the store. Alongside Vanessa's experiences, this reinforces the idea that being a black customer is deemed inappropriate or perceived as incongruous in a high-end store. Instead, even middle-class blacks who are professionally dressed are assumed to occupy the position of a service provider, arguably a lower status position. So, while in their workplaces their stylistic choices and efforts—such as Robert wearing glasses and Vanessa straightening her hair—are oriented toward minimizing perceptions of racial difference, when they are out shopping, stylistic modifications do little to buffer them from racism. Their style might even fuel white customers' perceptions that they are there to serve, not shop.

The racial hierarchies and cultural racism evident in society function in market and leisure settings, too. In some sense, the only occasions when middle-class blacks are free from racial hierarchies are occasions where they are in black settings or in the company of other blacks. Middle-class blacks indicate that in addition to engaging and cultivating black cultural capital, patronizing black-owned establishments can serve to buffer them from discriminatory treatment. Black-owned establishments can provide rest and relaxation and cater to their racialized cultural tastes and consumer preferences, while also being refuges from racism.

When I ask Erica, a 29-year-old membership manager for a nonprofit, if she has experienced differential or unfair treatment while out at a restaurant or bar, she replies that she had not recently. She had been living in a predominantly black neighborhood for a few years and frequenting black-owned restaurants. Not only are these places where blacks are treated with respect but they are also places where the racial and class hierarchy might even be flipped. As Erica explains, in her neighborhood, "the whole paradigm was inverted. There were lots of black-owned restaurants that I went to, particularly Peaches and the coffee shop, where it was the opposite. You had a lot of white servers serving more uppity black people." In Chapter Seven, I explore blacks' attraction to black-owned businesses, and it is important to note that part of the attraction is that in black establishments a different racial order prevails, one in which blacks are deemed worthy of service and their needs satisfied.

Beyond freedom from racism, my respondents' attraction to black-owned venues or predominantly black clubs or lounges is also due to these places celebrating black cultural capital in ways that can be seen and heard. One recurrent theme that respondents mention is that they perceive predominantly black clubs and lounges to be places where they can reliably enjoy the music. These places play music that they like, while predominantly white clubs often do not. Angela, the corporate attorney, loves to dance, especially to hip-hop, in predominantly black clubs with her friends. Sharon tends to frequent places where the patrons are "usually mostly brown people." When they have to choose venues to venture to with the goal of having fun, respondents often choose to go to black establishments or social events that cater to black people.

That said, not all predominantly black settings are viewed as the same; some, particularly when they are seen as catering to poor or working-class blacks, are often deemed undesirable. That is, there is also a class dimension to the type of black spaces and places that my interviewees frequent. Even if the crowd in a club is mostly black, Janae doesn't like a raucous situation: "If I go to a club, and it's majority people of color, and it's wild, it's not my scene." Regardless of the racial makeup, she prefers places that cater more to her middle-class notions of decorum.

Erica enjoys hanging around black people, but she prefers events that are "lighter" in mood, contrasting these with the black events in her former neighborhood of Bedford–Stuyvesant, which she found often put race at the center of the discussion. She adopts a raspy tone as she mockingly imitates an event organizer: "Sistahs of Color unite for my poetry night. . . . I'm thinking about black pain." Erica wants to let loose, relax, and have fun, and this means allowing her race, her blackness, to recede into the background. So she likes black venues where she can be treated with respect without simultaneously needing to focus on racial oppression. "I don't want to think about being black when I'm with other black people. . . . I don't need to talk about the struggle and the white man." She feels it is important at times to forget about racism and enjoy oneself. My middle-class respondents patronize black venues that vary in terms of both class composition and ideological intention. But even though not all black settings are the same, they still represent places where middle-class blacks can expect to be treated with respect and not have to anticipate potential unfair and exclusionary treatment because of their race.

The middle-class blacks I interviewed see patronizing black-owned businesses as connecting to their idea of racial progress and, perhaps just as importantly, providing them access to uniquely black cultural products and services. Black-owned clubs, restaurants, and shops are thus viewed as instrumental cultural producers, offering objects and services that are key to cultivating black cultural capital, but they are also places where black people can expect to be treated with esteem.

Black Buying Power

7

EVERY YEAR BLACK AMERICANS spend an estimated $1.2 trillion.[1] This combined spending power exceeds several nations' gross domestic product (GDP). Given this scale, leaders within the black community, both historically and today, have heralded blacks' collective buying power as a powerful tool to advance the race. Javon, like many of my interviewees, deeply believes that *buying black* and supporting black entrepreneurs is one way to mobilize economic resources for the purpose of racial uplift, and that through their consumption, blacks can help one another to build wealth.

Javon imagines blacks' collective purchasing power as a vital tool that can potentially create opportunities for blacks to experience prosperity. Over time, he has devoted time, money, and energy toward efforts that will advance the race, improve the financial well-being and status of blacks, and contribute to thriving black communities. This commitment to racial uplift separates him from his white colleagues at the private equity firm where he works, and it reflects a core value that is shared by many of the middle-class blacks in my study. Their belief in giving back and helping other blacks succeed is imbued in their black privilege. It is both a benefit of their economic position and a by-product of it.

Javon's dedication to empowering blacks financially stems from his own experience of upward mobility, and his realization that he is where he is today because of the investment of others in his development. Growing up, his family was poor. He has vivid memories of unpaid bills scattered on the kitchen table and nights spent in the dark because the electricity was cut off. Though his mother had a relatively secure, full-time job at an insurance agency, she never earned enough. His parents weren't married, and his mother was the sole provider. Back then, his mom never had a dependable car; today, Javon drives a Maserati.

Javon has worked hard to ensure his own financial security, but he also readily acknowledges that his upward mobility has been contingent on the involvement of a varied group of actors—many black, some white—in his early life. At critical junctions, as he strove to improve his family's circumstances, he benefited from the support of black organizations like the NAACP and his church. Institutional forms of black cultural capital sustained him during his youth, provided him with opportunities for personal development, kept him out of trouble, and were instrumental in expanding his worldview. Because he understands what it is like to struggle, but also recognizes the critical role that other blacks and black organizations played in his own rise to success, he feels connected to blacks still struggling and a sense of duty to help them.

Javon believes wealth can have a powerful role in changing blacks' future outcomes and outlooks. Having it could open doors that education never could. He contends that Bill Gates and Warren Buffet are powerful not because of their credentials, but because of the vast amounts of wealth they have accumulated. Predictably, then, Javon doesn't see degrees and accolades as the end goal, for himself or his people, though he is cognizant of the fact that "black people have to jump higher, spit farther, run faster." For example, the black people at his firm all have far superior and more prestigious credentials than the whites in the same positions have. Most whites at his office have gone to local universities and state colleges, but the few black men who work for his firm have prestigious Ivy League credentials and multiple degrees. As he notes: "All of the black people that have ever worked here have been way more educated. Way [*he prolongs the word for emphasis*] more prepared than their white counterparts." He acknowledges that a college education is necessary for blacks' advancement, but fervently believes that education alone is not sufficient to achieve racial equality. For him, black wealth is the answer. So he works both to enrich himself and to use the skills and knowledge he has gained from a decade in the finance industry to improve black neighborhoods. He envisions racial progress that will be accomplished by creating and concentrating economic capital in black communities.

Javon's belief that black economic empowerment is achievable through self-help and wealth creation is consistent with the historically persistent, racialized political ideology of black nationalism. Buying black is one tenet of black nationalism, which calls for blacks to cultivate racial pride and solidarity as well as social, political, and economic independence. Although the scope of black nationalism extends well beyond consumption and interactions in the market, various articulations of black nationalism share a consistent thread of proscriptions and prescriptions pertaining to blacks' economic life. Though Javon does not support calls for separatism (political or otherwise), he firmly believes in financial solidarity and leveraging blacks' spending power. Like other middle-class blacks in my study, Javon expresses moderate support for black nationalist ideologies in general, but strong support for black self-sufficiency and efforts that will increase black access to and control over economic resources. The economic principles outlined in black nationalism resonate with many of the middle-class blacks in my study, who, like Javon, want to see racial advancement and who endorse the idea of collective self-determination. When black dollars are spent in the black community, blacks' consumption is seen as a tool to achieve self-sufficiency and generate black wealth.

The call to buy black provides middle-class blacks, those with the most discretionary money to spend, with specific directives pertaining to their financial decision-making. The U.S. Census Bureau's Survey of Business Owners defines a black-owned business as a firm with African American owners holding at least a 51 percent or greater stake in the business.[2] Though the participants in my study did not use this technical definition, they understood a black-owned business to be one established and led by a black entrepreneur. The influence of ideological calls to buy black is evident in the fact that two-thirds of those I interviewed see buying black as essential, emphasizing that their support of black-owned businesses is a means of contributing to economic development and to the creation of black wealth.

Racial ideologies are often described as a tool used by the dominant group to exert power and influence over subjugated groups.[3] Racial ideologies enable the dominant group to maintain control over valued resources and deploy racist ideological frames to rationalize and justify the persistence of racial inequality.[4] Among blacks, racialized counter-frames and ideologies are often promulgated. These frames and ideologies contest negative assessments of the group and articulate demands for racial equality. Yet we know comparatively little about how racialized counter-frames and ideologies, like black nationalism, inform middle-class blacks' everyday lives and their efforts to contest anti-black bias and racism in the market. A few exemplary studies exist evidencing that black political ideologies have important implications for black consumers, but many questions remain pertaining to the role that racially specific, ideologically driven consumption plays in blacks' economic lives and economic activities.[5]

To understand how ideologies influence behavior, it's useful to start by describing what an ideology is. An *ideology* is an explicit and structured meaning system, with interrelated ideas and values, that forms a generalized worldview.[6] More than a mere commonsense understanding, an ideology functions as a "filter," or lens, that helps people to make sense of the social world and how they should operate within it.[7] An ideology provides a menu of styles to choose from and a curtailed set of strategies of action and proscribed behaviors.[8] When trying to motivate a group to achieve some objective, whether political, social, or economic, ideologies are often useful and strategic cultural tools to deploy.[9] Beyond one individual's belief system, an ideology can facilitate collective action and provide the cultural framing necessary to form mass movements,[10] to connect to allies, and to establish coalitions. Ideological belief systems are often characteristic of a particular group and shared among its members.[11] One arena in which the unifying potential of ideological beliefs is evident is in the consumer market. An ideology can structure consumption, producing purchasing patterns and shared consumer preferences among group members.

Long-standing political ideologies, like black nationalism, emerge as a response to shifting sociopolitical contexts and conditions. Black nationalism has been called "the most important determinant of black public opinion." It calls for blacks to buy black as part of an effort to achieve economic independence.[12] While blacks are not monolithic in their ideological leanings and often maintain conflicting perspectives on the question of how to achieve racial progress, the members of the middle class that I interviewed widely supported the idea of buying black. In this chapter, we see how the collective interest of the group is one factor that motivates and directs middle-class blacks' consumption. My respondents, like Javon, believe that together with other blacks they can change the status quo through mobilizing their collective consumption, and they are committed to the idea that racial progress requires racial solidarity and the leveraging of black spending power.

Endorsing an ideology can impact people's attitudes, values, and behaviors. In fact, a black person's ideological beliefs can constitute a form of black cultural capital, particularly if as a belief system it helps to forge relationships and is widely shared among blacks. Thus, by endorsing the idea of buying black, middle-class blacks cultivate a form of black cultural capital that asserts a common understanding, even intuitive insight, about the power of the market and their spending, which can function to unite and help to advance blacks.

Black Solidarity and Black Spending

Fundamentally, black nationalism calls for self-determination, cultural pride, self-reliance, and to various degrees, autonomy and control over resources in the black community. Those who have promoted claims about the utility of blacks' collective economic power include historic figures from diverse political traditions, all united in the goal of black racial progress. For example, W.E.B. Du Bois and Marcus Garvey, who diverged in many respects, both articulated strategies of racial advancement that required black economic solidarity. Du Bois outlined a program of cooperative economics stemming from the long-standing practice of blacks relying on one another for survival.[13] Creating an alternative black economy based on cooperative economics was, to him, a means of eliminating blacks' reliance on whites and, if implemented correctly, it could dramatically reduce black unemployment. By buffering black businesses and service providers from competition, blacks could capitalize on racial segregation. The emergence of a self-contained black economy would eliminate the exploitation of black consumers by producers, thus making an "advantage of the disadvantage."[14]

Garvey promoted a black nationalist philosophy that emphasized group empowerment through cultural pride, economic development, and social separation. Economic self-determination was a key principle, and in a famous speech delivered circa 1924, Garvey declared, "Be Black, Buy Black, Think Black, and all else will take care of itself!"[15] Garveyites in the 1940s and 1950s heralded campaigns to "Buy Black."[16] To both Garvey and Du Bois, blacks' economic solidarity was critical to the advancement of the race.

Throughout the twentieth century, black nationalist leaders and spokespersons have advocated for African American consumers to spend money in the black community. In the 1960s, Elijah Muhammad and Malcolm X, prominent leaders of the Nation of Islam, called for the development of black businesses and encouraged blacks to patronize black-owned businesses located in black neighborhoods. This, they argued, would create a loop of continuous reinvestment. In outlining the "economic philosophy of black nationalism," Malcom X specifically argued that only through ownership of businesses could blacks' retain control over the economic resources in their communities.

Black entrepreneurs, black business associations, and the black press have also broadcast calls to support black businesses, both as a means to advance the race and as an expression of black pride.[17] The idea of buying black is not a relic of the past but has retained its popularity over time. In their analysis of the 1980 National Survey of Black Americans, Brown and colleagues found that 63 percent of blacks agreed with the statement that "blacks should shop in black-owned stores whenever possible."[18] Evidence suggests that idea remains salient among black Americans today. For example, in 2009, a black family in Chicago, the Andersons, working collaboratively with researchers at Northwestern University, launched the Ebony Experiment in which they committed to spending their money only with black-owned businesses for an entire year. Maggie Anderson described the experiment as doing their part to solve "the crisis in the black community" and fervently expressed her belief that buying black was "the best way to demonstrate your love and pride for the community."[19]

In 2016, popular, Atlanta-based rapper Killer Mike vehemently entreated one million blacks to each deposit $100 into a black-owned bank, launching the #BankBlack challenge as a form of protest against a system of racial oppression and as a means to assert black control over their community.[20] More recently, hip-hop artists and businessmen Jay-Z and Sean "P. Diddy" Combs launched a collaborative venture, designing an app to help users locate black-owned and black-friendly businesses. In a 2018 interview with *GQ* magazine, Combs explained, "the application will make it possible for us to have an economic community. It's about Blacks gaining economic power. . . . At some point there has to be some kind of fight. I feel like we've done a lot of marching. It's time to start charging."[21] Combs was emphasizing strategically spending money ("charging"), as a perhaps more viable alternative to "marching" with the goal of promoting blacks' economic well-being and advancement. From clothing to alcohol to makeup, black entertainers have long been moguls of marketing consumer goods to black buyers, but their calls to support all black businesses on a much broader basis demonstrate that the appeal for economic racial solidarity remains a part of conversation about how to achieve racial progress and that this idea is deeply infused in black popular culture.

In speaking with my study respondents about why they try to buy black, I learned that this effort represents a group-specific ideological belief that not only calls for racial solidarity but is also seen as a real way to move the race forward. It reflects a self-imposed but often shared sense of responsibility to other blacks that is part of their being black and privileged.

Buying Black

When making everyday decisions, some middle-class blacks, like Kenneth, adhere to logics consistent with the racialized ideology of black nationalism. Kenneth says of his purchasing choices, "I'm supporting the community, for a certain level of uplift." Now, buying black is not relevant in every transaction; at times, Kenneth's commitment to buying black could conflict with his tastes or needs. Nonetheless, he endorses a logic of black consumer power and advocates for racial advancement, or "uplift," through his patronage of black-owned businesses.

When interviewing the comparatively small contingent of middle-class blacks who do not agree with the mandate to buy black, I found they prefer to see the market as a place where they are free to exert control and express "consumer sovereignty." Put differently, they prioritized "unbridled consumer choice" over racial allegiance.[22] These respondents in many instances believed in racial uplift and often maintained a collective orientation in other spheres, whether volunteering or giving back financially. That is, their lack of enthusiastic support of black-owned business is not their way of saying they shouldn't help other blacks or that blacks do not share a collective fate. Instead, they emphasize that to truly enjoy the rewards bestowed by their class status, they should experience the market as an arena free from the inflection of race and racial obligations; they prioritize the function of the market as a sphere in which black economic advancement is realized, rather than as an avenue for black economic advancement in and of itself.

Rationales for Buying Black

Consistent with the tenets of black nationalism, middle-class blacks articulate that keeping money in the community is a way to retain black control over economic resources, to contribute to the current and future successes of black entrepreneurs, and to ensure that their specifically black tastes and needs as consumers are met. Yet, of all the possible rationales given for endorsing buying black, the most frequent is the perception that such spending is a form of racial uplift. Rather than being driven by sheer self-interest, many of my respondents told me their consumption is one way to realize their commitment to the collective.

Not only is buying black desirable but the idea that blacks often fail to patronize black-owned businesses is seen as shameful. Blacks' dollars, when leveraged, could contribute to the personal income of black entrepreneurs, keep capital within the black community, and ensure the continued production of black cultural products. Blacks who fail to mobilize their collective economic resources within the community are thus seen as part of the problem. Often respondents drew comparisons between blacks and members of other ethnic or religious groups, who, they believe, more readily support one another. Kevin, a native New Yorker, sees black neighborhoods as suffering from a lack of the sort of solidarity in spending he perceives to exist in other ethnic enclaves:

> In New York you realize that really, outside of the African American areas, you will see certain enclaves, like the Jewish community [and] even if you go to Chinatown, you can tell it is close-knit. They support each other. . . . They invest with each other, their money stays in the community. When I grew up, you just learn that the money in Harlem does not stay in the community. You just don't see it. . . . Whenever I go to these [other] communities and I see nice neighborhoods. I'm like, "man, why can't we have that?"

Kevin's comparative assessment reveals that for him the disinvestment in black neighborhoods is something that is, in part, blacks' fault, or at least it is their responsibility to repair. One way he sees blacks could improve black neighborhoods would be to "support" and "invest" in other blacks. Similarly, Vanessa remarks:

> I think it's really important to support black-owned businesses, and one of the problems with Harlem, for example, is that we do not support our businesses, but at the same time, there has to be a quality component to it. Take Jewish neighborhoods. You know, thriving. Everything is Jewish-owned and Jewish-supported, and no black neighborhood in New York is like that at all.

Vanessa is not alone in feeling that one way to eliminate the underdevelopment in black communities, like Harlem, is to support "quality" black-owned businesses. Such respondents realize that black businesses vary in size, do not exist in all domains, and for a number of reasons, cannot compete with national chains. But with these caveats, Vanessa believes that blacks should look to

Jewish neighborhoods as models of what is possible. Perhaps because of Jewish people's history of social exclusion and ghettoization, they are seen as similar to blacks. However, it is interesting that while study respondents see Jewish communities as exemplars, they do not delve deeper to consider how differences, for example in access to capital, might contribute to divergent outcomes that disadvantage blacks, while simultaneously allowing Jewish entrepreneurs and merchants to compete on a different scale.

"Hell, yeah!" replies Wayne, a 28-year-old salesman for a major media company, when I ask if he patronizes black-owned businesses. While Wayne is the child of Jamaican immigrants, he still indicates that he believes strongly in buying black, which for him generates a sense of personal connection between himself and black entrepreneurs. He likes "putting money in other peoples' pockets," and when he spends his money with black-owned businesses, his dollars fatten another black person's pockets. It is empowering to think that through his consumption, he enables a black person to provide for their family. Erica, the nonprofit manager, also indicates that if given a choice, she would "privilege" a store owned by blacks: "I would be directly supporting black people and their income earning potential." For Wayne and Erica, patronizing black-owned businesses provides a clear means to direct their consumption to the advancement of black entrepreneurs.

Damon, who had recently purchased a condo in Harlem, tries to buy black whenever possible, too: "If I know there's a black-owned business, I'll try to spend my money there before I spend my money elsewhere." He sees such choices as giving back to the community, but also as allowing him to access unique cultural wares. For example, he frequents a black-owned boutique that sells graphic t-shirts with quotes and adages that celebrate black intellectuals and draw on black iconography. One of his favorite shirts features the slogan "the talented tenth," referencing Du Bois's idea of a class of educated black leaders who use their wisdom and wit to change the lot of their race. For Damon, purchasing and wearing his "talented tenth" t-shirt displays his black pride and allows him to express a form of black cultural capital, but his purchase also contributes in some small way to the entrepreneurial efforts of another black person, and is therefore also a form of economic upliftment.

Tasha reasons that beyond direct purchases, it is important to support black designers, business owners, and film directors, because their success ensures that future opportunities will be available for other blacks. Supporting black artisans and artists provides them with much-needed financial support so that they can continue to create art, films, literature, dance, and other forms of creative expression. This sentiment mirrors the thoughts of the middle- and upper-class black art collectors described in sociologist Patricia Banks's study, who feel a special duty to support black artists, frequently marginalized in the art world and struggling financially, through their consumption.[23] While there is a financial component to the idea of buying black, here we also see the underlying idea that by contributing to the survival of blacks with goods to sell, no matter the domain, one can ensure that the cultural producers who cater to blacks' tastes continue creating. As Lamar, a 34-year-old bank vice president, notes, when he spends his dollars with black businesses, he contributes to their ability to stay in business.

Lisa, like Vanessa and Kevin, argues that members of the Jewish community don't let each other fail. She grew up around Jewish friends and believes that blacks should similarly ensure that black businesses succeed. Lisa actualizes this belief by supporting a diverse array of retail and service providers, including her favorite bookstore owner, her hairdresser, her private banker, and her real estate broker, all of whom are black. Along with Tasha, she is passionate about patronizing black professionals across these various domains because she feels that their survival depends on other blacks' continued economic support.

Jabari, a job counselor, supports a black-owned dry cleaner, despite the fact that it is more expensive to have his clothes cleaned there: "If we don't support them, how will they stay in business?" he asks. He feels an obligation to support the long-standing business to ensure that it can prosper in a gentrifying part of a black neighborhood. Lance, a child of Jamaican immigrants, also remarks on supporting black-owned businesses in order to retain control over economic resources in the black community and to ensure those businesses' continued existence. He explains,

> I feel like for years, we didn't have our own. . . . Now that we have our own, I gotta try to make sure that we keep our own. 'Cause if I don't help, and nobody else helps, we outta business, and we're back to where we were before, [with] only the white folks owning everything. I can't complain about black folks not owning anything, if we black folks own something and I don't support it.

For Lance, a reality in which black people own and control the commercial activities in the community is much preferred to "white folks owning everything." Others told me that their support of black-owned businesses is centered in their desire to spur further economic development in black communities.

As Brittany points out: "Economics and money fuels the rest of the world. And so, if you invest your dollar back in your community, you create more resources and amenities for your [community], which, makes it a more enjoyable place to live." For middle-class blacks, this community development and improvement is often seen as conditional on their support for existing black-owned businesses. "[I]t's good to keep money in our community, because I feel that's the best way for us as a community to thrive, if we support each other with our dollars," Ashlee, the HR administrator, summarizes.

Angela returns to the idea that wealth building is essential for racial progress. For her, it makes sense that supporting black-owned businesses contributes to this objective: "You know, the more you support black-owned businesses, they stay in business and that's good." She believes that, whether individual or corporate, "ownership" of businesses and property is a sign of economic progress, not just for individuals but for blacks collectively. Building black wealth could be facilitated, these respondents argue, by the strategic deployment of black consumers' economic capital.

Black businesses are seen as catering to the black community's racially distinct needs and filling a racially specific market demand. Unlike the other rationales respondents offer for preferring to buy black, this one is less indicative of their commitment to racial progress—it is practical. In Chapter Three, I illustrated the plethora of ways that middle-class blacks maintain a constellation of black practices and indicate race-specific tastes and proclivities in a diverse array of categories. Cultivating black cultural capital requires the consumption of material objects, services, and spaces, and so it often means middle-class blacks need to develop relationships with and patronize black entrepreneurs and service providers—think, for instance, of Damon's favorite t-shirt, "the talented tenth," which is made by a local black-owned shop. Middle-class blacks' consumption of racialized products and services is one way of engaging and celebrating black culture. Many fear that these businesses might not keep their doors open without black financial support; for whatever reason—lack of familiarity, fear, or outright bias—whites are seen as unlikely patrons of black-owned businesses. (Many assume that anti-black bias and negative views about blacks are also applied to non-blacks' perceptions of black-owned businesses.) To counter white aversion or avoidance, study respondents assert that black support of black-owned businesses is crucial for sustaining enterprises that cater to blacks' specific tastes and needs.

Jada, the marketing manager who has a "side hustle" as a makeup artist, declares such businesses understand "our community and our culture." In her own entrepreneurial efforts, she tries to be aware of and on the lookout for products that work for her; if they work for her then they will work for her clients:

> I love doing makeup for black women. I'm not exclusive. Trust me. I have the
> skills to do anyone's hair or makeup, but there's something special about being
> the same. I understand what you need, because I share a lot of your needs. . . .
> I try to keep abreast of what my black clients might need. . . . I try to patronize
> black businesses because at the end of the day, this is our community. This is
> our culture.

Jada actively works to address the needs specific to black women. Because makeup companies have often neglected the variation in complexions that exists on the brown side of the spectrum, Jada's awareness of products that provide coverage for darker skin tones is knowledge that might not be widely available to or cultivated by all makeup artists. Jada realizes that as a makeup artist, her ability to cater to black women and to address issues related to their diverse skin tones qualifies as a unique form of cultural knowledge that she maintains as a black entrepreneur. She perceives that black businesses, like hers, are better equipped than others to cater to blacks' needs because of this cultural knowledge. Scholars have demonstrated that in certain industries and fields, the "racial abilities" of minority workers are linked to organizational goals and facilitate better outcomes for their customers and clients.[24] Studies of black patients, for example, demonstrate that blacks indicate greater satisfaction when cared for by black doctors, and that black physicians do not exhibit, or exhibit less, bias in their treatment of black patients and produce better health outcomes.[25] Thus, the racial matching of producers and consumers that Jada is referencing is a valid and legitimate consideration for black customers. Her support of black businesses is both a means of recognizing black artisans and professionals who cater to black consumers' needs and a means of acknowledging black culture and cultural knowledge as having value in the marketplace.

Among the most common black-owned businesses that respondents indicate they support are hair salons, barbershops, restaurants, entertainment venues, nightclubs, and lounges. Each provides a culturally specific product or service. For example, when it comes to socializing, many respondents report that they choose a club or lounge based on the music. As a consequence, they often frequent venues that are black-owned or that cater to a majority black crowd. Tasha, who vividly described to me an incident of racism at a club (related in Chapter Six), indicates her preference for black venues succinctly: "I tend to choose black establishments, or at least, you know, a black place, a black crowd, for the music, for the people you're going to be around, like the fun you're going to have. I tend to choose black-geared events." Spending her money in these venues is a market-based expression of her preference for black music and for a uniquely black social-interactional and cultural experience. It also makes it far less likely that she will be hassled by some bouncer or club manager reluctant to admit a group of black club-goers.

"I go to Broadway shows, museums, restaurants, people watching, the zoo, and cultural centers. I pretty much do it all." Paul, the strategist for a health insurance company, illustrates that he frequents diverse cultural spaces. But when he goes to a nightclub, you will find him, in his words, at "black-oriented" clubs. He prefers rap, rhythm and blues, and reggae—all instantiations of his black cultural capital—and he reports feeling out of place in most bars. "When you go to a bar, it's usually predominantly white, and there's a lot of, I wouldn't say, not binge drinking, but binge drinking of beer. I don't really drink a lot of beer, so it's kind of awkward for me." Paul associates bars with white people and beer; even with his diverse tastes, these are not his preference for a night out on the town.

The sorts of discriminatory treatment at nightclubs described in Chapter Six also serve as a deterrent to venturing to entertainment venues in certain parts of town or venues where blacks are few in number. When attempting to get into nightclubs in certain trendy areas of the city, many, particularly middle-class black men, feel they run the risk of being profiled and discriminated against. The "push" away from such areas and clubs is met with a "pull" toward black-owned venues trusted to be welcoming to blacks, to cater to black cultural tastes, and to make middle-class blacks feel comfortable.

In reality, people buy black for a range of reasons. Like all consumers, my respondents first sought to satisfy their individual needs, but many also sought to achieve collective ends through leveraging their consumer purchasing power. Their spending habits reveal their ideological commitment to the collective project of racial uplift. Among the roughly one-third of those interviewed who do not prioritize buying black, most emphasize the market as a place where their middle-class status should result in certain entitlements:

freedom to choose, attentive service, and access to high-quality products or services. For them, the market is a space where money should matter more than race, even if it often does not.

The Market Logic: Prioritizing Choice, Service, and Quality

As consumers with money to spend, most middle-class blacks feel they should, first and foremost, operate in the market with the goal of satisfying their needs. For some, this means that they feel they should be free to choose, without consideration of their race, the products and services they consume. Those who fall into this camp are like Michelle, who notes that even though she often purchases clothing made by black fashion designer Tracey Reese, she does not take a designer's race into consideration before making a purchase. Rather, as she remarks, "I buy what's worth me buying." Michelle is not interested in the racial symbolism of supporting a black entrepreneur in the fashion industry, an industry known to restrict blacks' opportunities for entry and participation.[26] Rebuffing the idea of buying black, she remarks, "I don't seek out that kind of stuff. I buy what I like."

Those who endorse the idea of buying black agree that the quality of products or services purchased or procured is important, and many state that they would only return to a black-owned business if the product and service is of decent quality. That is, their support of black-owned businesses is not unconditional; it is contingent on quality. Still, those who express ambivalence about the idea of buying black place far greater emphasis on their ability to freely choose—without any constraints—and buy the best quality product they can afford. They think of the market, in principle, as a sphere free from politics, but this stance is a reflection of an ideology that privileges the market.

A critique leveled by some middle-class blacks who do not believe it is important to support black-owned businesses, is that black businesses simply lack the capacity to compete, to provide the best product at the best price. These negative assertions are based on the idea that black-owned businesses cannot provide the level or quantity of services offered by large corporations. Larry, the library technician, notes that he mostly patronizes big-box stores and large retailers, such as Target and Macy's. Shopping is about convenience and ease, and for Larry, one-stop-shopping fits the bill. He does not believe that black businesses can operate on the same scale, so they don't get his patronage. Larry is correct in associating black-owned businesses with small businesses: nearly

96 percent of black-owned firms have only one employee,[27] and in 2012, the average sales receipts for black-owned businesses totaled $58,000, compared to $546,000 for non-Hispanic white-owned businesses.[28] Black-owned businesses are almost always small businesses, rarely occupying a market position that allows them to compete with national retailers. Because Larry prizes a certain practicality that comes from frequenting a big-box store over a small specialty store or boutique, black businesses are usually excluded from his marketplace experience.

The old adage "the white man's ice is always colder" also seemed to lurk in respondents' reasons for not seeking out black-owned businesses and artisans. Hesitance to support black-owned businesses at times seemed imbued with the idea that black-owned business are inherently inferior, often providing goods or services that are of poor or unreliable quality. The perception that products or services made by black-owned companies are of inferior quality, as compared to those produced by whites, can be attributed to internalized racial inferiority. It may also reflect a very real, though unfair, set of structural conditions that disadvantage black businesses—for example, a comparative lack of access to capital.[29] It may also reflect negative stereotypes (for example, that blacks have bad attitudes or lack the soft skills necessary to provide outstanding customer service). Regardless of the underlying justification, middle-class blacks are not immune from the belief that black businesses are not up to snuff. No one said it outright, but I detected hints. Michelle, for instance, mentioned that she often shops at a black-owned boutique in Brooklyn and had recently purchased a Tracey Reese dress that she absolutely loved. But she also declared that she had "issues" with black-owned businesses, citing a black theater company's outdated website, indicative of a lack of care and attention to detail and a failure to modernize, which is emblematic, for Michelle, of black businesses more broadly. She seemed both unsurprised and irritated to find black businesses and organizations poorly run. While Michelle does not object to buying something sold by a black-owned firm or produced by a black-owned brand, the ideology of buying black does not resonate with her. She tends to think that, with few exceptions, black-owned companies just could not get their act together.

Ideology Versus Practice

Proclaiming support for the idea of patronizing black-owned businesses and actually buying products and services from black entrepreneurs are, in reality, two separate things. In fact, the actual range of businesses that interviewees describe when asked what types of black-owned businesses they support is limited. As noted earlier, the most commonly mentioned businesses were barbershops and hair salons, restaurants, and entertainment venues—all business that provide services conditioned by race-specific cultural skills or know-how, catering to blacks' specific tastes and preferences, and requiring producers to have black cultural capital. These types of businesses are seen as reliably and readily accessible in almost any black neighborhood. Thus, they are also connected to racialized ideas of place, rather than being businesses that compete in the larger marketplace.

Some middle-class blacks mention patronizing black professionals. Black doctors, realtors, and even bankers are sought out, perhaps because in each sphere—health care, real estate and mortgage lending—research indicates that black consumers often receive inferior service and face discrimination.[30] It might be advantageous for blacks to seek out co-ethnic service providers to avoid costly and disadvantageous treatment as a consequence of racial bias. However, only one person mentioned avoiding discrimination or racially exclusionary treatment as a reason for buying black. Instead, it is far more popular to ground such support in claims of racial solidarity and the objective of racial uplift.

Even those who do not endorse the idea of buying black, in practice often seek out black service providers and businesses when they believe they have race-specific knowledge. Again, black cultural capital contributes to this attraction. Amare mostly shops at designer stores and remarks that he cares little about whether a business is black-owned, yet he is remarkably loyal to his barber. Amare tries to get his hair cut once a week. As a professional in the finance industry, he perceives it is critical that he is always clean shaven. For him, grooming is racialized, and the idea that he would exclusively patronize a barber who shares his race just makes sense. Like several interviewees, Amare sees the ease of patronizing commercial establishments that cater to a black clientele (such as barbershops and hair braiding salons) and that offer uniquely black cultural products (such as soul food restaurants) as a distinct advantage of living in a black neighborhood. "I like the fact that I can go and get a haircut in my neighborhood, that's big for me, because if I lived in, like say, midtown or any other place, I might have to go to Brooklyn or Harlem to get a haircut." Even though he does not see a need for racial solidarity in spending, he acknowledges that for certain services he feels compelled to patronize black service provider, in a black part of town. In practice he is tremendously loyal to the black barber that he frequently patronizes.

Similarly, Brandon, a 28-year-old manager of a big-box retail store, quickly replies, "no, not really," when asked if he believes it is important to support black-owned businesses. Then he goes on to explain that he does go out of his way to patronize at least one black-owned business: "My barbershop is black-owned. I still drive to Newark to get my hair cut. My barber's been my barber since I was a sophomore in high school. I still go to him. You know, it's still that home feeling. When you get in a barbershop, you know everybody that goes in there. You know the owner." This deep commitment goes beyond racial affiliation and affinity; his barber has race-specific knowledge about maintaining a black man's mane, and his shop is a space of connection, where Brandon feels at home because of his long-standing relationship with the owner and the fellow patrons. Though he does not endorse the ideology of buying black, the intimacy of his barbershop experience combined with the barber's racialized knowledge are central factors shaping Brandon's decision to be fiercely loyal and to patronize a black-owned business in practice.

For and Against Buying Black

What separates middle-class blacks who endorse and promote the idea of buying black from those who don't? Research on black nationalism finds few differences between those who do and do not endorse the ideology, though one notable difference is that blacks who are more group-centered, rather than individualistic, tend to subscribe to black nationalist beliefs.[31] My inquiry into differences among those who subscribe to the idea of buying black versus those who do not had similar results: the fault lines that exist among blacks seem not to follow traditional demographic characteristics, such as gender. The children of immigrants are just as likely as blacks who are multigenerational native-born to support or reject the idea of buying black, and HBCU grads were just as likely as alums of predominantly white schools. So, what separates those who support the idea from those who do not?

Given the research on black nationalism that suggests those who do not endorse the idea of buying black may be less collectively oriented, I thought that belief in racial uplift and commitment to group progress might be a determinant driving modern middle-class blacks to back buying black. However, the responses of middle-class blacks in my study do not necessarily support this hypothesis. Darryl, who early on in his interview expressed the importance of blacks helping each other to get ahead, sees blacks' willingness to help each other as something that separates his generation from previous generations. He maintains a group orientation in many respects:

> I don't want my race to be at the bottom of the totem pole because all of us are in prison, or all of us got bogus jobs. We all wanna keep excelling. So I think it's important and I think my generation realizes it's important to continue to build up our communities and reaching out to folks and making sure folks are connected. It's like, "Oh, I have a job here and you wanna job? You know, give me that resume!"

When I ask, later in the interview, about whether it is important for him to support black businesses, Darryl is ambivalent. He argues that a vendor's race matters little; if he buys something, it is because he likes the style or quality of the product. Being connected to and willing to help other blacks is not necessarily associated with a willingness to support black-owned businesses. The two are not linked, in part, because Darryl values the market and his ability to consume in ways that are not driven by his race.

I did see a divergence depending on respondents' exposure to the idea of buying black and whether their social ties expressed support for it. That is, when buying black is socially embedded, people are more likely to express support for the idea. My respondents often reported learning about the idea and practice through their interactions with family and friends, and that gave it weight. Historical figures and celebrities further promoted the idea, helping it to maintain its relevance in their eyes.

Kevin, who lamented that the black dollar did not stay in the community, feels that it is the duty of the black middle class to correct years of disinvestment in black neighborhoods. The idea of utilizing blacks' collective spending as a form of uplift was cemented for him as an undergraduate at Morehouse College. There, he developed strong social ties to other middle-class blacks and ideas about racial uplift were reinforced. Kevin spoke passionately about his efforts to save each year, with the goal of combining his resources with like-minded blacks and investing in entrepreneurial activities that he imagines will provide commercial services in the black community. He feels strongly that he and other "smart black folks" need "to pool our resources together. We need to do something positive with this money, with the money that we're making, and make something that could be long-sustaining and help out our people." Kevin believes in the power of the black dollar, particularly when aggregated, and this belief is reinforced by his peers: other college-educated blacks.

Javon is reinvesting his resources in the black community through several initiatives he leads at his church. He sees black neighborhoods as the ideal target for investment because they are full of "untapped assets." If leveraged properly, these assets could be used to reduce racial disparities and improve blacks' economic prospects. Javon envisions an investment fund that would select small and mid-size black businesses, provide them with start-up capital, and help them grow in black communities. His leadership role in his church's efforts enables him to actualize racial uplift by doing just that, making capital available to black entrepreneurs.

Both Kevin and Javon are embedded in social and institutional networks that embrace and encourage the idea of buying black, and they support such efforts because they represent a means of racial uplift. Among Kevin's group of friends and fellow Morehouse graduates and among the leadership at Javon's church, the idea that blacks should mobilize resources within the black community and capitalize on their collective economic and purchasing power to create opportunities for other blacks is encouraged. Thus, it is not surprising that they, too, support the idea enthusiastically.

Celebrity role models are often influential in the positive associations people have with black entrepreneurialism. The philosophies promoted by black public figures from Du Bois and Malcom X to Jay-Z and P. Diddy support the idea of collective advancement through black entrepreneurship and reinvesting in the black community. Jay-Z had many fans among middle-class blacks in my study. Beyond his music, he is admired for his business savvy and entrepreneurial spirit. As one of his lyrics attests, "I am not a businessman, I am a business man."[32] Damon, the fan of the talented tenth, describes Jay-Z as having opened "up a myriad of doors" for other blacks, while Shante, who is currently reading Jay-Z's autobiography, *Decoded*, is fascinated by Jay-Z's life as a testament to blacks' resilience and creative productivity. "Jay-Z, he understands that hip-hop is a black American cultural contribution and that we can take ownership of that," Shante reflects. Isaiah attributes his admiration for people like Jay-Z, 50 Cent, and P. Diddy as due to "the businesses that they have set up, the wealth that they have set up." He references P. Diddy specifically, proud of the fact that he is a black man with a billboard in Times Square promoting his brands Sean Jean and Cîroc.

Javon points out that P. Diddy is one of the few large-scale generators of black wealth, and he decries the scarcity of multi-million-dollar black corporations:

There are very few institutions that are uniquely owned by the black people. We don't have multi-billion-dollar corporations like other folks do. We've got BET, which no longer belongs to us. It's now owned by Viacom. We've got Harpo. We've got Johnson Publishing. We've got P. Diddy and maybe five or six others. We don't have a whole bunch of multi-million-dollar corporations.

In fact, while P. Diddy earned an estimated $64 million in 2018, Jay-Z out-earned him by taking in $76.5 million.[33] Both are among the wealthiest entertainers and hip-hop artists in the world, a testament to their business acumen. If one is looking for examples of how relatively young black men have generated wealth through business ownership, black celebrities like Jay-Z and P. Diddy stand out. Oprah, too, is an iconic figure, representing the possibilities for black women. Black celebrities are highly visible and frequently named figures, perhaps in part because so few blacks are part of the top 1 percent. In 2016, only 1.9 percent of all black households had a net worth over a million dollars, compared to 15 percent of all white households.[34] When blacks, whether celebrities or entertainers or corporate executives, enter the echelon of the very affluent, they are celebrated by the black middle class. Their success is a credit to the race and indicates the economic power that could potentially be generated by black entrepreneurship.

Variation in middle-class blacks' level of support for the idea of buying black also seems connected to the timing of their exposure to the directive: that is, when the idea is introduced and its implications are made real. Sharon, the daughter of Ghanaian immigrants, grew up in a majority white suburban community outside Washington, DC. It was not until she moved to a black neighborhood that she realized supporting black-owned business is important: "[I] never really thought about it before, until I was in an all-black community and then it started to be important to me." Sharon describes being "surrounded by black businesses and black people" which made her feel, "Oh, I should definitely build up the community." The idea of buying black did not become real and its everyday ramifications felt, until Sharon moved to a majority black neighborhood.

Even though not all middle-class blacks endorse the idea of buying black, the idea of supporting black businesses, particularly as a form of uplift, is pronounced among my respondents. Comparatively, among the small sample of working-class blacks I also interviewed (adults who were working but did not have a college degree), there was relatively little support for the idea of buying black. They did not reject the idea, but seemed unfamiliar with the many rationales articulated by the black middle-class for endorsing it, even the idea that it is a means of racial uplift. Melanie, an administrative assistant who grew up in the projects in Brooklyn, admits that she tries "to look at the product more than who made it." But she also notes that she would rather buy Cîroc, a vodka affiliated with the hip-hop mogul P. Diddy, than the pricey champagne Cristal, because, as she explains, the makers of Cristal do not want their product associated with rappers, which, in other words, means black people. Melanie indicates that blacks may avoid brands or companies they see as holding or maintaining prejudice. In the case of Cristal, one of the company's managers commented in the *Economist* that they were dismayed that rappers drank the champagne in their videos and mentioned it in their songs. This comment caused Jay-Z to call for a boycott of the pricey champagne.[35] Melanie, heeded that call, and indicates that she does not want to support a brand associated with discriminating against blacks, but more broadly, she does not report actively seeking out or wanting to support black-owned businesses.

Patrick, another working-class interviewee, employed in finance, is the same. Drawing on the example of the iPhone, he notes:

> I'm more focused on the product itself. Like, you know, the iPhone. Does anybody care if a white man is the CEO of Apple? You know, nobody cares. They just love the iPhone, basically because of how it operates and what it does, and it does everything that they want, so they buy it. I'm that kind of person.

Patrick sees himself as a rational actor whose purchases are not swayed by social considerations. If he likes the object, its functionality, quality, and performance, he buys it. For him, the market is not a place where racial loyalties matter. Patrick's rationale is more complete than those offered by most of the working-class interviewees, who were often ambivalent about buying black. The underlying ideological rationales that might be drawn on or refuted in discussing calls to buy black were not salient for them. This contrasts with the idea of racial solidarity in spending as a form of racial uplift, which is almost intuitive for many members of the black middle class. Class differences appear to be a relevant factor impacting blacks' familiarity with the various logics and rationales behind endorsing the ideological commitment to buy black.

The idea that one's consumption could constitute a tool used for the benefit of the race alters how some middle-class blacks view their consumption and the meaning they attribute to their participation in the market. How might this ideology compare to others commonly endorsed by members of the middle class? A comparison between buying black and being green reveals that middle-class black consumers might support an ideology consistent with their racial status, such as buying black, but not endorse an ideology common among members of the middle class more generally.

Being Black and Green

Being green, an umbrella term for adopting an assortment of environmentally friendly practices and consumption preferences, has been argued to be an expression of middle-class consumer sensibilities and tastes.[36] Research indicates that while there are racial differences in support for environmentally driven consumption, these differences are reduced when controlling for class status. However, among the middle-class blacks interviewed for this study, concern for the environment is infrequently a motivation for consumer choices. In contrast to the common and well-thought-out rationales they offer for their endorsement of the idea of buying black, my respondents often lack a clear cultural script to coherently articulate why they might value consumption driven by environmental conservation.

Kevin, who advocates for pooling economic resources and reinvesting in businesses in black communities, feels that being green is not a financial priority. Jada advocates for supporting black entrepreneurs, who, like herself, are dedicated to "our community, and our culture." Contrarily, she implies that a company's environmentally friendly policies are not an important consideration for her. And for Ashlee, being green requires the accompaniment of a certain cultural knowledge she feels she lacks: "I guess I am not as evolved in my choices when it comes to, you know environmental sustainability. . . . I think I'm just not very educated in it." She elaborates, saying, "You know, I don't really know exactly why I should be buying certain products, as opposed to another, what effect it's having on the environment." When I ask specifically about her inclination to purchase organic foods, Ashlee's response suggests that her choice is not due to her firm agreement with a belief system that promotes environmental conservation, as she states: "I will purchase organic foods, but I don't really understand necessarily what that really means for me, you know, or for the environment. It just kind of something that sounds nice, but I don't really get the difference." Ashlee does not have a compelling reason for purchasing organic foods, but she does for buying black: she believes blacks should "keep money in our community" to help the group thrive. Kevin, Jada, and

Ashlee indicate an ambivalence about consuming in ways that might benefit or preserve the environment. However, they all articulate logics consistent with the idea that buying black is important. They see supporting black-owned businesses as a means of directing their spending toward the benefit of the race, but feel no compelling ideological commitments driving their consumption with regard to the environment.

Amare admits with a little embarrassment that he litters and does not recycle. When I ask why, he explains that he occasionally litters because "it wasn't ingrained in me that I shouldn't, but I'm conscious about it now." Similarly, recycling is not a practice he had learned about growing up: "if I lived in an environment where I had to, that's what I would be doing. I'd be recycling." Jada's upbringing was also relatively free of environmental consciousness, and she hadn't really thought much about recycling until she moved into an apartment building in which it is mandatory. She notices that where she lives now: "People are really gung-ho about recycling up here. I like that, that's cool. But I had never habitually done it. So it was something that took some getting used to." For Jada, recycling is a practice that is learned and that reflects a change in her normative environment—it is not connected to her sense of self, nor is it ideologically driven.

Lisa and Javon are outliers in their commitments to being black and being green. Lisa mentions that she learned the importance of being green early on, having grown up in a place where consciousness about the environmental impact of human activity is encouraged. Now that she is an adult, that awareness remains relevant:

> I grew up in San Francisco, where that's just kind of the norm. And it was something that we learned a lot in school, and then I was a part of a lot of clubs that focused on composting or recycling or preserving the rain forest. And then, you know, having spent some time in parts of the world where all of our waste ends up, I see the impact that it has.

Within the company where she is a managing partner, Lisa is the chief advocate for using biodegradable and compostable packaging. She has been successful in her efforts, even though the change added to the costs that the company's customers would have to bear. But she feels the long-term impact is just that important. Javon similarly notes that growing up in Oregon, which he describes as a "very environmentally progressive part of the country," contributed to his being "very green." With ease, he rattles off his green bona fides: "I buy organic. I don't litter. I use minimal water. I recycle." Environmentalism, like buying black, is the result of a belief system that is learned and integrated into one's worldview over time, though for many middle-class blacks, the ideology attached to being green is not deeply incorporated into their consciousness. However, through consistent exposure, ideologies relating to the environment could become commonsense, expected, and habitual practices.

Ideologies are powerful drivers of middle-class blacks' consumption. Whether one is considering environmental ideologies, like being green, or racialized ideologies, like black nationalism, wholesale support for ideologies is not evident among all blacks, reflecting the fact that blacks are heterogeneous in their ideological beliefs. However, support for ideological beliefs that is evident in a person's consumption is more salient among those who encounter an ideology early and often. To understand the salience and relevance of ideological commitments and their impact on consumption, it is important to remember that such commitments are socially embedded. For some blacks, cultural ideas about collective advancement and racial progress influence their views of the role and function of their consumption. Consumption allows middle-class blacks to express long-standing, racially specific, ideological beliefs and cultivate black cultural capital through purchasing race-specific goods, patronizing black service providers, and seeking out venues that cater to blacks' taste. Their desire to use their economic power to benefit the black collective reveals that race and racialized ideologies condition their economic action. However, middle-class blacks in my study also made a choice about how they view the market. For some, the market is a place where they prioritize their personal needs. Nonetheless, from examining the logics used to justify the idea of supporting black-owned businesses, it becomes clear that many middle-class blacks share the goal of advancing the race. In this way, their consumption is motivated by their race and what they perceive are the needs of the collective.

Black American Dreams

8

IF CONSUMPTION IS TREATED AS A CYCLICAL PROCESS rather than a singular act, the first stage is dreaming and longing. When middle-class blacks think about making it big, do they wish for the same types of things as other Americans? Does their black cultural capital affect their aspirational consumption? How do their race-based affinities and sensibilities—their black cultural capital—influence the types of consumer goods and experiences that make it onto their wish lists? Middle-class blacks today have undeniable access to economic resources and opportunities that no generation of blacks has experienced before. This is a key part of the modern middle-class black experience. While cultural and financial capital does not free them from anti-black bias in the marketplace, their consumption remains an essential practice and an important indicator of their attitudes and values, as well as their racial identity and class standing.

To gauge middle-class blacks' aspirational consumption, each participant in the study was asked to list five things they would do or purchase if they won the lottery and had nearly inexhaustible financial resources. In other words, how would they use a windfall? What emerged is a depiction of their aspirational consumption that connects middle-class blacks to broader tropes about the American Dream and its material manifestation. But they also demonstrate their commitment to racial uplift, prioritizing group advancement and financial progress as aspects of their Black American Dreams.

Lori is confident in her position as a member of the middle class. She has a college education and a professional job. This means she could begin to enjoy—to consume—the rewards associated with a middle-class lifestyle. Lori's response to my windfall scenario illustrates how being part of the black community meaningfully impacts her vision for her financial future. The first thing Lori imagines she would buy is a brownstone in Harlem, then a second home in North Carolina, where she and her family are from. For Lori, owning a brownstone is like owning an iconic piece of the city: "That's a part of New York culture; brownstones are architectural staples in New York. And they're beautiful. If I didn't live in New York right now and I wouldn't be familiar with brownstones, I probably would say I want to buy a mansion." Local context clearly shapes her tastes and desires. Lori's connection to black people is reflected in the way she situates her imagined future home not on the Upper West or East Side but in Harlem, a place that holds racialized meaning. She currently lives in Harlem and values the neighborhood's symbolic import as a home to black cultural, commercial, and religious institutions. For Lori, these are "staples" of the black community. She ascribes value to these unique neighborhood assets, and that would not change if she won the lottery. But she also wants a home in the place where her family is from, a place tied to her southern roots. These choices show how black cultural capital is embedded even in my respondents' aspirational consumption.

Another reason Lori gives for dreaming of owning a brownstone is that a home is an asset. Indeed, homes are the primary and most significant asset most Americans will ever own. Lori's choice is consistent with widely held societal norms about homeownership, middle-class values, and achieving the American Dream. It is also about having wealth to pass on to the next generation. As she explains, "I want to have equity and to be able to have something I can give to my kids, and they can give to their kids, you know? I want to build wealth that I can pass down." Lori's vision is connected to her future family and their long-term well-being. She even notes that, after purchasing a house for herself, she would buy new homes for her grandparents: "they have great homes now," she quickly adds, but she wants them to have better homes and to be more "comfortable." The idea of taking care of family members by spending some of their imagined windfalls on purchasing homes, cars, and other consumption goods and experiences—of bringing other in-group members joy and comfort—is one way that middle-class blacks in this study demonstrate their obligation to the collective.

That obligation extends beyond family: Lori dreams of owning property, including lots of commercial property. She figures she could resell it to other blacks so that they could to set up businesses. She explains why this matters to her, stating:

> It's important to help people to live their best lives. And I think it's so great when you can help somebody fuel their dreams. To help people be happier and to be in a place that they want to support other people. . . . So, if I can invest in someone else so they can do something great, that's what I should be trying to do.

In her aspirational consumption, Lori feels that if she could, she should contribute to the welfare of the group and "invest" in others. As discussed in Chapter Seven, supporting black-owned companies and entrepreneurs is one way respondents aim to facilitate racial progress, but this sentiment is manifested even in how middle-class blacks imagine their financial futures.

Living the (Black) American Dream in the Consumer Republic

In American life, what we buy is indicative of our standard of living and quality of life. Such outlays indicate our material well-being. In analyzing interviewees' aspirational consumption, it becomes clear that they are embedded and active agents in a materialistic society that values positional, competitive consumption, linking the achievement of the American Dream to specific material acquisitions.

American society has been described as a consumer republic, in which consumer culture is so pervasive that it is widely adopted and expressed even among young children in their quest to belong.[1] There are two dimensions of consumption to note in relation to its social and symbolic function in the United States. First, full inclusion in American society requires market engagement. Social equality is signaled by a person's ability to spend money without restriction.[2] Second, attaining the American Dream and a middle-class lifestyle is widely understood to have material requisites. One way to examine whether middle-class blacks consider themselves incorporated into American society is to determine whether they feel they can freely participate in the consumer republic, whether they perceive that their spending capability reflects their middle-class standing, and whether they desire to acquire the material requisites encoded in the American Dream.

Americans maintain an intense belief in the equation of the freedom to consume with the achievement of social equality. Researchers have found that

Americans think consumers are entitled to rights and should be free to engage in the market without barriers or restrictions. The idea of protecting these rights is not organic, but the result of a concerted state effort to promote the idea that "democratic access to consumer goods implie[s] a broader democracy of life chances."[3] During the late 1940s and early 1950s, the federal government proactively encouraged (and sometimes subsidized) household consumption. Historian Charles McGovern notes, the "advent of the consumer society" meant the American people began to "equate the consumer with the citizen, a consumer standard of living with democracy, and the full participation in such an economy of spending and accumulation with being an American."[4] Citizenship and the right to vote became deeply connected with a person's right to choose what to purchase, owing in part to the advertising industry's efforts, starting at least as far back as the 1930s, to link "ideas of freedom, sovereignty, and rights with consumption." Consumption is used as both "a symbol of American social democracy and the engine of social equality."[5] To be American increasingly means to be a consumer.

Second, consumption plays a unique symbolic role in U.S. society as it is embedded in the idea of the "American Dream." The American Dream conveys not only information about the vastness of opportunity and prospects of upward mobility but also an idea about the material requisites of a middle-class lifestyle, which is seen as desirable both for the individual to obtain and as a shared societal goal. Being perceived as and feeling legitimately like a member of the middle class means possessing material objects—owning a home—and being able to enjoy leisure, such as going on vacation. Intrinsically, if blacks are to be recognized as legitimate members of the American middle class and are to feel truly middle class, they, too, must own certain objects and have particular experiences. For example, owning one's home is often celebrated as an indication of a person's level of success, and research finds that features of homes, such as size, layout, and granite countertops, are evaluated as further representations of their owners' social position.[6] In this way, we might expect middle-class blacks' aspirations for material comforts and engagement in positional consumption to be a means of asserting and affirming full membership in the larger society. Like other Americans, they might be driven by the idea that "bigger is better, more is better still, and if you can't afford it, then charge it."[7]

Middle-class blacks in my study understood that consumption is a symbolic tool in the quest for equal treatment, and that their consumption made their middle-class standing real. However, the question remains whether they

really subscribe to the belief that their consumption entitles them to full inclusion in U.S. society. In fact, it seems that middle-class blacks have not entirely
bought into the promises and entitlements that consumers are said to enjoy as
members of the consumer republic. Research finds that middle-class blacks are
less likely than middle-class whites to feel that the American Dream applies to
their life experiences. Scholarship has identified discrimination and stigmatization as central factors that detract from middle-class blacks' perception that
the American Dream is realizable.[8] Additional research suggests that feelings
of racial alienation, which range along a continuum from feeling entitled to
societal resources to feeling entirely excluded from such benefits, are strongest
among blacks and increase as blacks' incomes rise.[9] If middle-class blacks see
discrimination and racially biased and exclusionary treatment as a barrier to
their realization of the American Dream and generally indicate high levels of
racial alienation even when they have economic resources, then what role does
consumption play in the construction of their black American Dreams?

Americans are frequently portrayed as individualistic and materialistic, engaging in competitive consumption to convey and improve their social standing relative to similarly positioned others,[10] and scholars have long theorized
the role of acquiring and displaying material goods in people's efforts to demonstrate their status. Thorstein Veblen described how consumption is one way
that people make class differences visible.[11] Blacks, being part of a society in
which competitive consumption is customary, have also been characterized as
seeking out material objects that are emblematic of the social standing they
so desire. E. Franklin Frazier famously argued that the newly emerging, pre–
civil rights era, black middle class was almost obsessed with procuring material goods.[12] For him, "conspicuous consumption" was a defining feature of
the emerging black bourgeoisie.[13] He depicts an earlier generation of middle-
class blacks as "constantly buying things—houses, automobiles, furniture and
all sorts of gadgets, not to mention clothes" to cope with a profound sense of
inferiority.[14] He writes that middle-class blacks' belief that "wealth will gain
them acceptance in American life" results in their "fetish of material things or
physical possessions."[15] This harsh critique of the members of the black middle
class and their status-oriented consumption reflects his belief that prioritizing expenditures is short-sighted: amassing material possessions might very
well signify the acquisition of a middle-class lifestyle, but it also might worsen
blacks' economic position by diverting energies and resources from increasing
real wealth and gaining true economic power and influence.

Frazier was one of the first, but certainly not the last, to argue that middle-class blacks' expenditures are largely status oriented and driven by the goal of enhancing their perceived social standing. Economists, too, have argued that blacks are conspicuous consumers, offering a more recent analysis that finds that blacks use their economic capital in ways that ameliorate their low societal standing.[16] In one study, even when controlling for socioeconomic characteristics, blacks were found to spend roughly 30 percent more on visible goods than whites, a rate that held relatively constant from 1986 to 2002. The relative status of one's reference group is, in this conception, a key factor driving the consumption of visible goods (ones that are both portable and easily perceptible to others, like cars, clothing, and jewelry). Arguing that blacks' reference group is composed of other blacks, these economists write that blacks gauge their status by comparing themselves to other blacks. They find that in states where more blacks are impoverished, blacks engage in the purchase of visible goods at higher levels; this pattern holds for other racial groups, including whites.

In sociologist Elijah Anderson's ethnographic work examining the lives and lifestyles of the black professionals, he stresses that middle-class blacks prefer expensive, high-end goods because these clearly convey their owners' class status.[17] Anderson describes a near obsession among middle-class blacks with being well-dressed when traveling through and interacting in public spaces, and suggests it is an effort to differentiate themselves from poor blacks.

Yet, research indicates that economically disadvantaged blacks are also caught up in competitive consumption. The black poor consume in order to prove "themselves to be worthy," often in ways that resist dominant norms.[18] In historian Carl Nightingale's vivid account of poor black inner-city youth, he observes that "African American inner-city kids have also become eager practitioners of America's ethic of conspicuous consumption." He argues that their "conspicuous consumption" is a reaction to their marginalized position, resulting from the stigma attached to both being poor and being black: "to counter feelings of humiliation and frustration derived from poverty and racial exclusion, kids like the ones described in this book have enthusiastically embraced the American consumer culture—hundred dollar sneakers, sports jackets, gold and all."[19] Psychologist Richard Majors and sociologist Janet Billson similarly argue that black men use "coolness" to preserve a sense of themselves in the face of "daily insults and oppression," maintaining a "show and prove" composure resulting in stylistic choices that reconfigure clothing and other consumer goods as props.[20] Majors and Billson argue that for black men, "dignity and recognition are bound up with the immediate rewards of money and material goods."[21] Even the young mothers depicted in Anderson's *Code of the Street* adorn their babies with expensive clothing and footwear: "the teenage mother derives status from her baby; hence her preoccupation with the impression that the baby makes and her willingness to spend inordinately large sums toward that end."[22] Taken together, this scholarship asserts that both poor and middle-class blacks participate in consumption to achieve competitive, status-oriented ends. While middle-class blacks' spending patterns are said to draw boundaries, distinguishing middle-class blacks from the black poor, poor blacks are assumed to purchase goods to lessen the stigma attached to being black and poor.

A fundamental flaw of this research is that it projects blacks as unidimensional and solely self-interested, ignoring how blacks use their expenditures to achieve collaborative and collective ends. It also overlooks numerous other ways that consumption can maintain expressive and experiential functions. Blacks and black consumption are described in overly simplistic terms and as driven by status alone. Sociologist Elizabeth Chin offers an alternative account. Her examination of the material desires of poor black children finds that their consumption is "deeply social, emphasizing sharing, reciprocity, and mutual obligation."[23] While they might want a Barbie doll, they also want to buy things to help their families, and feel that they should contribute to the household. Chin's work importantly demonstrates that even as children, blacks' consumption is not just a symbolic communicator of status but also a means for building and sustaining ties to significant others. It follows that these patterns are reproduced in adulthood.

Indeed, as I have noted throughout this book, the middle class blacks in this study indicate that their everyday spending attempts to satisfy their personal desires, while also keeping an eye on goals of racial advancement. Because American society is one in which positional, competitive spending is the norm, it is not surprising to find that middle-class blacks subscribe to the idea that having a subset of goods and experiences means they are living the dream. When it comes to their aspirational consumption, Americans tend to maintain a preference for luxury cars, palatial residences, and exotic vacations[24]—all forms of consumption that are highly individualized, reflecting the pervasiveness of cultural scripts that emphasize the self over the collective, and promote "material success, social status, competitiveness and the privatization of risk (or self-reliance)," ideas that are argued to have become increasingly pervasive with the rise of neoliberalism.[25]

From analyzing middle-class blacks' aspirational consumption, one can gain an understanding of the full spectrum of objects and activities they covet—the things they associate with living the good life. While acknowledging that middle-class blacks' American Dreams are motivated by the desire for material comforts associated with a middle-class lifestyle, the discussion in this chapter inserts race into the matrix of meaning to demonstrate that the mix of objects and experiences that most middle-class blacks long for and dream of acquiring expresses not only their individual desires but also their sense of collective obligation and commitment to other blacks' material well-being.

Material and Experiential Desires

When I asked my respondents about their wish lists, I heard about both material desires and experiential desires. Purchasing a home came up most frequently, beating out all other items, and this shows how deeply these black professionals have bought into the idea of the American Dream. Homeownership has, historically, been unattainable for a sizable proportion of the black community. Only 41 percent of blacks in the United States today are homeowners, compared to 71 percent of whites.[26] Some researchers argue that a city's level of black homeownership is a key metric indicating the degree of black prosperity and opportunity evident at the metropolitan level.[27] Places like Atlanta, Georgia, and Washington, DC, and its suburbs, are viewed as meccas for the black middle class, in part because they have high levels of black homeownership, with rates of 44.8 and 48.8 percent, respectively. In New York City, the rate of black homeownership is just 31.9 percent;[28] owning a home for most blacks, even middle-class blacks, is understandably aspirational for the New Yorkers I spoke to.

Jabari, who describes himself as "not that materialistic," does not hesitate to indicate the value he places on homeownership: if he came into a large sum of money, the first thing he would do is purchase a condo. For him, as for many middle-class blacks, homeownership epitomizes the achievement of the American Dream. Beyond the financial benefits that homeownership represents, many respondents in my study see purchasing a home as symbolic of their strong connections with family members and friends. Indeed, they hope to one day be in a position to purchase a home for their loved ones. In addition to taking a vacation, writing a check to her church, and paying off her siblings' debts, Jada notes, "I would want to buy my mother a beautiful house. She has never owned a home. That would be an amazing thing, to buy her a home." It is common for middle-class blacks in this study to maintain a sense of financial obligation to the collective, and this is evident in their hopes of purchasing a home or homes for their intimate others. For them, truly "making it" means being in a position to provide other blacks with material comforts and to improve their loved ones' financial well-being.

Renee extends her generosity to her grandmother: "I'd probably buy my grandmother another house. She's paid off her house, but it's just, it's old. I mean, it's in good shape, but it's like 30-something years old. So I'd buy her another house." Lamar similarly admits that his loved ones could purchase a home without his help: yet, "I would love to buy my parents a house at some point." He reflects that, additionally, "a number of my relatives I know are in bad situations, and so I'd try to buy them all homes . . . that would be great." Economic struggle is not foreign to Lamar, though he isn't struggling these days, and he does not see the material welfare of his family as separate, apart, or distant from his own. He clearly maintains a sense of solidarity with family members and feels a responsibility to help them improve their "situations."

Cars are also highly sought-after material objects. Damon justifies his desire for a luxury sedan by stating plainly, "Status. It's one of those indicators. It's like, wow, like he's rolling in, you know, like an Ashton Martin, a Benz, or a Lamborghini." Car companies spend millions to convey what Damon denotes: cars are markers of status. Damon wants to drive a car that would leave an impression, that would "wow" others. Desiree, too, could easily imagine herself in a luxury ride—an Audi or a Porsche Cayenne. She thinks their design is eye-catching and "sleek." For Desiree and Damon, a car's style and physical appearance says something about its owner. Cars should reflect and, when possible, improve their owners' perceived social rank.

Cars also maintain an experiential function. Lori finds it relaxing to drive. She imagines driving her new car with the windows down and the weather holding steady at 75 degrees. She would be riding along with her "favorite songs playing, a strawberry shake in the dash, and French fries in the seat." She smiles at the thought of it. The car is a crucial part of the experience, but only one part. For Lori, the purchase of a luxury car is part of a bigger picture of what living the good life entails—having the autonomy, freedom, and space to enjoy simple pleasures without any outside incumbrances.

Middle-class blacks' imagined generosity is also evident when it comes to purchasing cars, again extending their consumption aspirations beyond themselves. After rattling off her hopes to buy property, perhaps a condo, and a brand-new, two-door Audi sports sedan, Renee pauses for a moment to clarify: "Does this have to be for me or for others?" I reply that she can use her windfall for whatever she desires. Without hesitation, she then states, "I'd buy my mom a car. She needs a car. I don't know what she wants . . . so whatever kind of car she wanted." Jasmine also thought about purchasing her mother a special gift: "I would buy my mom the Mercedes she's been dreaming of her whole life." Though lavishing their mothers with gifts of expensive cars is demonstrating an active engagement in consumer culture that emphasizes visible indicators of status, this dream also offers an emotional return that makes clear the experiential component of even material purchases. Their imagined generosity is a means to convey appreciation and love.

Travel comes up a lot, too. In addition to taking luxurious, international vacations, middle-class blacks envision traveling with ease. Damon muses about being "able to just get up and go whenever, wherever; it's gotta be the most beautiful thing in the world." Similarly, Lori remarks, "I love to travel, and I want to be able to travel wherever I want quickly." While they are able to travel now, it is not hassle-free. Traveling on a more luxurious scale means globally trotting on first-class flights and staying at the finest accommodations. For example, Vanessa wants to be able to take part in "unlimited international travel" and to stay only in "fabulous boutique hotels." Traveling in this aspirational way is about pampering oneself and being free from the daily grind. Middle-class blacks want to be able to see the world, with few restrictions, in maximum comfort. Some even imagined they would fly on a private plane or take a cruise on a yacht, both personalized and relaxing experiences and symbolic ones denoting wealth and exclusivity.

Owning a home, driving a nice ride, and vacationing around the world are aspirations that middle-class blacks in my study share with other Americans. Their material desires are plugged into those pervasive in the society of which they are members. The things they imagine buying and doing reflect status considerations, but are not solely devoted to improving their individual standing. They imagine consuming things for the pleasure doing so might bring but also consuming things that would benefit others and improve the material well-being of their family members and friends. Their black American Dreams include uplifting others, both family and friends and the broader black community.

Racially Imbued Aspirational Consumption

In their aspirational consumption, the middle-class blacks in my study demonstrate their ideological beliefs about how racial progress and uplift could be achieved. They also indicate that their tastes and imagined consumption are, at times, racially imbued. Race is primarily evident in that my respondents see affluent blacks as referents—they want to live like influential, well-to-do black celebrities and public figures—and they indicate preferences for objects and experiences tied to ideas about a middle-class lifestyle but also encoded with racial meaning. For example, in favoring international travel, respondents may do so in ways that reveal their black cultural capital. For most, like Lori, coming into a windfall does not mean abandoning racially imbued tastes and preferences or leaving behind the black community but indulging those tastes while also uplifting other blacks.

Like Lori, Sharon envisions owning two homes. The child of Ghanaian immigrants who grew up visiting Ghana regularly, she states that—again, just like Lori—she wants to own a brownstone in Harlem and then a home where she has family roots. Her desire for a home in Harlem is infused with racial symbolism, as is her desire to put down roots in her parents' homeland and express her proud Ghanaian heritage. With unlimited resources, these racial connections would be amplified. Sharon's imagined future consumption, her black American Dream, is infused with her ethnic and racial identities.

Darryl also wants to own a brownstone, but his would be located in Fort Greene, Brooklyn. "I wanted to say a brownstone in Harlem, but I just have the image of *Cosby Show* in my head, you know?" The *Cosby Show* was a groundbreaking sitcom, and its iconic house (in which the patriarch also ran an OB/GYN practice) had impressed a vision of a black middle-class life that had powerfully affected Darryl even into adulthood.[29] For Darryl, the purchase of a home would be most meaningful when that home was tied to his pride in his racial identity and his ability to live like the Huxtables. Others made the same reference: they wanted to own a brownstone in Brooklyn because they dreamed of living as though they were on the *Cosby Show*. Curtis envisions living on a grander scale. He would buy rapper and actor 50 Cent's 50,000-square-foot, 19-bedroom Connecticut property, a home so extravagant it features a helipad, an indoor pool, an indoor basketball court, a recording studio, and a nightclub.[30]

The Huxtables and 50 Cent embody different ideas of what black prosperity looks like, yet holding either in high regard indicates that my respondents are looking to other blacks as their points of reference. They aim to emulate the lives of black people who are richer than they are. Again, this demonstrates how their consumption is racially informed.

Their desires for travel also bring race into the mix: several long to travel to their imagined ancestral homeland or places that maintain cultural significance for blacks, like West Africa and Egypt. It is worthwhile to note that research demonstrates that tourists who set out to visit heritage sites (termed cultural or heritage tourism) are typically well-educated and high-earning.[31] This was particularly true among blacks traveling to Ghana to visit ports and castles that were once central sites in the mid-Atlantic slave trade.[32] Traveling is about leisurely seeing the world, but it can also be driven by a desire to reconnect to a racial and cultural past.

While exceptions exist, middle-class blacks' imagined future consumption appears to occur in ways that satisfy their class tastes and aspirations while simultaneously expressing their racialized tastes. Their aspirational consumption at times connects them to other blacks through expressing their black cultural capital and their shared black American dreams. This is what black privilege looks like on the ground. It reflects both their class sensibilities and their racial identity.

For the Benefit of the Collective

As discussed throughout the previous chapters, giving back and working toward racial uplift are highly salient beliefs among study participants. This underlying ideological belief system also informs their aspirational consumption. Through their consumer dreams and desires, these respondents seek to share resources and to work toward the benefit of other blacks, and this finding complicates the popular narrative that middle-class blacks are individualistic, materialistic consumers motivated by personal status alone.

Kendra loves her current job as an account executive, but her dream is a job that incorporates her desire to advance the race, where she would "work for a nonprofit to help to send kids to college, specifically African American kids to historically black colleges." When I ask why this is something she values, she tells me, "because of my family and the way that I was raised." Her parents had stressed that she needed to be aware of the opportunities she was afforded and work to help others, particularly other blacks. She recalls her parents telling her, "There are a lot of people out there that don't have the privileges you have, and it's your responsibility to at least give as much to them as you can." For Kendra, improving blacks' educational opportunities and contributing to the preservation of HBCUs is something that she sees as part of being black and being middle class. Most respondents, in fact, report that they learned from their parents, grandparents, and other family members that they should work not just to advance personally but also work to benefit the race.

Religious beliefs also inform their orientation to the collective. Vanessa reveals that her "leading scripture in life is Luke 12:48, 'to whom much is given, much is expected.'" She is motivated by her faith to give back, which she does financially and through mentoring. "I was blessed to have really great jobs, so I happened to have a really great income. So I've tried to be a good steward of that," Vanessa informs me. She feels she should be a blessing to others, particularly other blacks. For Kendra and Vanessa, their sense of what it means to be middle class and of the advantages afforded to them because of their position of economic privilege is always inflected by a morally driven and social reinforced obligation to the race. Their sense of collective obligation and their deep commitment to work toward the advancement of the race, in turn, finds its way into their dreams and aspirations.

When they try to explain why they feel obligated to help other blacks get ahead, many of my respondents return to the idea that their privileged positions are possible only because of the help of others. Along the way, many people sacrificed for and invested in them. Jabari says he wants to "live comfortably," but he also feels that "the ability to lift other[s] up" is vital. Jabari, the only one of five siblings to earn a college degree, had a difficult childhood: his parents barely had enough money to buy them school clothes, and his mother, who abused drugs, died of AIDS when he was only 19. Jabari, who describes himself as a survivor, had dropped out of high school and only later in life earned a GED and then enrolled in a local community college. Because he has experienced his share of struggle, he feels compelled to "lift others up." As he explains, "it is because I've experienced it firsthand and I know what the struggle looks like." Now working as a job counselor at a social services agency, he finds meaning in his work because it incorporates giving back to the black community. Still, he wishes he could do more, give more, and reach more people. Jabari strongly adheres to the idea that opportunities should be shared, not hoarded.

Natalie, also feels an obligation to give back to the black community because she has benefited from efforts of other blacks along her journey. "I feel like I'm, in some sort of way, a successful by-product of people helping me out when I was coming up. I just feel like it would be selfish of me not to help out the other person, the next person, especially someone who comes from a similar background," she remarks. Natalie wants to ensure that other blacks who grew up working class or in extreme poverty—"even living in the projects"—have access to an education that will enable them to be upwardly mobile. She wants blacks to have the opportunity to compete for and secure competitive, professional jobs, and feels that she has a part to play to make sure that happens.

Robert's motivation to work for collective uplift is similar, but he adds that success is more gratifying when shared with others. "I'm one of those dudes where if something good happens, I want people to enjoy it with me. It won't feel good if it's just you at the top. . . . I want my people to be there with me to say, you know, 'Look at what we did.'" Robert's advancement to the "top" of the economic ladder would be meaningless to him if other blacks could not also share in his good fortune. True solidarity means progressing together and sharing the rewards and victories.

Time and again, racial uplift and solidarity are ideals revealed to be deeply embedded in my interviewees' aspirational consumption. Jeff told me that if he ever amassed an almost endless amount of money, his singular objective would be to give to others. As he explained, "That is my wish, to be able to have and to give. That's enough for me, just to be able to have, to give. That's a luxury." Jeff imagines that the act of giving is an extravagance in and of itself, and it is something that he finds deeply meaningful. Larry reveals that in addition to buying himself "lots of cars," which he admits is a form of self-indulgence, he would "give back to the community," and Curtis, who wants to purchase 50 Cent's stately Connecticut home, underscores "doing my part for the community." Personal success and financial security are central shared goals, but so, too, are efforts that would uplift other blacks.

Some middle-class blacks are dedicated to giving back not just to other individuals but also to institutions, particularly when they feel that black institutions and organizations have significantly contributed to their success or provided them with support or opportunities along their own journey. The black church is chief among those institutions my respondents would shower with their imagined cash. Jada imagines gifting herself an extended vacation first, but writing a check to her church ran a close second—"a big check to my church [to] finish the construction on it. . . . Just one check. Like, I don't know what you're going to do with this, but pick it up." Jada had benefited tremendously from the work of her church. Her pastor has been instrumental in her development not just as a Christian but as a person. She believes that giving to her church is both giving back and a form of paying her imagined good fortune forward. Other interviewees imagine committing funds to build community centers and to establish organizations that provide disadvantaged blacks with opportunities for social advancement.

Connected to the idea of giving back is a desire to open the door of opportunity for friends and family members currently burdened with debt. Javon, who cites building wealth as central to black community progress, thinks eliminating debt is equally important. For him, eradicating the harmful effects of debt for his family is a priority: "Pay off all of the debt of everyone in my entire family. Any debt that is associated with them in any way, form, or fashion. . . . Car, college, home. My father is a minister. His church has debt. I'd pay it all off." When asked why eliminating family members' debt is so important to him, he explains, "Because debt is the crippling factor of building net worth." What Javon imagines would be gained by paying off the debts owed by his significant others is their financial freedom. He hopes to release his family members from financial strife and insecurity and to provide a path for them to accumulate wealth—to transform his loved ones' financial position from fragility to security to generational wealth.

Jada is the youngest but also the most financially successful among her siblings, and she feels it her duty to help her brother and sister with their finances. This sense of responsibility is evident, too, in her aspirational consumption:

> I would clear my brother and sister's debt. That's a big thing for me. They're older than I am, and I've been offered a lot of opportunities through education and stuff that they haven't. And you know, they have financial burdens on their backs that have kind of kept them from advancing as fast as they would like in their lives. And if I could clear that away and just kind of free them, that would be awesome.

Like Javon, Jada sees freeing family members from debt as a means of liberating them so they could advance. Jada is cognizant that she has experienced opportunities that her siblings did not enjoy. She realizes that other blacks, even her family members, face barriers from which she has been lucky enough to be buffered. Since she was afforded opportunities that enabled her to move up the class hierarchy, she believes it would only be right, if she could, to help her siblings do the same.

The value of education for the middle-class blacks in my study is closely linked to ideas of collective gain and racial uplift and is reflected in their aspirational consumption as well. Why is education prioritized? Similar to owning a home, obtaining a college education is seen as essential to achieving the American Dream. Educational opportunities for blacks are also seen as necessary for racial uplift. Long-term prosperity and advancement of the race are achievable through investments in education. Jabari attained his college degree later in life than most, with the help of many others who mentored and invested in him. He is proud of his bachelor's degree and hopes to keep going to receive a master's degree, but the expense has delayed him. If he came into a windfall, he would use the money in part to pay for his education. Lamar, who wants to buy homes for his parents and his struggling family members, feels strongly about the importance of an education: "A passion for me is ensuring that as a people we understand the importance of education. I thank God that I was able to get an education. But if there was anything that I could give a lifetime to, it would be that." Lamar does not see his educational attainment as a result of only his individual efforts or merit, rather he thanks God for it. Helping others gain such educational opportunities reflects his faith, but also his belief in the importance of education for other blacks.

The few interviewees who have children mentioned investing in their children's education as a paramount objective. Amare wants to secure his daughter's future by covering the cost of her education, which he imagines will be prohibitively costly:

> I'd have a college fund for my daughter. Because I want her to be at a point where—she's five, I got thirteen years—you get into Harvard, I'll pay. I don't want to discuss in my head; I don't want to hem and haw; I don't want to think about it. You get in, how much is it, here's a check. . . . I feel like if she can get in, then she deserves for me to pay. It's that simple. If you can work your ass off and get into the best school in the world, or in America, at least, then you don't have to ask; we will pay.

Amare believes a college degree is a gateway to financial security, so he wants his daughter to have unfettered educational opportunities. He does not want money to affect her college choices—if she can get into an elite university like Harvard, he wants to pay for her to attend. This emphasis on education reveals how my respondents' aspirations embody a core American middle-class value, but also a path to racial uplift for themselves, their children, and the black community at large.

Overall, it is agreed by these middle-class black Americans that if they came into a large windfall, they would take care of themselves and their people.

Me, Myself, and I: The Bad and Bougie

There is one group whose members are unlike other middle-class blacks in this study, in that they not only articulate their consumption fantasies with ease, but their wish lists highlight personal indulgence and extravagance, and lack a collective orientation. The slang phrase made popular by the rap trio Migos, "bad and bougie," seems apt, considering that this group is nearly exclusively middle-class black women who have grown up in upper- and upper-middle-class homes. Not only are their wish lists well-formulated, but they tend to feature highly sought after, status-laden goods that these women imagine express their personalities while also demonstrating sophisticated tastes and sensibilities. Their aspirational consumption does not include engagement in racial uplift or an allegiance to the collective.

Lisa indicates that she would love to own a designer dog (an English bulldog), a vintage Jeep Grand Cherokee Wagoneer, a Steinway grand piano, and a $600 pair of boots she has been lusting after but that feels she cannot afford at the moment. Lisa has clearly been thinking of these items for some time and they point to her discerning taste. The Wagoneer trim model, an upscale version of the Jeep, was revolutionary in that it was the first ever luxury SUV.[33] It is a much sought after collectible today. Her Steinway piano would have to have "a matte finish, not a glossy finish." Her discriminating taste, knowing which of the possible finishes she prefers, reveals her longing for material goods that she thinks would be pleasing to own and expressive of her unique personality and taste. Imagining her future consumption is about a well thought out sense of self; it is highly individualistic and personal, but also indicative of her taste for the finer things.

When asked about what she would do with a windfall, Amber, a 32-year-old school recruiter, is ready with an answer, too; she would pay a visit to "the most exclusive jeweler in the world." This jeweler is based in Paris, and his custom pieces are "literally masterpieces, like on the level of, like, Fabergé in our time." Given her administrative job, this type of cultural knowledge might seem superfluous. But for Amber, aspirational consumption is not constrained by her current economic reality. Her consumptive dreams reflect and indulge her elevated aesthetic sensibilities. When I ask Amber how she learned about the jeweler, JAR, she tells me:

> I love design, I love interior design. . . . [And] catalog[s] for auctions . . . occasionally [list his jewelry]. . . . There was a famous jewelry auction a few years ago by this woman who divorced her billionaire husband. . . . [S]he sold this

JAR jewelry and the stuff is just like, I just, I've never seen anything like it. Like, after seeing that, it made me like, I don't want to ever go to Tiffany's again, or Cartier, or Harry Winston. I just have no interest in that. . . . [N]ow those [are] places which I think a lot of people would consider, like, this is the best jewelry you could get, you know, Tiffany's or Cartier or Harry . . . After seeing [JAR's jewelry] it's like, no, I don't even want it.

Amber's "love" of design and sophisticated taste in jewelry fit with her intimate knowledge of high culture. Unlike Darryl and Curtis, who aim to be like the Huxtables and the rapper 50 Cent, Amber does not describe wealthy, well-known blacks as reference points. Instead, she refers to an obscure, former wife of a billionaire who had amassed a collection of rare jewelry. While she might not ever buy a piece of JAR jewelry, just knowing about his collection demonstrates that her tastes are aligned with the most exclusive class of elites.

Tasha also differs from Darryl, Curtis, Lori, and the other middle-class blacks who, even in their windfall scenarios, maintain their preference for living in a black neighborhood. When Tasha imagines purchasing a home, it is "a Soho loft, like a huge, big Soho loft in a pre-war building." Even though she values and appreciates the sense of community she gets from living in Harlem at present, Tasha still desires a more prestigious address, one in a trendy, upmarket neighborhood. She also longs for a collection of designer shoes and an expensive handbag: "A Chanel bag, a leather, black Chanel bag, and not the, like, small, quilted, 255. Like a big, nice, really soft leather Chanel bag." Tasha is well versed in the styles of handbags the Chanel brand offers, and knows exactly what she would buy. Tasha hopes to one day indulge herself with posh goods that would bring tactile and aesthetic pleasure while also signaling exclusivity and status.

Amber, Tasha, and Lisa all grew up in upper-middle-class homes. Tasha's father works as a corporate attorney and her mother is a high-ranking administrator in the local school district. Though her parents had not themselves grown up middle class, they made sure to provide Tasha with everything she ever imagined she would need. Both of Amber's parents are corporate executives, and Lisa describes a childhood filled with frequent family vacations, "nice" cars, and a debt-free Ivy League college education. Their membership in the black middle class is generational, and this is the most commonly shared variable expressed by those in my study who emphasized material objects, nearly exclusively, on their wish lists. There are too few men of similar backgrounds in the study to give a sense of whether the same might be true for men who grew up upper-middle or upper class. However, as Jasmine's answer suggests, the phenomenon of focusing on handbags and jewelry seems gendered: "I guess I would probably be a girl and buy like a really nice, expensive purse . . . or a really nice piece of jewelry," she said. She would love to own a "Louis" (Louis Vuitton) or a Gucci bag, and perhaps a Cartier or Rolex watch.

Race, for black women who grew up in upper-class homes, is still relevant in the other spheres of their lives. At times, in other parts of our interviews, they demonstrated an ideological commitment to the collective. Racial uplift was noticeably absent only when it came to their "bougie" aspirational consumption, which is free from race and family obligations. These consumption scenarios are steeped in class-based tastes and individualistic indulgences, reflecting their (elite) cultural capital and their willingness to think solely about what they find personally pleasing and expressive. They possess the liberty to dream and long for only things that they find titillating. This could be thought of as a unique form of advantage or as a way in which they are even more deeply embedded than other middle-class blacks in a culture that emphasizes materialistic and individualistic values. It could also be that having grown up in well-to-do families they feel free to think of how to spoil themselves and are able to elaborate their consumptive fantasies with ease. However, if they actually came into a windfall, perhaps they would behave in ways more closely aligned with racial uplift ideologies consistent with research that has illustrated the significant role middle-class black women have played in efforts to advance the race throughout US history.

Black American Dreams

In U.S. society today, materialism, individualism, and competitive consumption are the norm. Ideas about success, social mobility, and prosperity are all embedded in the American Dream. Like other Americans, most middle-class blacks in this study wanted a brownstone and a BMW and to travel the world on a private jet. The consumption of objects and experiences, and the pleasure those things could bring, represented living "the good life." However, they also want to give back to their churches and communities. Most maintained deep-rooted ideas about racial uplift and collective responsibility that were revealed even in their aspirational consumption.

Sociological theories of consumption posit that, on the aggregate level, it is a means by which people demonstrate their social standing and group membership. On the individual level, objects and goods are acquired partially for their symbolic value—their utility in "construct[ing] identities and relations with others who inhabit a similar symbolic universe."[34] Middle-class blacks' unique position within race and class hierarchies means that they inhabit specific symbolic universes. A few, particularly those who have privileged backgrounds, reveal aspirational consumption that is free from racial obligation and racialized tastes. But for most, their aspirational consumption reflects their combined class and racial tastes and affinities; for example, having a desire to vacation in international destinations, especially those where African and African diasporic culture are rooted. Their black American Dreams also reflect their collective orientation, as many middle-class blacks express deep-rooted ideas about the importance of collective responsibility. On the whole, I found that aspirational consumption diverges from the pervasive idea that blacks are conspicuous consumers and excessively materialistic; my respondents, in most cases, may have desired to purchase luxuries for themselves, but they also prioritized giving to family, friends, black cultural institutions, and their community. Black cultural capital and racialized ideological commitments are deeply infused in the ways many dream about consuming.

Striving and Surviving

9

ON A FUNDAMENTAL LEVEL black privilege is shaped by middle-class blacks' increased access to economic and cultural resources, combined with the fact that their increased access does not buffer them from the challenges that result from a racial order in which blacks are considered culturally and socially inferior to whites. Modern middle-class blacks have been granted access, but they are not fully integrated into the consumer republic. This raises an important question about black privilege and how blacks experience the advantages that come with middle-class status. Certainly, there are benefits: more avenues to earn prestigious credentials, cultural capital, and economic resources, all rewards that often accompany a college degree. But when trying to use this capital, when taking this privilege into the marketplace, middle-class blacks may be met with hostility and denied entitlements that are seemingly race-neutral, granted to all with money to spend. This book offers insight into what being black, middle class, and a consumer is like for those living and working in New York City. It demonstrates how some middle-class entitlements are curtailed for racial minorities. Yet blacks can still enjoy a middle-class lifestyle.

Maya Angelou, a famous American writer and poet, once commented that she did not aim merely to get by but to thrive, living her life "with some passion, some compassion, some humor, and some style." My respondents, too, aimed to thrive, to enjoy themselves and have a good time, while also being compassionate to other blacks who do not enjoy the same financial advantages.

They also aimed to creatively and often strategically display their distinctly black cultural tastes and sensibilities.

Thriving and surviving aptly describes their effort to reap the fruits of their labor, while still contending with bias against their racial group. Analyzing their daily lives reveals the extent to which racial prejudice, though often masked, remains a burden they bear. Yet the findings of my study suggest that consumption is a unique tool that modern middle-class blacks can wield in both challenging the idea of their cultural inferiority and relishing the material comforts of the world. Consumption practices are deeply ingrained in middle-class blacks' perceptions of a middle-class lifestyle, but how they think about buying, spending, and engaging in leisure is also tied to their racialized ideological commitments, cultural preferences that affirm their race-based tastes, and practices that strengthen racial identity. While blacks who are members of the middle class have little control over encounters with racism and the prevalence of anti-black biases, this book demonstrates that they strategically employ their cultural knowledge and financial resources with the goal of improving their circumstances, individually and collectively. This skillful deployment of cultural resources to gain social acceptance and respect is a key characteristic of those who enjoy black privilege.

The Limitations of Black Privilege

Analyzing the stories and experiences of the middle-class blacks who agreed to participate in my study quickly debunks the assumption that once blacks have gain access to educational opportunities and experience some degree of economic security, they will enjoy full social and economic inclusion and equality of lifestyles. Middle-class blacks have certainly come to experience unprecedented symbolic integration in the public sphere: prominent black political figures gain widespread admiration and acceptance. Cultural figures like Beyoncé achieve global dominance while consciously drawing upon black cultural iconography, and the institutionalization of cultural centers, such as the Smithsonian Institution's National Museum of African American History and Culture, which opened in 2016, suggests increasing recognition of the value and valor of black cultural traditions. However, as middle-class blacks attempt to be unapologetically black *and* live a middle-class lifestyle—to be full members of the consumer republic—they find that spending means contending with barriers to their enjoyment of all the privileges they associate with their middle-class status and cultural sensibilities. Their cash, credentials, and cultural capital cannot free them from racism reliant on stereotypes of blacks as poor, criminal, poorly educated, and financially irresponsible. Economically advantaged and culturally dexterous, modern middle-class blacks nonetheless experience a sort of truncated privilege, particularly as consumers in the marketplace.

This book provides insight into the often subtle forms of racism that pervade public spaces: prejudice evidenced in poor service, the inability to get into a club as white patrons stream past, and being steered to the sale section of a store under the assumption that *they* can't afford the finer things in life. This is how, in part, contemporary racial alienation is experienced, and this is a type of modern exclusionary practice. When middle-class blacks face anti-black bias, discrimination, and cultural racism, they undoubtedly pay a cost, as discriminatory treatment can limit or prevent them from gaining access. Due to a racial hierarchy evident in the market, middle-class blacks are rarely afforded all the rewards people expect from achieving entry into the American middle class. One way that the market underserves black consumers, outside of outright discrimination, is in the many instances where their needs, wants, and cultural tastes are not catered to or met. Middle-class blacks are not free to walk into any store, restaurant, or club in any neighborhood and be accommodated, let alone guaranteed to leave satisfied.

Mass consumption is often theorized as having a homogenizing and democratizing effect, yet the experiences of my study respondents illustrate how the consumption of middle-class blacks is impacted by their race, both as they demonstrate racialized tastes and preferences and also as they perceive the risk of being evaluated as undesirable or unwanted customers because of racial stereotypes and stigma.[1] Black consumers *are* distinct and are *treated as* distinct within a racial consumer hierarchy made evident to them. The market does not upend the racial hierarchy of society, but proves to be a venue in which cultural racism operates and is revealed. The character and scope of racial stigma, evidenced in middle-class blacks' marketplace transactions and interactions, has significant implications for our understanding of how consumers' status and worth are determined along racial lines and how social hierarchies are perpetuated in the market.

Despite middle-class blacks' potential as consumers, stereotypes about blacks being poor and criminal influence the degree to which black consumers are judged as legitimate and worthy of service. Experiences of racism that result from stigmatization are distinct from those that result from discrimination.[2] Stigmatizing events result in assaults on worth, while discrimination results in a denial of access to opportunities. The unfair treatment that blacks describe as consumers may be due to either stigma or discrimination or to both. In my research, most middle-class blacks are allowed the opportunity to spend their money, but are subject to exclusionary treatment and deemed unworthy of first-rate service. The nature of the treatment experienced by black consumers is evidence of modern-day racism.

Race, my respondents find, often renders their middle-class status imperceptible in the fertile ground of the marketplace. These modern middle-class blacks identify interactions that conform with the definition of status misrecognition. The idea that class status provides little buffering from retail racism supports research that finds that middle-class blacks are more likely than working-class blacks to say that they have been "underestimated or stereotyped as poor, low-status, or uneducated."[3] If you also happen to be black, being middle class and an active consumer does not guarantee entry into an ideal middle-class American life, nor will it give you access to all the rewards and entitlements associated with middle-class status. Middle-class blacks experience privilege attenuated by race. It is a distinctly black privilege.

Refuting the commonplace assumption that money is the great equalizer, many of the middle-class blacks in my study describe patron-staff interactions and patron-patron interactions reflecting socially pervasive racial hierarchies. In contrast, research shows that white customers enjoy a comparatively advantaged position in the market.[4] Arguably, whites' experiences as consumers contribute to their sense of entitlement, as marketers actively seek out and aim to satisfy middle-class whites and actively work to influence and shape whites' desires. While the middle-class blacks in my study describe occasions where the pleasure that theoretically comes with shopping and engaging in leisure is significantly reduced by the actual experience, nonetheless, their objective to look good and dress to impress, whether for the workplace or for their lives outside of work, as well as to enjoy the rewards associated with a middle-class lifestyle, necessitates shopping and engaging in certain forms of leisure. Barring market abstinence, middle-class blacks have to learn to cope with the less-than-optimal circumstances that result from the reproduction of the racial order in the marketplace.

Race also impacts middle-class black consumers in another way. Anti-black bias, operating in retail settings, restaurants, and nightclubs, conditions how the status, honor, and prestige associated with owning high-status goods or engaging in leisure is interpreted. Due to their black bodies, blacks' attire, for example, can be reinterpreted in ways that "confirm" and conform to stereotypes. For example, a black woman dressed nicely and shopping in a high-end store might be assumed to be a salesperson rather than a customer. A black man living in a luxury high-rise apartment building might be assumed not to be a successful entrepreneur but a drug dealer. High-status goods may not bestow prestige on black owners. And if blacks anticipate that the status associated with goods or activities might be reinterpreted in ways that are consistent with racially biased views, they might see the "status function" of consumption objects or leisure activities as only marginally useful in their efforts to convey their middle-class status or tastes and sensibilities. Their consumption of high-status goods and leisure activities may be *altered* by knowing that the pleasure and status reaped from consuming might be restricted due to encounters with racism.

Historical evidence suggests that well-to-do blacks have forfeited the purchase of preferred items in order to mitigate racism and heed a perception that certain types of goods are, in a marketplace structured by assumptions of white normativity or superiority, inappropriate for blacks to own. For example, in the past, blacks might have purchased older car models rather than new cars in order to prevent white resentment of black success, which could prove dangerous.[5] Despite middle-class blacks' spending potential, stereotypes about blacks being poor and criminal, being inappropriate owners of certain types of goods, or being illegitimate and unworthy of service function as barriers to blacks' consumer satisfaction. Blackness, then, can function as a kind of tax on material pleasure. In some instances, it may cost more for blacks to enjoy the same things that whites do.

To the extent that anti-black bias is pervasive, being black can negatively impact the experiential dimension of consumption. One of the most popular responses study respondents adopt when encountering racially prejudiced treatment in the market is to leave the shop or restaurant and refuse to return. When they are facing longer wait times, are treated as if serving them is a low priority, or are made to feel out of place or unworthy of service, the negative treatment not only takes away from the experience but also reduces the benefits that are supposed to accrue as they relate to the experiential dimension of consumption.

One way that frequently encountering service failure reproduces racial inequality is by restricting blacks' acquisition of cultural knowledge. A store's sales staff are at times critical teachers, who inform prospective customers about the qualities of products and the differences between brands.[6] The market performs this added function, being a site for the transmission of cultural knowledge. This process is restricted for racial minorities marginalized in retail and commercial settings, reducing their ability to gain an in-depth understanding of the subtle differences in products' aesthetics and attributes, as well as their opportunities to learn what meanings to associate with goods or how to distinguish between the users of different types of goods. Racially biased sales staff are unlikely to exchange privileged information about products when customers are black. This is particularly true in luxury stores, where staff perform a curatorial function, offering prospective customers "guidance and knowledge."[7] The "pre-acquisition" activities, including browsing, researching, and comparison shopping, that facilitate the accumulation of cultural capital are off-limits when middle-class blacks are restricted in terms of when and where they shop and in whether they participate in "window shopping." Consumers learn to distinguish goods, in part, by browsing and shopping around,[8] thus marketplace racism can function to disempower black consumers in yet another way by limiting the transference of this specialized knowledge. In a multitude of ways, retail racism imposes an added burden on black consumers, raising the costs and reducing the rewards of consumption.

The experiences of middle-class black consumers documented by my study also shed light on questions on inequality by illustrating how subtle discrimination can be. Middle-class blacks are not regularly barred from entry, but their access is at times *restricted*. Often, middle-class blacks encounter gatekeepers, salespeople, club bouncers, and restaurant staff who determine the scale and scope on which they can cash in on the benefits of their middle-class status, and to what extent they will be included and treated as social equals. These gatekeepers have the discretion to recognize black consumers as legitimate and worthy of service or to treat them in accordance with pernicious stereotypes—that blacks are poor, poorly educated, criminal, and undesirable. To manage the burdens associated with their race—or more properly, others' responses to their race—while also engaging their middle-class tastes and preferences, they have to become astute observers of their surroundings, reading subtle cues and moderating their behavior to appropriately use consumption objects[9] to gain respect and acceptance, and also recognizing when it might be best to withdraw and conserve their energies.

Strategically Striving and Surviving the Market

Recognizing that their middle-class status will not buffer them from exclusionary experiences, whether at work, at home, or in the market, the middle-class blacks in my study often take proactive stances to prevent discriminatory treatment. Some work, for instance, to develop personal connections with retail store staff. The utility of drawing on social capital in order to prevent racial exclusion parallels Lauren Rivera's finding that the only black club-goers who are able to escape negative evaluations of their racial status are those with strong social ties to club regulars or nightclub staff.[10] In her work, Rivera notes how the doormen at an elite nightclub scrutinized and negatively evaluated potential black patrons, using race as the sole criterion for rejection, because they viewed blacks as "troublemakers," with limited spending potential. In line with her study, while recognizing that they might be treated unfairly, black patrons in my study did not just give up if they were stymied by racist treatment; many utilized other means (social capital) or paid a higher cost to procure the goods or services they were looking for. They navigated the system in part by picking their battles but also by establishing networks with trusted allies, who might be able to prevent or mitigate mistreatment.

The findings of my study also demonstrate that middle-class blacks use goods strategically. For example, Curtis describes how at work he is buttoned up. He wears dark blue or grey suits, and on the one occasion he went without a tie, he quickly learned that the only black man in the office could not get away with such casual dress. When shopping or hanging out with friends, though, Curtis can be cavalier about how he dresses. He curates his style and the way he is dressed depending on the stakes, using consumption objects to convey his class status in some but not all settings. As quoted in Chapter Six, he says, "I don't really care about what I'm dressed like when I'm not trying to make a power move." The agency and tactical employment of goods for status enhancement purposes is important for many of my respondents, in ways that undermine the popular assertion that blacks use consumption of high-status goods as a way to assert equality. Rather than being status obsessed, the middle-class blacks in my study determine when to use material goods to mitigate the negative impact of racial stigma, with the goal of preventing status misrecognition. They are not always engaged in an effort to project their various social identities or preoccupied with the task of using material objects to assert their class and racial group memberships, even when they perceive that doing so might prove beneficial. Surviving and striving in the market and beyond requires middle-class blacks to adopt a dynamic approach to combating stereotypical assumptions, including drawing strategically on their cultural resources, deploying them at times and reserving them other times.

Striving in and surviving the market often also means relying on black service providers and black-owned businesses. Middle-class blacks realize that their racialized tastes will rarely be satisfied by mainstream institutions. To engage their black cultural capital, they often have to seek out businesses that cater to black consumers, value black cultural production, and produce products and services with black consumers in mind. Many also patronize black-owned enterprises because they see their mere existence as aligned with the racialized ideological commitments they maintain. Through their support of black businesses, they affirm their racial pride and engage in racial uplift, while also enjoying freedom from anti-black bias. When they buy black, they can expect to be recognized as worthy consumers.

Implications

Despite the relevance of consumption and the important symbolic function objects play in almost every sphere of life, scholars of inequality rarely consider consumption as a contributing factor to and an indicator of inequality in the United States. Further, empirical research is needed to improve our understanding of the connection between consumption and economic inequality, and to supplement what we know about racial inequality. In part, this means research is needed to determine the extent to which racial groups in a society have equal access to social status and class-inflected lifestyles. Having to strategically deploy cultural, social, and economic resources while consuming to mitigate the negative repercussions of cultural racism negates the idea that unfettered rewards accompany middle-class status. Race conditions the middle-class experience for blacks, as well as the ways in which blacks perceive, construct, and live out their classed lifestyles. Racism, retail or otherwise, helps to fuel the unequal experiences of blacks in the market. Their degree of inclusion in the market also has larger implications for efforts to measure societal inclusion, because consumption plays such a vital role in U.S. society.

In many instances, the market has failed to meet the needs of black consumers, even those with money to spend. Middle-class blacks are rarely able to satisfy both their racial and class-based tastes at the same time. Time and time again, companies' missteps underscore racial insensitivity and reinforce the racial order. In other instances, products marketed to blacks or widely available in black neighborhoods have been harmful to blacks' health and well-being.[11] Even the push for multicultural marketing may come at the expense of addressing and catering to the specific needs and taste profiles of black consumers.[12] A more equitable market would aim to satisfy the unique tastes and preferences of all consumers, rather than seeking merely to satisfy and to appeal to the dominant group. As the vignettes throughout this book imply, those black Americans who have worked hard to get to the middle class often find they have to work harder on the job and then work even harder to experience the pleasures that come with having economic resources.

While my study focused on the experience of members of the black middle class and how they maneuver in diverse social contexts by drawing on their cultural consumption, future research should examine how other racial groups, including whites, learn to do the same. Learning more about how racialized cultural knowledge is cultivated and used to forge connections across racial lines could shed light on how to improve race relations, while also demonstrating how middle-class status is experienced differently across racial groups. What does it mean to be unapologetically Chicano or unapologetically Chinese American? What happens to racialized and ethnically specific cultural tastes and practices over successive generations of upward mobility? As American society moves toward a minority majority, cultural flexibility may become increasingly necessary for people of all races—even those who enjoy white privilege.

By painting a picture of how those who are both middle class and black traverse the different domains of everyday life, the trials, tribulations, and *triumphs* innate to a broader black experience can be highlighted. Many sociological accounts have focused on blacks' encounters with discrimination and racial oppression, but have failed to address blacks' agency. They do not reveal blacks as strategic cultural actors navigating racial hierarchies. We have seen throughout this book that middle-class blacks are quite strategic, not only in defying stereotypes but also in actively working to enjoy life in their neighborhoods and their workplaces and to engage in leisure. Modern middle-class blacks, as a consequence of having cash, credentials, and black cultural capital are able to experience black privilege. Amid cultural racism and discrimination, the members of today's black middle class really *are* thriving as they keep one eye on the advancement of all black Americans. They are working to advance the race while simultaneously living life with "some passion, some compassion, some humor and some style." They are realizing the power of being black with credentials and cash to spend. Black privilege is, despite its limitations, a privilege.

Acknowledgments

Growing up, I was always an enormous fan of Oprah Winfrey. Who, fate would have it, was the commencement speaker the year I received my PhD. Something I always remember Oprah saying is that *nobody ever makes it alone.* I have found that this has been profoundly true, particularly in my experience while writing this book. I have been blessed to have many people who have in various ways contributed to its completion.

I am enormously grateful for the wonderful people whom I met while completing this research, my study respondents, who gave so freely of their time. They offered up their opinions and shared with me their worldviews, and without them, this project would not have been possible! Additionally, thanks are due to Stanford University Press for its support and efforts in publishing this book, and a special thanks to my editor Marcela Maxfield. I am truly grateful for all of your guidance, as well as your patience throughout the various stages of the publishing process.

Beyond the project itself, arriving at this point would not have been possible without the endless support and encouragement of my social network, composed of people both in my academic community and many family members, friends, and loved ones.

Within the academy, I must first thank my dissertation committee members at Harvard, who provided me with exceptional feedback at every stage of the research design and implementation, as well as during the preliminary analysis. I feel honored to have been mentored and advised by such an exceptional group of faculty. I have deep respect and admiration for each and every one of my committee members. My advisor, Professor William Julius Wilson, receives my unremitting praise. He is a true intellectual, and I am forever grateful for his constant nudging, demanding that I think more deeply and broadly about the theoretical implications of my work. I learned many lessons, too, about how to be a passionate, thoughtful, and kind member of an academic community from him. I additionally must thank my committee members. Professor Michèle Lamont, who has always extended herself and her wealth of knowledge, facilitating my professional development, offering me opportunities to cultivate my skills as a qualitative researcher, and helping me to evaluate my work at various stages. I know that I have benefited from her direction and advice and am grateful to have received it. Professor Orlando Patterson, who has been a constant source of intellectual stimulation, providing critique when needed, while demanding that I be bold in my assertions. Last, and certainly not least, I would like to thank Professor Juliet Schor. I am enormously indebted to her, as she has so often taken time to advise me and offer her insight, and I have benefited immensely from her expertise and genius.

The broader academic community that nurtured my growth as a scholar includes faculty and staff at the University of Pennsylvania, where I earned my undergraduate degree, especially Professors Camille Charles, Tukufu Zuberi, and Herman Beavers. Since the time I was an undergraduate, I have benefited from the constant support of the Mellon Mays Undergraduate Fellowship Program. Being a Mellon Mays Fellow is a distinct privilege and honor. Through their programming and continued investment in my intellectual development, the staff and scholars affiliated with the Mellon Mays program have immensely shaped what it means for me to enter academia and have provided me with resources to help me reach my full potential. I would especially like to thank Vice Provost Dr. Valarie Swain-Cade McCoullum and Patricia Ravenell.

I must also thank the many people who made up my community at Harvard, including my fellow graduate students who were my allies during this lengthy process: Patricia Banks, Kevin Lewis, Eunmi Mun, Nicole Hirsh, and Tracey Scollenberger Lloyd, who were officemates or roommates at various points in time. I must especially thank Jessica Welburn and Ernesto Martinez for their constant support and encouragement every step along the way. I could not have asked for better mentors and friends. Thank you for offering to read my work and subsequently providing me with excellent feedback, and for attending my conference and workshop presentations over the years. Few graduate students are as lucky as I have been to receive the genuine support of colleagues who take their scholarship seriously and truly share in their success. I must also thank Chana Teeger for her constant brilliance and endless willingness to help me work through various conundrums that arose during the writing process. Members of my various writing account-ability groups over the years—Marie Brown, LaToya Tavernier, Jennifer Jones, Christy Smith, Jennifer Eaglin, and Kara Young—were instrumental in keep-ing me on track and helping me to maintain a viable time frame for complet-ing all the small tasks that eventually add up to published research. During my time at The Ohio State University, it was a privilege and honor to work with Rachel Dwyer and Ruth Peterson. While at OSU, I also benefited from receiv-ing advice and feedback from Devin Fergus, Korie Edwards, and Townsand Price-Spratlen, for which I am truly grateful. I would also like to thank my colleagues at Case Western Reserve University, and the Fellows who were tre-mendously supportive during my time at the Hutchins Center of the DuBois Institute as the Sheila Biddle Ford Foundation Fellow, where much of the final writing for this book was done.

This work has benefited from the support of a team of bright and diligent research assistants who also helped make this project possible. I must thank Alysha Johnson, Jarrell Lee, and Sharron Jeffries who dedicated time during their undergraduate careers to work on this project as research assistants; Alicia Smith Chan, Delia Su, Reema Sen, Jacob Rivera, Marissa Gilbert, and Amber Byrd, who worked as graduate assistants; and Tracey Baker, who served as my transcriptionist and provided me with exceptional service and first-rate work.

As the book advanced to a more substantive draft, I received feedback from a broader community of scholars. I am forever thankful for the thoughtful, critical feedback offered by Mary Pattillo, Tyrone Foreman, and Cory Fields. Each provided insight and commentary that was enormously impactful in the framing of this book. I must also thank the anonymous reviewers who pro-vided helpful and constructive feedback.

Beyond academia, I have friends and loved ones who have been a constant source of positivity and encouragement. They have never failed to have my back and to make me smile. Through all the trials and tribulations, they never stopped believing in me and were always there to provide me with social, emo-tional, and at times financial support, without which I do not believe I could have made it through to the other side! Thank you from the bottom of my heart, my dear husband, Adam; Mom; Dad; Jordan; Nolan; and my dear sis-ter, Sholah; Kia and Matt; Zahra; Oyebisi; Lauren; Carmelita and the Johnson

Family; Aunts Joni, Toni, and Willeen; Uncles Robert and Ronald; my cousin Earl; and my fantastic grandparents, Everett and Raffie Durham, who every step of the way have let me know how enormously proud they are, which was often just the encouragement that I needed to keep moving upward and onward. I love and thank you all enormously.

Appendix

Profile of Study Respondents

Pseudonym	Sex	Age	Education	Occupation	Income
Alysha	F	26	Bachelor's	Financial analyst	$50,000 to 74,999
Amare	M	30	Bachelor's	Financial analyst	$100,000+
Amber	F	32	Master's	School recruiter	$50,000 to 74,999
Angela	F	28	J.D.	Corporate attorney	$100,000+
Antoine	M	36	Bachelor's	Firefighter	$75,000 to 99,999
Ashlee	F	28	Bachelor's	HR administrator	$50,000 to 74,999
Brandon	M	28	Bachelor's	Manager of retail store	$50,000 to 74,999
Brittany	F	28	J.D.	Attorney	$50,000 to 74,999
Bryson	M		J.D.	Attorney	
Crystal	F	29	Master's	Executive assistant	$50,000 to 74,999
Curtis	M	34	Bachelor's	Director of community relations	$100,000+
Damon	M	29	Bachelor's	Associate in legal department	$100,000+

Daniel	M	35	Bachelor's	Training specialist	$100,000+
Darryl	M	28	Bachelor's	Bank associate	$100,000+
Desiree	F	29	Bachelor's	Marketing professional	$50,000 to 74,999
Eric	M	27	Bachelor's	Director of strategy	
Erica	F	29	Bachelor's	Membership manager	$50,000 to 74,999
Eve	F	32	Bachelor's	City worker	$50,000 to 74,999
Heather	F	29	Bachelor's	Deputy director	$75,000 to 99,999
Isaiah	M	31	Bachelor's	Entrepreneur	$100,000+
Jabari	M		Bachelor's	Job counselor	
Jada	F	28	Bachelor's	Marketing manager	$75,000 to 99,999
James	M	39	Bachelor's	Firefighter	$75,000 to 99,999
Janae	F	32	Bachelor's	Freelance television Producer	$50,000 to 74,999
Jasmine	F	30	Master's	Teacher	$75,000 to 99,999
Javon	M	32	Master's	Associate at private equity firm	$100,000+
Jeff	M	28	Bachelor's	Sales manager	$100,000+
Jennifer	F	31	J.D.	Lawyer	$75,000 to 99,999
Jordan	M	29	Bachelor's	Actor and model	$50,000 to 74,999
Kendra	F	28	MBA	Account executive	$50,000 to 74,999
Kenneth	M	27	Bachelor's	Advertising	$50,000 to 74,999

Kevin	M	27	Bachelor's	Accountant	$50,000 to 74,999
Lamar	M	34	Bachelor's	Banking VP	
Lance	M	30	Bachelor's	Tax preparer	$25,000 to 49,999
Larry	M		Bachelor's	Library technician	
Leah	F	32	Bachelor's	Analyst for government	$50,000 to 74,999
Lisa	F	32	MBA	Managing partner	$100,000+
Lori	F	28	Bachelor's	Recruiter	
Marcus	M	30	Bachelor's	Director of a nonprofit	$50,000 to 74999
Michelle	F	28	Master's	Event planner	
Natalie	M	25	Bachelor's	Senior banking analyst	$50,000 to 74,999
Nate	M	33	Bachelor's	Parole officer	$50,000 to 74,999
Paul	M	28	Bachelor's	Health care strategist	$75,000 to 99,999
Renee	F	32	Master's	Digital marketing professional	$75,000 to 99,999
Robert	M	28	Bachelor's	Senior banking associate	$100,000+
Shante	F	25	Bachelor's	Marketing professional	$25,000 to 49,999
Sharon	F	27	Bachelor's	Advertising account manager	$75,000 to 99,999
Sheila	F	47	Bachelor's	Clinical researcher	$100,000+
Stacey	F	28	Bachelor's	Advertising	
Tasha	F	28	J.D.	Attorney	$50,000 to 74,999

Tatiana	F	31	Bachelor's	Broker contract specialist	$25,000 to 49,999
Vanessa	F	29	Bachelor's	Consultant	$100,000+
Wayne	M	28	Bachelor's	Advertising sales	$25,000 to 49,999
William	M	32	Master's	School administrator and teacher	$75,000 to 99,999

In addition to pseudonyms, identifying information (the name of the college or university where they graduated, for example) may have been altered to preserve respondents' anonymity.

This study examines the experiences of blacks living and working in the New York City metropolitan area. Middle-class respondents constituted the majority of the sample interviewed for my study, though I also interviewed a small contingent of working-class participants for comparative purposes. Working-class respondents typically had some college or had attended a trade school. The background information for the two working class respondents quoted in the work is detailed below.

| Melanie | F | 27 | High School | Administrative Assistant | |
| Patrick | M | 28 | Associate's | Finance Analyst | $50,000 to 74,999 |

Notes

Chapter 1: Black and Privileged

1. Barnes 2015; Pattillo-McCoy 2000; Anderson 1999b; Jackson 2001; Taylor 2002; Banks 2006; Landry and Marsh 2011; Wingfield 2013; Landry 2018; Fleming and Roses 2007; Wilson 1980.
2. Du Bois 2004.
3. Lacy 2007, 1.
4. Neckerman, Carter, and Lee 1999.
5. Barnes 2015, 27; Banks 2012.
6. Auer 1988.
7. Young 2009.
8. Sharkey 2008.
9. Sharkey and Elwert 2011.
10. Pfeffer and Killewald 2019.
11. McIntosh 1989.
12. Carter 2003.
13. Carter 2003.
14. Bourdieu 2007; Fleming and Roses 2007.
15. Imoagene 2017.
16. Rollock et al. 2011; Rollock, Gillborn, and Vincent 2015; Wallace 2017.
17. Fleming and Roses 2007.
18. DiMaggio 1994.
19. Valluvan 2016.
20. Mukhopadhyay and Chua 2008.
21. Bonilla-Silva 2003.
22. Carter 2010.
23. Carter 2010.
24. Khan 2012.
25. Wingfield 2015.
26. Schor 1999.

27. Marsh et al. 2007.
28. U.S. Census Bureau 2018a.
29. U.S. Census Bureau 2015.
30. Stoute 2011; Miller and Kemp 2005.
31. Logan and Alba 2002.
32. Frey 2010.

Chapter 2: The Emergence of a Modern Black Middle Class

1. Marable 2001.
2. Joseph 2009.
3. Van Deburg 1993.
4. Meier, Rudwick, and Broderick 1985.
5. Banks 2017.
6. Hill 1985.
7. "Long-Term Black Student Enrollment Trends at the Nation's Highest-Ranked Colleges and Universities," 1996.
8. Davis 2017; *Black Students at Stanford*, 1970s, 8.
9. Daniels 1970.
10. Nawi 2000.
11. Cowan and Maguire 1995.
12. Rooks 2007.
13. Rooks 2006, 8.
14. Collins 1997.
15. Landry 2018.
16. Landry 2018.
17. Collins 1997.
18. Collins 1997.
19. Collins 1997.
20. Landry 2018.
21. Dimock 2019.
22. Brown and Shaw 2002.
23. Bourdieu 2007.
24. Holt 1998.
25. Shavitt and Cho 2016.
26. Ridgeway 2011.
27. Landry 1987.
28. U.S. Bureau of Labor Statistics 2019.
29. Landry and Marsh 2011.
30. Hout 2012.
31. Lacy 2007.
32. Oliver and Shapiro 2006; Conley 2010.
33. Oliver and Shapiro 2006; Oliver and Shapiro 2019; Conley 2010.
34. Avery and Rendall 2002.

35. Oliver and Shapiro 2019.

36. Aliprantis and Carroll 2019.

37. Keister 2005.

38. Killewald 2013.

39. Boshara 2017.

40. Alston and Kelly 2015.

41. Pfeffer and Killewald 2019.

42. Heflin and Pattillo 2006.

43. O'Brien 2012; Heflin and Pattillo 2006; Chiteji and Hamilton 2002.

44. Chiteji and Hamilton 2002.

45. O'Brien 2012.

46. See the discussion of Pullman porters in Gaines 1996, 15.

47. Ray and Hunt 2012.

48. Frazier 1962.

49. Twitchell 1999.

50. Crockett and Wallendorf 2004.

51. Political scientist Michael Dawson theorizes "linked fate" as the idea that racial group interests are critical to shaping blacks' political attitudes and behavior. See Dawson 1994.

52. Lewis 2004; Edwards 2008.

53. Edwards 2008.

54. Lewis 2004.

55. Alexander 2016; Mukhopadhyay and Chua 2008.

Chapter 3: Unapologetically Black

1. Sandberg and Scovell 2017.

2. Abelson and Holman 2017.

3. Hunt 2007; Gay 2004.

4. Dawson 1994.

5. Hyra 2016.

6. Lamont et al. 2016.

7. Fields 2016.

8. Charles et al. 2015.

9. Charles et al. 2015.

10. Brown and Shaw 2002.

11. Gaines 1996, 76.

12. Fleming and Roses 2007.

13. Landry 1987.

14. Higginbotham 1997.

15. Cole and Omari 2003.

16. Higginbotham 1997, 189.

17. White 2001; Wolcott 2001; Harris 2003.

18. Yaish and Katz-Gerro 2010.

19. Arnould, Price, and Zinkhan 2005, 872.

20. Lamont and Molnár 2001; Lamont and Molnár 2002; Banks 2010.

21. Donahoo 2019.

22. Byrd and Tharps 2014; Craig 2002; Greene 2011; Yoshino 2006; Donahoo 2019.

23. Randle 2015.

24. Donahoo 2019; Ellington 2015; Gill, 2015; Randle 2015.

25. Randle 2015.

26. Randle 2015.

27. Donahoo 2019.

28. Byrd and Tharps 2014.

29. Rahman 2011; Green 2009.

30. Rahman 2011.

31. Rickford and Rickford 2000.

32. Massey and Lundy 2001.

33. Because the word is potentially offensive, in this section I will use "n-word" in place of spelling out the actual word.

34. Other "ethnically colored terms" used for the goal of "establishing solidarity and rapport" with other blacks include *brother* and *sister*, although I did not investigate these because they emerged only rarely during the course of the interviews.

35. Randall 2003.

36. Henderson 2003.

37. Rahman 2011.

38. Allan 2016.

39. Rahman 2011.

40. Randall 2003.

41. Chideya 1999.

42. Williams 2007.

43. Bridges 2018.

44. In 2013, the Museum of African Art underwent a name change and is now called the Africa Center.

45. Banks 2018.

46. Fleming and Roses 2007.

Chapter 4: Represent Your Hood and Your Hood's Rep

1. Zukin 2008.

2. Bourdieu 2005.

3. Lacy 2007.

4. Drake and Cayton 1945, 385–87.

5. Barnes 2015; Lacy 2007; Pattillo 2007.

6. Hunter 1974.

7. Charles 2000; Charles 2006.

8. Charles 2000; Shlay and DiGregorio 1985; Zubrinsky and Bobo 1996; Charles 2003; Krysan 2002; Harris 1999; Emerson, Chai, and Yancey 2001; St. John and Bates 1990; Clark 1992.

9. Sampson and Raudenbush 2004.

10. Pattillo 2007; Lacy 2007.

11. Strivers Row is an area of Harlem consisting of two picturesque blocks of 142 rowhouses known for both their architectural grandeur and their famous and renowned black residents, who were thought of as "strivers," blacks who were ambitious and determined to be upwardly mobile. See Dolkart and Sorin 1999.

12. Boettner et al. 2018.

13. Rottenberg 2013.

14. Krysan et al. 2009.

15. Anderson 2015.

16. Sampson and Raudenbush 2004.

17. Miller, Middendorf, and Wood 2015.

18. Du Bois 1903. Du Bois was not the first to coin the phrase "the talented tenth," but he is most famously associated with it. He used the term in an essay that appeared in *The Negro Problem: A Series of Articles by Representative American Negroes of Today*, edited by Booker T. Washington, and originally published in 1903.

19. Kanter 1977.

20. Grier and Perry 2018.

21. Rivera and Lamont 2012.

22. Charles 2006; Ellen 2000; Galster 1988; Zubrinsky and Bobo 1996; Charles 2003.

Chapter 5: Work, Work, and More Work at Work

1. Wingfield 2010; Bell, Edmondson, and Nkomo 2001; Feagin 2006.

2. Skrentny 2014.

3. Wingfield 2010; Collins 1997; Kraiger and Ford 1985; Greenhaus, Parasuraman, and Wormley, 1990; Forman 2003.

4. Anderson 1999b, 9.

5. Anderson 1999b.

6. Kanter 1977.

7. Kanter 1977; Yoder 1991; Jackson, Thoits, and Taylor 1995; Turco 2010; Zimmer 1988.

8. Shaw 1990.

9. Stowe 2019.

10. Stowe 2019.

11. Rivera 2012.

12. Rivera 2012, 1008.

13. Zimmer 1988.

14. Erickson 1996, 221.

Chapter 6: Policing Black Privilege

1. Kusmer and Trotter 2009, 364.

2. Wilson 1980.

3. Landry 2018.

4. Givhan 2005; Obama 2013.

5. Lee 2006; Weems 1998; Pittman 2017; Feagin and Sikes 1994; Essed 1990; Crockett 2017; Crockett, Grier, and Williams 2003.

6. Schreer, Smith, and Thomas 2009.

7. Williams et al. 2015.

8. Gabbidon and Higgins 2007.

9. Feagin 1991; Lamont et al. 2016; Lee 2006.

10. Small and McDermott 2006.

11. Mukherjee, 2011.

12. Charron-Chénier, Fink, and Keister 2017.

13. Mukherjee 2011.

14. McGovern 1998.

15. Austin 1994.

16. Austin 1994, 150.

17. Wherry 2008.

18. Wherry 2008.

19. Brewster and Rusche 2012; Brewster, Brauer, and Lynn 2015.

20. Dirks and Rice 2004.

21. Brewster and Rusche 2012.

22. Brewster, Brauer, and Lynn 2015.

23. May 2015; May 2018.

24. May and Goldsmith 2018.

Chapter 7: Black Buying Power

1. Neilson 2018.

2. U.S. Census Bureau 2018b.

3. Bonilla-Silva 2017; Omi and Winant 2014.

4. Bonilla-Silva 2017; Feagin 2006.

5. Crockett and Wallendorf 2004, 511; Brown 2015.

6. Crockett and Wallendorf 2004; Dawson 2001, 4.

7. Dawson 2001.

8. Swidler 1986, 278.

9. Skocpol 1985.

10. Dawson 2001.

11. Gaines 1996.

12. Dawson 2001, 67.

13. Du Bois 2004.

14. Du Bois 2004.

15. Garvey 1924.

16. Brown and Shaw 2002.

17. Tucker 1969.

18. Brown, Duncan, and Kettrey 2017.

19. "Buy Black," 2015.

20. "Killer Mike on Recent Murders of Black Men," 2016.

21. Sullivan 2018.
22. Crockett and Wallendorf 2004, 516.
23. Banks 2006; Banks 2010.
24. Skrentny 2014.
25. Skrentny 2014.
26. Mears 2011.
27. McManus 2016.
28. McManus 2016.
29. Quintana and McKown 2008.
30. Williams 2012; Pager and Shepherd 2008.
31. Price 2009.
32. West and Jay-Z 2005.
33. Greenburg 2008.
34. Collins et al. 2019.
35. Greenburg 2014.
36. Murphy, Kangun, and Locander 1978.

Chapter 8: Black American Dreams

1. Cohen 2003; Pugh 2012.
2. McGovern 1998.
3. Lipsitz 1998, 134.
4. McGovern 1998; Cohen 2003.
5. McGovern 1998, 46.
6. Dwyer 2009a; Dwyer 2009b.
7. Rank, Hirschl, and Foster 2016, 48.
8. Hochschild 1996.
9. Bobo and Hutchings 1996.
10. Packard 1959.
11. Veblen 2006.
12. Frazier 1962.
13. Frazier 1962.
14. Frazier 1962, 230.
15. Frazier 1962, 230.
16. Charles, Hurst, and Roussanov 2007.
17. Anderson 1999b.
18. Austin 1994.
19. Nightingale 1993, 10.
20. Majors and Billson 1992; see also George 1999.
21. Majors and Billson 1992, 50.
22. Anderson 1999a, 165.
23. Chin 2001, 4–5.
24. Fournier and Guiry 1993.
25. Lamont 2019, 666.

26. Brooks 2017.
27. Kotkin and Cox 2015.
28. McCargo and Strochak 2018.
29. This interview was conducted before Bill Cosby, the *Cosby Show*'s creator and star, was convicted of sexual assault, tarnishing much of his artistic legacy.
30. Miskin 2018.
31. Timothy and Boyd 2006.
32. Bruner 1996.
33. Foster 2014; Allen 2015.
34. DiMaggio 1994.

Chapter 9: Striving and Surviving

1. McGovern 1998.
2. Lamont et al. 2016.
3. Lamont et al. 2016.
4. Williams 2006.
5. Gabbidon and Higgins 2007.
6. Zelizer 2011.
7. Joy et al. 2014.
8. Zukin 2005.
9. Holt 1995.
10. Rivera 2010.
11. Singer 2008.
12. Rosa-Salas 2019.

References

Abelson, Max, and Jordyn Holman. 2017. "Black Executives Are Losing Ground at Some Big Banks." *Bloomberg Business Week*, July 27, 2017.

Advertising Age. 2012. *In Plain Sight: The Black Consumer Opportunity*. http://branded content.adage.com/pdf/CABblackconsumer.pdf.

Alexander, Claire. 2016. "The Culture Question: A View from the UK." *Ethnic and Racial Studies* 39 (8): 1426–35.

Aliprantis, Dionissi, and Daniel Carroll. 2019. "What Is Behind the Persistence of the Racial Wealth Gap?" *Economic Commentary* (Federal Reserve Bank of Cleveland), February 28, 1–6.

Allan, Keith. 2016. "Contextual Determinants on the Meaning of the N Word." *Springer-Plus* 5. doi:10.1186/s40064-016-2813-1

Allen, Jim. 2015. "1963 Jeep Wagoneer Custom—Backward Glances." *Four Wheeler*, January 9. http://www.fourwheeler.com/features/1502-1963-jeep-wagoneer-custom -backward-glances.

Alston, Alicia, and Dawn Kelly. 2015. "New Prudential Study Shows Greater Financial Confidence of African Americans, but Gaps in Retirement Planning Still Restrict Wealth Building." MarketWatch (Press release), August 6.

Anderson, Elijah. 1999a. *Code of the Street: Decency, Violence, and the Moral Life of the Inner City*. New York: Norton.

Anderson, Elijah. 1999b. "The Social Situation of the Black Executive: Black and White Identities in the Corporate World." In *The Cultural Territories of Race: Black and White Boundaries*. Edited by Michèle Lamont and Elijah Anderson, 291–320. Chicago: University of Chicago Press.

Anderson, Elijah. 2015. "The White Space." *Sociology of Race and Ethnicity* 1 (1): 10–21.

Arnould, Eric J., Linda L. Price, and George Martin Zinkhan. 2005. *Consumers*. New York: McGraw-Hill/Irwin.

Auer, Peter. 1988. *Code-Switching in Conversation: Language, Interacting and Identity*. New York: Routledge.

Austin, Regina. 1994. "'A Nation of Thieves': Consumption, Commerce, and the Black Public Sphere." *Utah Law Review* 1994: 147–77.

Avery, Robert B., and Michael S. Rendall. 2002. "Lifetime Inheritances of Three Generations of Whites and Blacks." *American Journal of Sociology* 107 (5): 1300–46.

Banks, Patricia A. 2006. *Art, Identity, and the New Black Middle Class: How Elite
Blacks Construct Their Identity through the Consumption of Visual Art*. New York:
Routledge.

Banks, Patricia A. 2010. *Represent: Art and Identity among the Black Upper-Middle Class*.
New York: Routledge.

Banks, Patricia A. 2017. "Ethnicity, Class, and Trusteeship at African American and
Mainstream Museums." *Cultural Sociology* 11 (1): 97–112.

Banks, Patricia A. 2018. "Money, Museums, and Memory: Cultural Patronage by Black
Voluntary Associations." *Ethnic and Racial Studies*. https://doi.org/10.1080/01419870
.2018.1540789.

Barnes, Riché J. Daniel. 2015. *Raising the Race: Black Career Women Redefine Marriage,
Motherhood, and Community*. New Brunswick: Rutgers University Press.

Bell, Ella, L. J. Edmondson, and Stella M. Nkomo. 2001. *Our Separate Ways: Black and White
Women and the Struggle for Professional Identity*. Boston: Harvard Business School Press.

Black Students at Stanford. 1970s. (Brochure.) Stanford University, Office of Admissions.
https://purl.stanford.edu/xz351ht5726.

Bobo, Lawrence, and Vincent L. Hutchings. 1996. "Perceptions of Racial Group Competition: Extending Blumer's Theory of Group Position to a Multiracial Social Context." *American Sociological Review* 61 (6): 951–72.

Boettner, Bethany, Christopher Browning, Catherine Calder, Jodi Ford, and Lesley
Schneider. 2018. "Racial Segregation, Exposure to White Areas, and Safety Percep-
tions among African American Youth." Paper presented at the annual meeting of the
American Sociological Association, Philadelphia, PA, August 9.

Bonilla-Silva, Edwardo. 2003. *Racism without Racists: Color-Blind Racism and the Persistence of Racial Inequality*. Lanham: Rowan and Littlefield.

Bonilla-Silva, Edwardo. 2017. *Racism without Racists: Color-Blind Racism and the Persistence of Racial Inequality*. 5th ed. Lanham: Rowan and Littlefield.

Boshara, Ray. 2017. "Does College Level the Playing Field?" *Federal Reserve Bank of St.
Louis Review* 99 (1): 1–5.

Bourdieu, Pierre. 2005. *The Social Structures of the Economy*. Cambridge: Polity.

Bourdieu, Pierre. 2007. *Distinction: A Social Critique of the Judgment of Taste*. Cambridge, MA: Harvard University Press.

Brewster, Zachary W., Jonathan R. Brauer, and Michael Lynn. 2015. "Economic Motiva-
tions and Moral Controls Regulating Discrimination against Black and Hispanic
Diners." *Sociological Quarterly* 56 (3): 506–38.

Brewster, Zachary W., and S. N. Rusche. 2012. "Quantitative Evidence of the Continuing
Significance of Race: Tableside Racism in Full-Service Restaurants." *Journal of Black
Studies*, 43 (4): 359–84.

Bridges, Brian. 2018. "African Americans and College Education by the Numbers." United
Negro College Fund, November 29. https://uncf.org/the-latest/african-americans
-and-college-education-by-the-numbers.

Brooks, Rodney. 2017. "Declining Black Homeownership Has Big Retirement Implications." *Forbes*, May 10.

Brown, Nicole M. 2015. "Freedom's Stock: Political Consumerism, Transnational Blackness and the Black Star Line." *Critical Sociology* 41 (2): 237–48.

Brown, Robert A., and Todd C. Shaw. 2002. "Separate Nations: Two Attitudinal Dimensions of Black Nationalism." *Journal of Politics* 64 (1): 22–44.

Brown, Tony N., Ebony M. Duncan, and Heather Hensman Kettrey. 2017. "Black Nationalist Tendencies and Their Association with Perceived Inefficacy of the Civil Rights Movement and of Black Elected Officials." *Sociology of Race and Ethnicity* 3 (2): 188–201.

Bruner, Edward M. 1996. "Tourism in Ghana: The Representation of Slavery and the Return of the Black Diaspora." *American Anthropologist* 98 (2): 290–304.

"Buy Black: The $50 Billion Empowerment Tour Coming to a City Near You & The Push to Create 1 Million Jobs." *NewsOne Now*. TV One. Silver Spring, Maryland. January 2, 2015. Television.

Byrd, Ayana D., and Lori L. Tharps. 2014. *Hair Story: Untangling the Roots of Black Hair in America*. 2nd ed. New York: St. Martin's Griffin.

Carter, Prudence L. 2003. "'Black' Cultural Capital, Status Positioning, and Schooling Conflicts for Low-Income African American Youth." *Social Problems* 50 (1): 136–55.

Carter, Prudence L. 2010. "Race and Cultural Flexibility among Students in Different Multiracial Schools." *Teachers College Record* 112 (6): 1529–74.

Charles, Camille Zubrinsky. 2000. "Neighborhood Racial-Composition Preferences: Evidence from a Multiethnic Metropolis." *Social Problems* 47 (3): 379–407.

Charles, Camille Zubrinsky. 2003. "The Dynamics of Racial Residential Segregation." *Annual Review of Sociology* 29 (1): 167–207.

Charles, Camille Zubrinsky. 2006. *Won't You Be My Neighbor? Race, Class and Residence in Los Angeles*. New York: Russell Sage.

Charles, Camille Z., Rory A. Kramer, Kimberly C. Torres, and Rachelle J. Brunn-Bevel. 2015. "Intragroup Heterogeneity and Blackness: Effects of Racial Classification, Immigrant Origins, Social Class, and Social Context on the Racial Identity of Elite College Students." *Race and Social Problems* 7 (4): 281–99.

Charles, Kerwin Kofi, Erik Hurst, and Nikolai Roussanov. 2007. *Conspicuous Consumption and Race*. Cambridge, MA: National Bureau of Economic Research. http://catalog.hathitrust.org/api/volumes/oclc/173816890.html.

Charron-Chénier, Raphaël, Joshua J. Fink, and Lisa A. Keister. 2017. "Race and Consumption: Black and White Disparities in Household Spending." *Sociology of Race and Ethnicity* 3 (1): 50–67.

Chideya, Farai. 1999. *The Color of Our Future*. New York: William Morrow.

Chin, Elizabeth. 2001. *Purchasing Power: Black Kids and American Consumer Culture*. Minneapolis: University of Minnesota Press.

Chiteji, N. S., and Darrick Hamilton. 2002 "Family Connections and the Black-White Wealth Gap among Middle-Class Families." *Review of Black Political Economy* 30: 9–28.

Clark, William A. V. 1992. "Residential Preferences and Residential Choices in a Multi-ethnic Context." *Demography* 29 (3), 434–48.

Cohen, Lizabeth. 2003. *A Consumers' Republic: The Politics of Mass Consumption in Post-war America.* New York: Knopf.

Cole, Elizabeth R., and Safiya R. Omari. 2003. "Race, Class and the Dilemmas of Upward Mobility for African Americans." *Journal of Social Issues* 59 (4): 785–802.

Collins, Chuck, Dedrick Asante-Muhammed, Josh Hoxie, and Sabrina Terry. 2019. "Dream Deferred: How Enriching the 1 Percent Widens the Racial Wealth Divide." Washington, DC: Institute for Policy Studies.

Collins, Sharon M. 1997. *Black Corporate Executives: The Making and Breaking of a Black Middle Class.* Philadelphia: Temple University Press.

Conley, Dalton. 2010. *Being Black, Living in the Red: Race, Wealth, and Social Policy in America.* Berkeley: University of California Press.

Cowan, Tom, and Jack Maguire. 1995. "History's Milestones of African-American Higher Education." *Journal of Blacks in Higher Education*, no. 7: 86–90.

Craig, Maxine Leeds. 2002. *Ain't I a Beauty Queen? Black Women, Beauty, and the Politics of Race.* New York: Oxford University Press.

Crockett, David. 2017. "Paths to Respectability: Consumption and Stigma Management in the Contemporary Black Middle Class." *Journal of Consumer Research* 44 (3): 554–81.

Crockett, David, Sonya Grier, and Jerome Williams. 2003. "Coping with Marketplace Discrimination: An Exploration of the Experiences of Black Men." *Academy of Marketing Science Review* 4 (7): 1–21.

Crockett, David, and Melanie Wallendorf. 2004. "The Role of Normative Political Ideology in Consumer Behavior." *Journal of Consumer Research* 31 (3): 511–28.

Daniels, Lee A. 1970. "Black Studies Department Reflects a Decade of Change." *Harvard Crimson*, September 24. https://www.thecrimson.com/article/1970/9/24/black-studies-department-reflects-a-decade.

Davis, Alison Carpenter. 2017. *Letters Home from Stanford: 125 Years of Correspondence from Students of Stanford University.* St. Louis: Reedy Press.

Dawson, Michael C. 1994. *Behind the Mule: Race and Class in African-American Politics.* Princeton: Princeton University Press.

Dawson, Michael C. 2001. *Black Visions: The Roots of Contemporary African-American Political Ideologies.* Chicago: University of Chicago Press.

DiMaggio, Paul. 1994. "Culture and Economy." In *The Handbook of Economic Sociology.* Edited by Neil J. Smesler and Richard Swedberg, 27–57. New York: Russell Sage.

Dimock, Michael. 2019. "Defining Generations: Where Millennials End and Generation Z Begins." Pew Research Center. https://www.pewresearch.org/fact-tank/2019/01/17/where-millennials-end-and-generation-z-begins.

Dirks, Danielle, and Stephen K. Rice. 2004. "Dining while Black: Tipping as Social Artifact." *Cornell Hotel and Restaurant Administration Quarterly* 45 (1): 30–47.

Dolkart, Andrew, and Gretchen Sullivan Sorin. 1999. *Touring Historic Harlem: Four Walks in Northern Manhattan.* New York: New York Landmarks Conservancy.

Donahoo, Saran. 2019. "Owning Black Hair: The Pursuit of Identity and Authenticity in Higher Education." In *Navigating Micro-Aggressions toward Women in Higher Education*. Edited by Ursula Thomas, 73–95. Hershey: Information Science Reference.

Drake, St. Clair, and Horace R. Cayton. 1945. *Black Metropolis*. New York: Harcourt, Brace, and World.

Du Bois, W.E.B. 1903. "The Talented Tenth." In *The Negro Problem: A Series of Articles by Representative American Negroes of Today*, by Booker T. Washington, W. E. Burghardt Du Bois, Paul Laurence Dunbar, Charles W. Chesnutt, and others, 31–75. New York: James Pott & Co.

Du Bois, W.E.B. 2004. *The Souls of Black Folk*. Boulder: Paradigm.

Dwyer, Rachel E. 2009a. "Making a Habit of It: Conventional Action, Positional Consumption, and the Standard of Living." *Journal of Consumer Culture* 9: 328–47.

Dwyer, Rachel E. 2009b. "The McMansionization of America? Income Stratification and the Standard of Living in Housing, 1960–2000." *Research in Social Stratification and Mobility* 27 (4): 285–300. Packard

Edwards, Korie L. 2008. "Bring Race to the Center: The Importance of Race in Racially Diverse Religious Organizations." *Journal for the Scientific Study of Religion* 47 (1): 5–9.

Ellen, Ingrid Gould. 2000. *Sharing America's Neighborhoods: The Changing Prospects for Stable, Racial Integration*. Cambridge, MA: Harvard University Press.

Ellington, Tameka N. 2015. "Social Networking Sites: A Support System for African-American Women Wearing Natural Hair." *International Journal of Fashion Design, Technology and Education* 8(1), 21–29.

Emerson, Michael O., Karen J. Chai, and George Yancey. 2001. "Does Race Matter in Residential Segregation? Exploring the Preferences of White Americans." *American Sociological Review* 66 (6): 922–35.

Erickson, Bonnie H. 1996. "Culture, Class, and Connections." *American Journal of Sociology* 102 (1): 217–51.

Essed, Philomena. 1990. *Everyday Racism: Reports from Women of Two Cultures*. Claremont: Hunter House.

Feagin, Joe R. 1991. "The Continuing Significance of Race: Antiblack Discrimination in Public Places." *American Sociological Review* 56 (1): 101–16.

Feagin, Joe R. 2006. *Systemic Racism: A Theory of Oppression*. New York: Routledge.

Feagin, Joe R., and Melvin P. Sikes. 1994. *Living with Racism: The Black Middle-Class Experience*. Boston: Beacon Press.

Fields, Corey D. 2016. *Black Elephants in the Room: The Unexpected Politics of African American Republicans*. Oakland: University of California Press.

Fleming, Crystal M., and Lorraine Roses. 2007. "Black Cultural Capitalists: African American Elites and the Organization of the Arts in Early Twentieth-Century Boston." *Poetics* (356): 368–87.

Forman, Tyrone A. 2003. "The Social Psychological Costs of Racial Segmentation in the Workplace: A Study of African Americans' Well-Being." *Journal of Health and Social Behavior* 44 (3): 332–52.

Foster, Patrick R. 2014. *Jeep: The History of America's Greatest Vehicle*. Minneapolis: Motorbooks.

Fournier, Susan, and Michael Guiry. 1993. "'An Emerald Green Jaguar, a House on Nantucket, and an African Safari:' Wish Lists and Consumption Dreams in Materialist Society." *Advances in Consumer Research* 20: 352–58.

Frazier, Edward Franklin. 1962. *Black Bourgeoisie*. New York: Collier Books.

Frey, William H. 2010. *New Racial Segregation Measures for Large Metropolitan Areas: Analysis of the 1990–2010 Decennial Censuses*. Brookings Institution and University of Michigan Social Science Data Analysis. https://www.psc.isr.umich.edu/dis/census/segregation2010.html.

Gabbidon, Shaun L., and George E. Higgins. 2007. "Consumer Racial Profiling and Perceived Victimization: A Phone Survey of Philadelphia Area Residents." *American Journal of Criminal Justice* 32 (1–2): 1–11.

Gaines, Kevin K. 1996. *Uplifting the Race: Black Leadership, Politics, and Culture in the Twentieth Century*. Chapel Hill: University of North Carolina Press.

Galster, George. 1988. "Residential Segregation in American Cities: A Contrary Review." *Population Research and Policy Review* 72: 93–112.

Garvey, Marcus. 1924. "Look for Me in a Whirlwind or a Storm." A partial recording and transcript of a speech. https://www.buyblackmovement.com/MarcusGarvey/AudioRecordings/index.cfm.

Gay, Claudine. 2004. "Putting Race in Context: Identifying the Environmental Determinants of Black Racial Attitudes." *American Political Science Review* 98: 547–62.

George, Nelson. 1999. *Hip Hop America*. New York: Penguin Books.

Gill, Tiffany M. 2015. "#TeamNatural: Black Hair and the Politics of Community in Digital Media." *Journal of Contemporary African Art* 37 (November): 70–79.

Givhan, Robin. 2005. "Oprah and the View from Outside Hermes' Paris Door." *Washington Post*, June 24.

Green, Lisa J. 2009. *African American English: A Linguistic Introduction*. Cambridge: Cambridge University Press.

Greenburg, Zach O'Malley. 2014. "The Real Story behind Jay-Z's Champagne Deal." *Forbes*, November 4, 2014.

Greenburg, Zach O'Malley. 2018. "Jay-Z's Earnings: $76.5 Million in 2018." *Forbes*, September 13, 2018.

Greene, D. Wendy. 2011. "Black Women Can't Have Blonde Hair . . . in the Workplace." *Journal of Gender, Race and Justice* 14 (2): 405–30.

Greenhaus, Jeffrey H., Saroj Parasuraman, and Wayne M. Wormley. 1990. "Effects of Race on Organizational Experiences, Job Performance Evaluations, and Career Outcomes." *Academy of Management Journal* 33 (1): 64–86.

Grier, Sonya, and Vanessa Perry. 2018. "Dog Parks and Coffee Shops: Faux Diversity and Consumption in Gentrifying Neighborhoods." *Journal of Public Policy & Marketing* 37 (1): 23–38.

Harris, David R. 1999. "'Property Values Drop When Blacks Move in, Because . . . ':

Racial and Socioeconomic Determinants of Neighborhood Desirability." *American Sociological Review* 64 (3): 461–79.

Harris, Paisley Jane. 2003. "Gatekeeping and Remaking: The Politics of Respectability in African American Women's History and Black Feminism." *Journal of Women's History* 15 (1): 212–20.

Heflin, Colleen M., and Mary Pattillo. 2006. "Poverty in the Family: Race, Siblings, and Socioeconomic Heterogeneity." *Social Science Research* 35 (4): 804–22.

Henderson, Anita. 2003. "What's in a Slur?" *American Speech* 78 (1): 52–74.

Higginbotham, Evelyn Brooks. 1997. *Righteous Discontent: The Women's Movement in the Black Baptist Church, 1880–1920.* Cambridge, MA: Harvard University Press.

Hill, Susan. 1985. "The Traditionally Black Institutions of Higher Education, 1860 to 1982." Washington, DC: U.S. Dept. of Education, Office of Educational Research and Improvement, National Center for Education Statistics.

Hochschild, Jennifer. 1996. *Facing Up to the American Dream: Race, Class, and the Soul of the Nation.* Princeton: Princeton University Press.

Holt, Douglas. 1995. "How Consumers Consume: A Typology of Consumption Practices." *Journal of Consumer Research* 22 (1): 1–16.

Holt, Douglas. 1998. "Does Cultural Capital Structure American Consumption?" *Journal of Consumer Research* 25 (1): 1–25.

Hout, Michael. 2012. "Social and Economic Returns to College Education in the United States." *Annual Review of Sociology* 38: 379–400.

Hunt, Matthew O. 2007. "African American, Hispanic, and White Beliefs about Black/White Inequality, 1977–2004." *American Sociological Review* 72 (3): 390–415.

Hunter, Albert. 1974. *Symbolic Communities: The Persistence and Change of Chicago's Local Communities.* Chicago: University of Chicago Press.

Hyra, Derek S. 2006. "Racial Uplift? Intra-Racial Class Conflict and the Economic Revitalization of Harlem and Bronzeville." *City & Community* 5 (1): 71–92.

Imoagene, Onoso. 2017. *Beyond Expectations: Second-Generation Nigerians in the United States and Britain.* Oakland: University of California Press.

Jackson, John L. 2001. *Harlemworld: Doing Race and Class in Contemporary Black America.* Chicago: University of Chicago Press.

Jackson, Pamela Braboy, Peggy A. Thoits, and Howard F. Taylor. 1995. "Composition of the Workplace and Psychological Well-Being: The Effects of Tokenism on America's Black Elite." *Social Forces* 74(2): 543–57.

Joseph, Peniel E. 2009. "The Black Power Movement: A State of the Field." *Journal of American History* 96(3): 751–76.

Joy, Annamma, Jeff Jianfeng Wang, Tsang-Sing Chan, John Sherry, and Geng Cui. 2014. "M(Art)Worlds: Consumer Perceptions of How Luxury Brand Stores Become Art Institutions." *Journal of Retailing* 90 (3): 347–64.

Kanter, Rosabeth Moss. 1977. *Men and Women of the Corporation.* New York: Basic Books.

Keister, Lisa A. 2005. *Getting Rich: America's New Rich and How They Got That Way.* New York: Cambridge University Press.

Kennedy, Randall. 2003. *Nigger: The Strange Career of a Troublesome Word*. New York: Vintage.

Khan, Shamus. 2012. *Privilege: The Making of an Adolescent Elite at St. Paul's School*. Princeton: Princeton University Press.

"Killer Mike on Recent Murders of Black Men." 2016. Aired July 7, WHTA-FM, Hot 97.9, Atlanta, GA. Radio.

Killewald, Alexandra. 2013. "Return to 'Being Black, Living in the Red': A Race Gap in Wealth That Goes Beyond Social Origins." *Demography* 50 (4): 1177–95.

Kotkin, Joel, and Wendell Cox. 2015. *Best Cities for Minorities: Gauging the Economics of Opportunity*. Orange, CA: Chapman University Press.

Kraiger, Kurt, and J. Kevin Ford. 1985. "A Meta-Analysis of Ratee Race Effects in Performance Ratings." *Journal of Applied Psychology* 70 (1): 56–65.

Krysan, Maria. 2002. "Community Undesirability in Black and White: Examining Racial Residential Preferences through Community Perceptions." *Social Problems* 49 (4): 521–43.

Krysan, Maria, Mick P. Couper, Reynolds Farley, and Tyrone Forman. 2009. "Does Race Matter in Neighborhood Preferences? Results from a Video Experiment." *American Journal of Sociology* 115 (2): 527–59.

Kusmer, Kenneth, and Joe Trotter. 2009. *African American Urban History since World War II*. Chicago: University of Chicago Press.

Lacy, Karyn R. 2007. *Blue-Chip Black: Race, Class, and Status in the New Black Middle Class*. Berkeley: University of California Press.

Lamont, Michèle. 2019. "From 'Having' to 'Being': Self-Worth and the Current Crisis of American Society." *British Journal of Sociology* 70 (3): 660–707.

Lamont, Michèle, Graziella Silva, Jessica Welburn, Joshua Guetzkow, Nissim Mizrachi, Hanna Herzog, and Elisa Reis. 2016. *Getting Respect: Responding to Stigma and Discrimination in the United States, Brazil, and Israel*. Princeton: Princeton University Press.

Lamont, Michèle, and Virág Molnár. 2001. "How Blacks Use Consumption to Shape Their Collective Identity Evidence from Marketing Specialists." *Journal of Consumer Culture* 1 (1): 31–45.

Lamont, Michèle, and Virág Molnár. 2002. "Social Categorization and Group Identification: How African-Americans Shape their Collective Identity through Consumption." In *Interdisciplinary Approaches to Demand and Its Role in Innovation*. Edited by Andrew McMeekin, 88–112. Manchester: University of Manchester Press.

Landry, Bart. 1987. *The New Black Middle Class*. Berkeley: University of California Press.

Landry, Bart. 2018. *The New Black Middle Class in the Twenty-first Century*. Newark: Rutgers University Press.

Landry, Bart, and Kris Marsh. 2011. "The Evolution of the New Black Middle Class." *Annual Review of Sociology* 37: 373–94.

Lee, Jennifer. 2006. *Civility in the City: Blacks, Jews, and Koreans in Urban America*. Cambridge, MA: Harvard University Press.

Lewis, Amanda E. 2004. "'What Group?' Studying Whites and Whiteness in the Era of 'Color-Blindness'" *Sociological Theory* 22 (4): 623–46.

Lipsitz, George. 1998. "The Hip Hop Hearings: Censorship, Social Memory, and Inter-generational Tension among African Americans." In *Generations of Youth: Youth Cultures and History in Twentieth-Century America*. Edited by Joe Austin and Michael Nevin Willard, 395–411. New York: New York University Press.

Logan, John, and Richard D. Alba. 2002. "Does Race Matter Less for the Truly Advantaged? Residential Patterns in the New York Metropolis." In *The New Politics of Race: From Du Bois to the 21st Century*. Edited by Marlese Durr, 71–88. Westport: Praeger.

"Long-Term Black Student Enrollment Trends at the Nation's Highest-Ranked Colleges and Universities." 1996. *Journal of Blacks in Higher Education*, no. 12: 10–13.

Majors, Richard, and Janet Billson. 1992. *Cool Pose: The Dilemmas of Black Manhood in America*. New York: Simon & Schuster.

Marable, Manning. 2001. *Race, Reform, and Rebellion*. Jackson: University Press of Mississippi.

Marsh, Kris, William A. Darity, Philip N. Cohen., Lynne M. Casper, and Danielle Salters. 2007. "The Emerging Black Middle Class: Single and Living Alone." *Social Forces* 86 (2): 735–36.

Massey, Douglas. 1985. "Ethnic Residential Segregation: A Theoretical Synthesis and Empirical Review." *Sociology and Social Research* 69 (3): 315–50.

Massey, Douglas, and Garvey Lundy. 2001. "Use of Black English and Racial Discrimination in Urban Housing Markets." *Urban Affairs Review* 36 (4): 452–69.

May, Reuben Buford. 2015. "Discrimination and Dress Codes in Urban Nightlife." *Contexts* 14: 38–43.

May, Reuben A. Buford. 2018. "Velvet Rope Racism, Racial Paranoia, and Cultural Scripts: Alleged Dress Code Discrimination in Urban Nightlife, 2000–2014." *City & Community* 17 (1): 44–64.

May, Reuben A. Buford, and Pat Rubio Goldsmith. 2018. "Dress Codes and Racial Discrimination in Urban Nightclubs." *Sociology of Race and Ethnicity*, 4 (October): 555–66.

McCargo, Alanna, and Sarah Strochak. 2018. "Mapping the Black Homeownership Rate." *Urban Wire: Housing and Housing Finance* (blog). Urban Institute. https://urbn.is/2FxMoYz.

McGovern, Charles. 1998. "Consumption and Citizenship in the United States, 1900–1940." In *Getting and Spending: European and American Consumer Societies in the Twentieth Century*. Edited by Susan Strasser, Charles McGovern, and Matthias Judt, 37–58. Cambridge: Cambridge University Press.

McIntosh, Peggy. 1989. "White Privilege: Unpacking the Invisible Knapsack." *Peace and Freedom* (July/August): 10–12.

McKernan, Signe-Mary, Caleb Quakenbush, Caroline Ratcliffe, Emma Kalish, and C. Eugene Steuerle. 2017. "Nine Charts about Wealth Inequality in America." Urban Institute. https://apps.urban.org/features/wealth-inequality-charts.

McManus, Michael. 2016. "Minority Business Ownership: Data from the 2012 Survey of Business Owners." Issue Brief no. 12. Washington, DC: U.S. Small Business Administration, Office of Advocacy.

Mears, Ashley. 2011. *Pricing Beauty: The Making of a Fashion Model*. Berkeley: University of California Press.

Meier, A., Rudwick, E., & Broderick, F. L., eds. 1985. *Black Protest Thought in the Twentieth Century*. New York: Macmillan.

Miller, Michael, Gerad Middendorf, and Spencer D. Wood. 2015. "Food Availability in the Heartland: Exploring the Effects of Neighborhood Racial and Income Composition." *Rural Sociology* 80 (3): 340–61.

Miller, Pepper, and Herb Kemp. 2005. *What's Black about It? Insights to Increase Your Share of a Changing African-American Market*. Ithaca: Paramount Market.

Miskin, Shaina. 2018. "See Inside 50 Cent's Multi-Million Dollar Mansion He Forgot He Had." *Money*, January 26.

Mukherjee, Roopali. 2011. "Bling Fling: Commodity Consumption and the Politics of the 'Post-Racial.'" In *Critical Rhetorics of Race*. Edited by Michael G. Lacy and Kent A. Ono, 179–93. New York: New York University Press.

Mukhopadhyay, Carol C., and Peter Chua. 2008. "Cultural Racism." In *Encyclopedia of Race and Racism*. Edited by John H. Moore, 377–83. Detroit: Macmillan Reference USA/Thompson Gale.

Murphy, Patrick E., Norman Kangun, and William B. Locander. 1978. "Environmentally Concerned Consumers—Racial Variations." *Journal of Marketing* 42 (4): 61–66.

Nawi, Rachel. 2000. "Minority Enrollment Shows Stagnation since the 1970s." *Daily Pennsylvanian* 116 (November 28).

Neckerman, Kathryn M., Prudence Carter, and Jennifer Lee. 1999. "Segmented Assimilation and Minority Cultures of Mobility." *Ethnic and Racial Studies* 22 (6): 945–65.

Nielsen. 2018. "Black Impact: Consumer Categories Where African Americans Move Markets." *Insights*, February 15, 2018. https://www.nielsen.com/us/en/insights/news/2018/black-impact-consumer-categories-where-african-americans-move-markets.html.

Nightingale, Carl H. 1993. *On the Edge: A History of Poor Black Children and Their American Dreams*. New York: Basic Books.

Obama, Barack. 2013. "Remarks by the President on Trayvon Martin." The White House (July 19). https://obamawhitehouse.archives.gov/the-press-office/2013/07/19/remarks-president-trayvon-martin.

O'Brien, Rourke L. 2012. "Depleting Capital? Race, Wealth and Informal Financial Assistance." *Social Forces* 91 (2): 375–96.

Oliver, Melvin L., and Thomas M. Shapiro. 2006. *Black Wealth/White Wealth: A New Perspective on Racial Inequality*. New York: Routledge.

Oliver, Melvin L., and Thomas M. Shapiro. 2019. "Disrupting the Racial Wealth Gap." *Contexts* 18 (1): 16–21.

Omi, Michael, and Howard Winant. 2014. *Racial Formation in the United States*. London: Routledge.

Packard, Vance. 1959. *The Status Seekers: An Exploration of Class Behavior in America and the Hidden Barriers That Affect You, Your Community, Your Future*. New York: D. McKay.

Pager, Devah, and Hana Shepherd. 2008. "The Sociology of Discrimination: Racial Discrimination in Employment, Housing, Credit, and Consumer Markets." *Annual Review of Sociology* 34: 181–210.

Pattillo, Mary. 2007. *Black on the Block: The Politics of Race and Class in the City*. Chicago: University of Chicago Press.

Pattillo-McCoy, Mary. 2000. *Black Picket Fences: Privilege and Peril among the Black Middle Class*. Chicago: University of Chicago Press.

Pfeffer, Fabian T., and Alexandra Killewald. 2019. "Intergenerational Wealth Mobility and Racial Inequality." *Socius* 5 (January 2019).

Pittman, Cassi. 2020. "'Shopping while Black': Black Consumers' Management of Racial Stigma and Racial Profiling in Retail Settings." *Journal of Consumer Culture* 20(1): 3–22.

Price, Melanye T. 2009. *Dreaming Blackness: Black Nationalism and African American Public Opinion*. New York: New York University Press.

Pugh, Allison J. 2012. *Longing and Belonging: Parents, Children, and Consumer Culture*. Berkeley: University of California Press.

Quintana, Stephen M., and Clark McKown. 2008. *Handbook of Race, Racism, and the Developing Child*. Hoboken: Wiley.

Rahman, Jacquelyn. 2011. "The N Word: Its History and Use in the African American Community." *Journal of English Linguistics* 40 (2): 137–171.

Randle, Brenda A. 2015. "I Am Not My Hair: African American Women and Their Struggles with Embracing Natural Hair!" *Race, Gender & Class* 22 (1–2): 114–21.

Rank, Mark R., Thomas A. Hirschl, and Kirk A. Foster. 2016. *Chasing the American Dream: Understanding What Shapes Our Fortunes*. New York: Oxford University Press.

Ray, Rashawn, and Matthew O. Hunt. 2012. "Social Class Identification among Black Americans: Trends and Determinants, 1974–2010." *American Behavioral Scientist* 56 (11): 1462–80.

Rickford, John R., and Russell John Rickford. 2000. *Spoken Soul: The Story of Black English*. New York: Wiley.

Ridgeway, Cecilia L. 2011. *Framed by Gender: How Gender Inequality Persists in the Modern World*. New York: Oxford University Press.

Rivera, Lauren. 2010. "Status Distinctions in Interaction: Social Selection and Exclusion at an Elite Nightclub." *Qualitative Sociology* 33 (3): 229–55.

Rivera, Lauren. 2012. "Hiring as Cultural Matching: The Case of Elite Professional Service Firms." *American Sociological Review* 77 (6): 999–1022.

Rivera, Lauren A., and Michèle Lamont. 2012. "Price vs. Pets, Schools vs. Styles: Residential Tastes and Inequality among the American Upper-Middle Class." Paper presented at the annual meeting of the Eastern Sociological Society, New York, February.

Rollock, Nicola, David Gillborn, and Carol Vincent. 2015. *The Colour of Class: The Educational Strategies of the Black Middle Classes*. Abingdon: Routledge.

Rollock, Nicola, David Gillborn, Carol Vincent, and Stephen J. Ball. 2011. "The Public

Identities of the Black Middle Classes: Managing Race in Public Spaces." *Sociology* 45 (6): 1078–93.

Rooks, Noliwe M. 2006. "The Beginnings of Black Studies." *Chronicle of Higher Education* 52 (23): 8.

Rooks, Noliwe M. 2007. *White Money/Black Power: The Surprising History of African-American Studies and the Crisis of Race in Higher Education.* Boston: Beacon Press.

Rosa-Salas, Marcel. 2019. "Making the Mass White." In *Race in the Marketplace.* Edited by Guillaume D. Johnson, Kevin D. Thomas, Anthony Kwame Harrison, and Sonya A. Grier. Cham: Palgrave Macmillan.

Rottenberg, Catherine. 2013. "Introduction: Black Harlem and the Jewish Lower East Side." In *Black Harlem and the Jewish Lower East Side: Narratives Out of Time.* Edited by Catherine Rottenberg, 1–15. Albany: State University of New York Press.

Sampson, Robert J., and Stephen W. Raudenbush. 2004. "Seeing Disorder: Neighborhood Stigma and the Social Construction of 'Broken Windows.'" *Social Psychology Quarterly* 67 (4): 319–42.

Sandberg, Sheryl, and Nell Scovell. 2017. *Lean In: Women, Work, and the Will to Lead.* New York: Knopf.

Schor, Juliet. 1999. *The Overspent American: Why We Want What We Don't Need.* New York: Harper Perennial.

Schreer, George E., Saundra Smith, and Kirsten Thomas. 2009. "'Shopping While Black': Examining Racial Discrimination in a Retail Setting." *Journal of Applied Social Psychology* 39 (6): 1432–44.

Sharkey, Patrick. 2008. "The Intergenerational Transmission of Context." *American Journal of Sociology* 113 (4): 931–69.

Sharkey, Patrick, and Felix Elwert. 2011. "The Legacy of Disadvantage: Multigenerational Neighborhood Effects on Cognitive Ability." *American Journal of Sociology* 116 (6): 1934–81.

Shavitt, Sharon, Duo Jiang, and Hyewon Cho. 2016. "Stratification and Segmentation: Social Class in Consumer Behavior." *Journal of Consumer Psychology* 26 (4): 583–93.

Shaw, David. 1990. "The 'Jackie Robinson Syndrome'—a Double Standard: Hiring: Many Newspapers Will Employ Minorities Only If They Are Superstars—Superior Performers—While Whites Are Held to a More Average Standard, Some Minorities Say." *Los Angeles Times*, December 14, 1990.

Shlay, Anne B., and Denise A. DiGregorio. 1985. "Same City, Different Worlds." *Urban Affairs Review* 21 (1), 66–86.

Singer, Merrill. 2008. *Drugging the Poor: Legal and Illegal Drugs and Social Inequality.* Long Grove: Waveland Press.

Skrentny, John David. 2014. *After Civil Rights: Racial Realism in the New American Workplace.* Princeton: Princeton University Press.

Skocpol, Theda. 1985. "Cultural Idioms and Political Ideologies in the Revolutionary Reconstruction of State Power: A Rejoinder to Sewell." *Journal of Modern History* 57 (1): 86–96.

Small, Mario Luis, and Monica McDermott. 2006. "The Presence of Organizational Resources in Poor Urban Neighborhoods: An Analysis of Average and Contextual Effects." *Social Forces* 84 (3): 1697–724.

Stoute, Steve. 2011. *The Tanning of America: How Hip-Hop Created a Culture That Rewrote the Rules of the New Economy*. New York: Gotham Books.

Stowe, Stacey. 2019. "New York City to Ban Discrimination Based on Hair." *New York Times*, February 18.

St. John, Craig, and Nancy A. Bates. 1990. "Racial Composition and Neighborhood Evaluation." *Social Science Research* 19 (1): 47?61.

Sullivan, John Jeremiah. 2018. "Diddy Opens Up about Biggie's Death and the Secret Project He's Working on with Jay-Z." *GQ*, March 18, 2018.

Swidler, Ann. 1986. "Culture in Action: Symbols and Strategies." *American Sociological Review* 51 (2): 273–86.

Taylor, Monique M. 2002. *Harlem between Heaven and Hell*. Minneapolis: University of Minnesota Press.

Timothy, Dallen J., and Stephen W. Boyd. 2006. "Heritage Tourism in the 21st Century: Valued Traditions and New Perspectives." *Journal of Heritage Tourism* 1 (1): 1–16.

Tucker, David M. 1969. "Black Pride and Negro Business in the 1920's: George Washington Lee of Memphis." *Business History Review* 43 (4): 435–51.

Turco, Catherine J. 2010. "Cultural Foundations of Tokenism: Evidence from the Leveraged Buyout Industry." *American Sociological Review* 75(6): 894–913.

Twitchell, James B. 1999. *Lead Us into Temptation: The Triumph of American Materialism*. New York: Columbia University Press.

U.S. Bureau of Labor Statistics. 2018. Current Population Study: Household Data Annual Averages. Washington, DC: U.S. Department of Labor.

U.S. Bureau of Labor Statistics. 2019. "Rising Educational Attainment among Blacks or African Americans in the Labor Force, 1992 to 2018." *The Economics Daily*, February 13. https://www.bls.gov/opub/ted/2019/rising-educational-attainment-among-blacks-or-african-americans-in-the-labor-force-1992-to-2018.htm.

U.S. Census Bureau. 2015. "Los Angeles County a Microcosm of Nation's Diverse Collection of Business Owners." Census Bureau Reports (Press release). https://www.census.gov/newsroom/press-releases/2015/cb15–209.html.

U.S. Census Bureau. 2018a. 2013–2017 American Community Survey 5-Year Estimates. https://www.census.gov/programs-surveys/acs/technical-documentation/table-and-geography-changes/2017/5-year.html.

U.S. Census Bureau. 2018b. Survey of Business Owners. https://www.census.gov/econ/overview/mu0200.html.

Valluvan, Sivamohan. 2016. "What Is 'Post-race' and What Does It Reveal about Contemporary Racisms?" *Ethnic and Racial Studies* 39 (13): 2241–51.

Van Deburg, William L. 1993. *New Day in Babylon: The Black Power Movement and American Culture, 1965–1975*. Chicago: University of Chicago Press.

Veblen, Thorstein. 2006. *Conspicuous Consumption*. New York: Penguin Books.

Wallace, Derron. 2017. "Reading 'Race' in Bourdieu? Examining Black Cultural Capital among Black Caribbean Youth in South London." *Sociology* 51 (5): 907–23.

Weems, Robert. 1998. *Desegregating the Dollar: African American Consumerism in the Twentieth Century*. New York: New York University Press.

West, Kanye, and Jay-Z. 2005. *Diamonds from Sierra Leone: Remix*. Grandmaster Recording Studios, n.d.

Wherry, Fred. 2008. "The Social Characterizations of Price: The Fool, the Faithful, the Frivolous, and the Frugal." *Sociological Theory* 26 (4): 363–79.

White, E. Frances. 2001. *Dark Continent of Our Bodies: Black Feminism and the Politics of Respectability*. Philadelphia: Temple University Press.

Williams, Christine. 2006. *Inside Toyland: Working, Shopping, and Social Inequality*. Berkeley: University of California Press.

Williams, Corey. 2007. "NAACP Symbolically Buries N-Word." *Washington Post*, July 9.

Williams, David R. 2012. "Miles to Go before We Sleep: Racial Inequities in Health." *Journal of Health and Social Behavior* 53 (3): 279–95.

Williams, Jerome, Geraldine Henderson, Sophia Evett, and Anne-Marie Hakstian. 2015. "Racial Discrimination in Retail Settings: A Liberation Psychology Perspective." In *Race and Retail: Consumption across the Color Line*. Edited by Mia Bay and Ann Vincent Fabian. New Brunswick: Rutgers University Press.

Wilson, William Julius. 1980. *The Declining Significance of Race: Blacks and Changing American Institutions*. Chicago: University of Chicago Press.

Wingfield, Adia Harvey. 2010. "Are Some Emotions Marked 'Whites Only'? Racialized Feeling Rules in Professional Workplaces." *Social Problems* 57 (2): 251–68.

Wingfield, Adia Harvey. 2013. *No More Invisible Man: Race and Gender in Men's Work*. Philadelphia: Temple University Press.

Wingfield, Adia Harvey. 2015. "Being Black—but Not Too Black—in the Workplace." *The Atlantic*, October 14.

Wolcott, Victoria W. 2001. *Remaking Respectability: African American Women in Interwar Detroit*. Chapel Hill: University of North Carolina Press.

Yaish, Meir, and Tally Katz-Gerro. 2010. "Disentangling 'Cultural Capital': The Consequences of Cultural and Economic Resources for Taste and Participation." *European Sociological Review* 28 (2): 169–85.

Yoder, Janice D. 1991. "Rethinking Tokenism: Looking beyond Numbers." *Gender and Society* 5(2): 178–92.

Yoshino, Kenji. 2006. *Covering: The Hidden Assault on Our Civil Rights*. New York: Random House.

Young, Vershawn Ashanti. 2009. "'Nah, We Straight': An Argument against Code Switching." *JAC*, 29 (1/2): 49–76.

Zelizer, Viviana. 2011. *Economic Lives: How Culture Shapes the Economy*. Princeton: Princeton University Press.

Zimmer, Lynn. 1988. "Tokenism and Women in the Workplace: The Limits of Gender-Neutral Theory." *Social Problems* 35 (1): 64–77.

Zubrinsky, Camille L., and Lawrence Bobo. 1996. "Prismatic Metropolis: Race and Residential Segregation in the City of the Angels." *Social Science Research* 25 (4): 335–74.

Zukin, Sharon. 2005. *Point of Purchase: How Shopping Changed American Culture*. New York: Routledge.

Zukin, Sharon. 2008. "Consuming Authenticity: From Outposts of Difference to Means of Exclusion." *Cultural Studies* 22 (5): 724–48.

Index

CULTURE AND ECONOMIC LIFE

Diverse sets of actors create meaning in markets: consumers and socially engaged actors from below; producers, suppliers, and distributors from above;
and the gatekeepers and intermediaries that span these levels. Scholars have
studied the interactions of people, objects, and technology; charted networks
of innovation and diffusion among producers and consumers; and explored the
categories that constrain and enable economic action. This series captures the
many angles in which these phenomena have been investigated and serves as a
high-profile forum for discussing the evolution, creation, and consequences of
commerce and culture.

CPSIA information can be obtained
at www.ICGtesting.com
Printed in the USA
JSHW011207030920
7645JS00003B/184